ART AND THE
CHRISTIAN INTELLIGENCE IN
ST. AUGUSTINE

For R. James Finlay,
— with warm thanks,

RJ O'Connell S.J.

ART AND THE
CHRISTIAN INTELLIGENCE IN
ST. AUGUSTINE

ROBERT J. O'CONNELL, S.J.

Harvard University Press
Cambridge, Massachusetts
1978

Library of Congress Cataloging in Publication Data

O'Connell, Robert J
    Art and the Christian intelligence in St. Augustine.

    Includes bibliographical references and index.
    1. Augustinus, Aurelius, Saint, Bp. of Hippo—
Aesthetics. I. Title.
B655.Z7026   111.8'5   78–546
ISBN 0–674–04675–7

For
Henri-Irénée Marrou
(1904–1977)
in grateful remembrance

CONTENTS

ACKNOWLEDGMENTS

THE NUMBER of those I must thank proves embarrassingly large. They include the legion of Fordham University faculty colleagues and students, graduate and undergraduate, who have borne with the long gestation of the views expressed here, with patience, interest, and probing questioning. Typists, like Brother Daniel Dempsey, S.J., Lee Ambriano, Susan Cardosa, Anne Florio, and Virginia Guarascio, must merit a special place in heaven, as must editors like Elizabeth Suttell and Joan Ryan of Harvard University Press. Thanks, as well, to Fr. Paul Kelly for his care in proofreading, constructing the index, and his serenity in coping with the million maddening details that attend such parturitions as this. To Frs. Elmer Henderson, S.J., and John Boyd, S.J., who read parts of the text, and to John J. O'Meara and Leonard Feldstein, who read the entire text, more thanks. All responded with helpful comment. But with the hope of not seeming ungrateful to all the above, I must avow my single greatest debt to A. Hilary Armstrong, who has always, and has now once more, gone well beyond the expected or hoped-for in reading, criticizing, encouraging, and, in general, providing information and insight that make this not nearly so flawed a work as it otherwise would have been. No one I have mentioned will find I have responded to their helpfulness so fully as to meet their generous expectations: the responsibility for that is my own.

One golden name I have deliberately omitted. The dedication may, I hope, remedy that lacuna.

FORMS OF CITATION

FOR SIMPLICITY of reference, the following forms of citation have been used throughout:

(*a*) Research instruments

Augustinus Magister, Acts of the Augustinian Congress, 3 vols. (Paris, 1954)=*AM,* I, II, III depending on the volume.

Real-Encyklopaedie der Klassischen Altertumswissenschaft, Pauly-Wissowa-Kroll-Witter (Stuttgart, 1894ff) = *RE.*

(*b*) Texts and translations

Bibliothèque Augustinienne series of *Oeuvres de Saint-Augustin* (Paris, 1933ff) = *BA* plus the volume number (e.g., *BA* 6).

Ancient Christian Writers series (Westminster, Md., 1946ff) = *ACW* plus the volume number (e.g., *ACW* 22).

Fathers of the Church series (New York [later, Washington, D.C.], 1948ff) = *FC* plus the volume number (e.g., *FC* 1).

The translations from the *Confessions* are my own; they follow the Skutella text reproduced, with minor emendations, in *BA* 13 and 14. I have found E. B. Pusey's translation (reprinted in Everyman's Library, London, 1953) particularly helpful in composing my own versions. Fr. Aimé Solignac's notes to the *BA* edition, as well as a number of other translations and commentaries, have also been of significant aid to me. They are mentioned where relevant; but any defects in my translations are my responsibility.

For the remainder of Augustine's writings, I have regularly worked from the texts recommended by the editors of the *Clavis Patrum Latinorum,* 2d ed. (= *Sacris Erudiri,* III), Steenbrugge: Eligius Dekkers and Aemilius Gaar, 1961.

Translations from Plotinus' *Enneads* I-III are taken from A. H. Armstrong's version in the Loeb Library series (Cambridge, Mass., 1966–67); for *Enneads* IV-VI, I have used the version of Stephen MacKenna, 3d ed., revised by B. S. Page

(New York, 1962). Reference is made in standard form, *Enn* I, 6, 8, 1–8, for example, indicating a quotation drawn from the *First Ennead,* sixth treatise, chapter 8, lines 1–8. The text of the *Enneads* has been that of the critical edition produced by Fr. Paul Henry and Hans-Rudolf Schwyzer (Museum Lessianum, Series Philosophica, volumes 33, 34, and 35 respectively; Paris, 1951, 1959, and 1973).

(*c*) Works of Saint Augustine

Latin titles (in chronological order as qualified below) and their corresponding abbreviations as used throughout the book are as follows:

Works composed prior to the *Confessions* (abbreviated as *Conf*):

Contra Academicos	*Acad*
De Beata Vita	*Vita*
De Ordine	*Ord*
Soliloquia	*Sol*
De Immortalitate Animae	*Immort*
De Moribus Ecclesiae et Manichaeorum	*Mor*
De Quantitate Animae	*Quant*
De Genesi contra Manichaeos	*GenMan*
De Libero Arbitrio	*Lib*
De Diversis Questionibus	*DivQQ*
De Musica	*Mus*
De Magistro	*Mag*
De Vera Religione	*Ver*
De Utilitate Credendi	*Util*
De Fide et Symbolo	*Symb*
De Genesi ad Litteram Opus Imperfectum	*GenImp*
Epistulae ad Romanos Inchoata Expositio	*RomInch*
Ad Simplicianum	*Simp*
De Doctrina Christiana, I-III, 35	*Doc*[1]
Contra Epistulam quam Vocant Fundamenti	*Fund*

Works composed after the *Confessions*:

Contra Faustum Manichaeum	*Faust*
De Natura Boni	*NatBon*
Contra Secundinum Manichaeum	*SecMan*
De Trinitate	*Trin*
De Opere Monachorum	*OpMon*
De Catechizandis Rudibus	*CatRud*
De Genesi ad Litteram	*GenLitt*
Ad Cresconium Grammaticum	*Cresc*

De Unico Baptismo	*UnBapt*
De Civitate Dei	*Civ*
In Epistulam Joannis ad Parthos	*JoParth*
Tractatus in Joannis Evangelium	*InJo*
Contra Sermonem Arianorum	*SermAr*
Questiones in Heptateuchum	*QQHept*
Ad Consentium contra Mendacium	*CMend*
Contra Adversarium Legis et Prophetarum	*AdvLeg*
Contra Julianum	*Jul*
Enchiridion	*Enchir*
De Doctrina Christiana, III, 36-IV	*Doc²*
Retractationes	*Retr*
Epistulae	*Ep*
Enarrationes in Psalmos	*Enar*
Sermones	*Serm*

Because of the peculiarities of their chronology, Augustine's *Epistles, Enarrationes in Psalmos,* and *Sermons* are regularly cited, in that order, after reference has been made to his other works. The reader is also reminded that *De Doctrina Christiana,* I-III, 35, was composed in 396/9, whereas the remaining sections date from 426/7.

In citing from Augustine's works, the chapter numbers are regularly omitted except for those works where they are indispensable (*Civ* and *Retr*); only book and section are given. Thus, for example, *Conf* V, x, 19, is shortened to *Conf* V, 19.

Anne de Vercors: Did you mean this world? Or is there another?
Violaine: There are two of them and I tell you there is only one of them and it is enough.

—Paul Claudel, *The Tidings Brought to Mary*

INTRODUCTION

THERE IS NO loosening Augustine's powerful hold upon the human spirit, no age that remains unmoved by his "philosophy of the heart." Central to his appeal, to the spell he works, is the invincible impression one gleans: here was a man with a passionate sense of beauty. *The Restless Flame*: that title may have been the finest feature of Louis de Wohl's novelistic life of Augustine.[1] For from first to last, he strives to fire our hearts with longing for the beauty that lured him throughout his life, the Beauty whose name, he ultimately was led to see, was God. "What do we love, if it be not beauty?" was the question that opened his youthful debut into the literary world, the lost *De Pulchro et Apto*.[2] And at the climax of his autobiography, he could find no better greeting for the haven that opened at the end of his pilgrimage than the exclamation: "Late have I loved Thee, Beauty, ever ancient, ever new, late have I loved Thee!"[3]

Man's restless quest for happiness: this, throughout his long career of writing and preaching, was Augustine's enduring preoccupation.[4] That quest has also been termed a "quest for Wisdom,"[5] but the difference is only one of terms: the wisdom Augustine's heart had always been seeking turns out to be nothing else than a world where Wisdom, Truth and Beauty are at one in God's own reality. *At illa veritatis et sapientiae pulchritudo*: it is the "beauty of truth and wisdom" that beckons the heart, at its topmost reach, to "embrace, and find joy."[6]

The ages have not been deceived. Augustine's sense of beauty was real, no less real than his unfailing power, in dialogue, sermon, or in that consummate work of poetic imagination, *The Confessions,* to awaken us to beauty's call. Yet he is full of surprises. Incomparable artist, he was ever turning to reflect on beauty's workings; like Plato and Plotinus before him, he was both artist and aesthete. How disconcerting, then, to read from so loyal an *augustinisant* as Henri-Irénée Marrou:

> I am well aware that there is an aesthetic, a theory of artistic beauty in the works of Saint Augustine . . . But it is necessary to see the role it plays: its function is not to ground the aesthetic experience in reason, to justify it; on the contrary, its function is to transcend [that experience] . . . to pass from art to science; it annihilates, to the soul's gaze, the fallacious magic of aesthetic sensation by reducing it to its rational elements.[7]

Sr. Joseph Arthur protests—a genuinely great artist, Augustine was concerned to make his art the loyal ally of truth.[8] But the paradox to which Marrou calls attention is very like the one that plagues the admirer of Plato: how could so great a literary artist, in his passion for truth, become the very same man whose theory of art amounts, at times, to the banishment of art?

In their contribution to *The History of Esthetics*,[9] Katharine Gilbert and Helmut Kuhn essay a partial explanation of the paradox: both Aristotle and St. Thomas, we are told, as against their predecessor counterparts, Plato and Augustine, "dealt with goodness and beauty for man . . . and not in the abstract . . . The later thinkers were more lenient toward the human hunger for recreation, and the place of art as food for that hunger."[10] They then add the interesting observation that "it is true that St. Augustine became more and more ascetic as he grew older."[11]

Gilbert and Kuhn are echoing the evaluation to be found in Karel Svoboda's *L'esthétique de S. Augustin et ses sources.*[12] Having admitted the substantial constancy of Augustine's aesthetic notions through his long career, Svoboda permits himself the estimate that

> nonetheless, even in Augustine's aesthetic researches, a certain evolution can be discerned. Over the long pull his ideas spiritualize, shuck off sensualist elements, turn from sensible to intelligible beauty, from

the artist here below to the Creator-artist: this, evidently, is due to Christianity's influence.[13]

Such a judgment replies, of course, to a notion of Christianity which not too long ago might have passed without serious demur. But in a century preoccupied with the relation of nature and supernature, human and Christian values, it presents an inviting challenge. What was, in fact, the influence of Christianity on Augustine's evaluation of art? Does Christianity require this turning from the sensible to the intelligible beauty? If it did so in Augustine's case, as Svoboda declares, then is this evolution inevitably linked with the Christianization of his views, or was it, rather, an outgrowth of Augustine's personal way of thinking out the implications of the Christian revelation?

On the face of it, another development is entirely imaginable: a deepening Christianity could gradually develop so "sacramental" a view of the universe—that phrase is LeBlond's in speaking of Augustine's evolution[14]—that the divine would be recognized "in" the sensible, God's presense and activity sensed in a manner alluded to in poets like Wordsworth, Hopkins, Claudel, or St. John of the Cross: *mi amado las montañas . . .* Was not Christianity's peculiar mystery the Incarnation, that epiphany of "God with us"?

Before these two possibilities, the Christian of our century still hesitates. Two tendencies, not always well defined, invite his allegiance. Grossly put, the so-called eschatologist would proclaim a world-negating asceticism as part and parcel of the perennial Christian message, while incarnationists contend for a more positive appreciation of the world, the sensible, the immanent human, or as they have come to be called, secular, values. The first would agree with Svoboda that the development he speaks of was indeed an evident outgrowth of Augustine's progressive assimilation of the world of Christian values; the second would suspect that other, not specifically Christian, factors may have been at work.

Such was the context in which I came to study Augustine's aesthetic theory some fifteen years ago. The initial result of that study was a thesis for the University of Paris on "The Christian Value of Art in St. Augustine," a tottering structure compounded of evidence, speculation, and conjecture, provoking Professor Jean Guitton's bemused query as to whether it was really one thesis after all, or two, or possibly even three. Three, I have come to think, would be a fair count. For a study of Augustine's art theory leads—as Svoboda's learned pages make abundantly clear —into the wider areas from which his art theory springs, and notably into his theory of man. Exploration of his theory of man, I became convinced, required in turn a fresh evaluation of its many parallels with Plotinus' view of man as fallen soul. So closely are the second and third of these questions bound together, however, that I have not found it possible to treat them separately. I have repeatedly found it necessary to develop my views of Augustine's theory of man in tandem with the evidence for his dependence on a wider array of Plotinian treatises than scholars of some years ago would have countenanced.

The resulting suggestion—that *St. Augustine's Early Theory of Man*, A.D. *386–391*[15] embodied a modification of Plotinus' view of man's inmost identity as that of soul, fallen from pre-existent bliss into the world of body, time, and action—has met with a not surprising mixture of criticism, reserved appreciation, and occasional agreement. To most of the criticisms that seemed to have point I have since replied;[16] whether well or ill, the reader must judge. I may be pardoned the presumption of thinking that the view I proposed remains substantially sound for the years enclosed in that study.

Those same years—386–391—are especially crucial for the issues involved in the first four chapters of this work, for they extend from the *De Ordine* of Cassiciacum where Augustine is brought around to make a number of specifically aesthetic observations, to the only formally aesthetic work we have from his pen, the *De Musica,* completed in 391. Since this is the work where Svoboda claimed to find the first and most tangible evidence for Augustine's turn away from earthly art toward the ascetic accent which he claims to detect in the saint's more mature view of art, one may hope to perpetrate no serious injustice by initially testing his "curve of spiritualization" over this relatively manageable span. That curve of spiritualization included, Svoboda finds Augustine's later aesthetic developing with substantial fidelity to the lines marked out earlier. On this estimate, too, this study will enter a number of reservations. But it is not my primary intention to redo what Svoboda has done, on the whole, both carefully and well; the reader must still consult him for a sober, comprehensive presentation of the texts that reveal Augustine's aesthetic theory from the beginning to the end of his long career.

The only serious rival to Svoboda's work, in its attempt to present a comprehensive view of Augustine's aesthetic, remains

Emmanuel Chapman's *St. Augustine's Philosophy of Beauty*.[17] Of his predecessor in the field, Chapman opines that Svoboda "is so concerned with sources and the reproduction of texts that he hardly attempts to give a systematic exposition of Augustine's aesthetic thought."[18] The severity of that judgment needs some tempering: Vernon Bourke is a shade gentler in suggesting of Chapman that it is obvious he is "working toward a personal theory of beauty which now and then intrudes upon the account" he gives of Augustine's theory.[19] Had it reached eventual formulation, that personal theory would, one suspects, have owed much to the influence of such masters as Maritain, Gilson, and Phelan,[20] formidable thinkers all, but not all of them, one guesses, equally effective in warning Chapman of the temptation that dogs, and at times overtakes him: to read his Augustine through the spectacles of a developed neo-Thomism.

Chapman's strictures on Svoboda come, then, from a man who would have Augustine's aesthetic thought be more systematic than it actually was. It will be my argument that the jagged edges, the tensions, and occasional inconsistencies of Augustine's thought, especially in its earlier stages, are partially, if not largely accounted for, by the disparate sources on which Svoboda chose to focus and by Augustine's brave attempt to bring their conflicting voices into sometimes forced unison. It is not always certain that Augustine read and was influenced by each and every source to which Svoboda points; it is, however, quite certain that he never read Aquinas, Maritain, or Gilson. For an initial accurate understanding of what Augustine actually said, Svoboda's approach, despite all its risks, clearly recommends itself. Only when this initial job is done, may one feel entitled to move to the second phase that engages Chapman's attention: that of eliciting from what Augustine actually said, the lines of a more coherent synthesis.

The understanding here presented of Augustine's actual aesthetic theory will, accordingly, depend far more closely on Svoboda's work than on Chapman's. But my purpose is to explore not so much that aesthetic theory as its roots and implications—the relationships Augustine sets up between art, aesthetics, and the perennial wider concerns of the Christian intelligence, and the underlying views that lend structure to those relationships. Something of the same purpose animates Josef-Matthias Tscholl's *Gott und das Schöne beim hl. Augustinus*,[21] which attempts, in a fashion more soberly repertorial than critical, to situate Augustine's aesthetic in the larger framework of his entire theology.

I find Cornelius P. Mayer more critical and suggestive, however, in his *Die Zeichen in der geistigen Entwicklung und in der Theologie des jungen Augustinus*,[22] a work that came to my attention only after all of what I had written here on Augustine's theory of signs had been composed. Perhaps it is because Mayer, too, views it as important to estimate Augustine's theologizing in terms of the philosophic instruments he brought to bear[23] that our conclusions and evaluations substantially coincide.

There are, as I see it now, two ways of conceiving of the task embarked on here. His aesthetic theory can be envisaged as growing out of Augustine's more general theory of man and of the human condition, hence as a kind of corollary emerging from a broader network of considerations, theological in the main but betraying a discernible philosophic framework. But there are strong reasons for holding an inverse view: that Augustine's sensitivity to beauty and the need he felt to understand, and by understanding, partially to exorcise its spell upon him, provided the entryway into the entire web of philosophic and theological questions that came to claim his attention. Looked at from this angle, Augustine's aesthetic and what I have elsewhere characterized as its "radically defective theory of sensibility"[24] may be said to lie at the very root of his philosophizing and to furnish the central strand knitting together all his thinking.

That may be an overbold way of stating the proposition of this study, however—reflecting an illusion of perspective that results from taking Augustine's aesthetic as focus for examination; whatever focus one chooses, the remainder of his thought almost inevitably tends to assume ancillary status. Avoiding the temptation to state my case that baldly, then, I can perhaps hope for at least this much: that the reader may come to acknowledge the strategic role that art, beauty, and the aesthetic endeavor played at the inception and in the gradual development of Augustine's thought. He may come to see, moreover, that these concerns never function as *mere* corollaries: only an organic image can begin to express their organic linkage with the fundamentals of his vision. Compare his aesthetic observations, then, to the foliage of a tree that owes its life to, yet contributes in its turn to the life, shape, and solidity of the roots from which it springs. For there is no doubt that Augustine's satisfaction with the aesthetic he found coherent with his broader theory of man commended that broader theory to his own mind, confirmed, even hardened it at certain points. Conversely, a contemporary thinker may feel entitled to find the frequently seductive power

and occasional tragic flaws of Augustine's broader thought reflected in, and often explained by, those very same qualities as
they mark his message concerning beauty, art, and their place in
a Christian understanding of human experience. The adequacy
of Augustine's aesthetic may be, accordingly, not an exclusive,
but a specially sensitive, indicator of the adequacy of his entire
philosophy. This, in the course of some fifteen years' study of
the man, has come to be my own conviction.

It is only fair to confess, as well, that the queries and criticisms
directed at, the "retranslations" suggested for Augustine's
"Christian philosophy," all emerge from my own personal philosophical outlook. That way of seeing things can lay only modest
claim to either profundity or originality: the influences that have
played upon its evolution are too numerous, too various to mention or indeed even to remember. But I would hope that the outlook presiding over these pages is not entirely foreign to Augustine's: it has developed in terms of my taking his own questions,
particularly his aesthetic questions, seriously, exploring his answers to those questions, and attempting to reform both questions and answers in such a way as to preserve or perhaps rescue
their original spirit, appeal, and life, even when violating the
Augustinian letter.

The first five chapters of this work constitute, along with my
two earlier books on Augustine's developing thought, what I
consider to be the indispensable first stage of any such *Wiederholung* (in Heidegger's phrase) or "retrieval" of a great man's
views. They represent my conviction that the attempt to ferret
out what the mediaevals termed the *vera intentio,* the underlying purpose of an author, imposes an initial, sober, self-effac-
ing step of finding out just what the man did actually say and
mean. Jean Guitton once spoke in terms of disengaging Augustine's "spirit" from the husk of "mentality" and "language" he
inevitably inherited from his philosophic predecessors.[25] I have
been brought to wonder if those distinctions do not already
imply an all too Augustian way of relating thought to the
language in which it is "bodied forth," as it were; a spirit can,
I am persuaded, have no other existence than as incarnate in a
language and a mentality. Hence the almost painful step of
scholarly detective work presented in Chapters 1 to 5, a step that
brings me at many points (as in my two earlier books) to take
a critical view of what I think Augustine said and, willy-nilly,
meant to say.

It was not until the year 391 that Augustine composed his *De*

Musica, again, the only formally aesthetic work we have from his pen. Chapter 4 is my attempt to elucidate that aesthetic theory and its implications. But Chapters 1 to 3, dealing with the Cassiciacum writings and then the works spanning the years from 386 to 391, present what I hold to be the necessary background for understanding the *De Musica.* In Chapter 5 I endeavor to show that the theory of art proposed in the *Confessions* remains substantially faithful to that contained in the *De Musica.*

This completes the first stage of my inquiry; Chapters 6 to 8 venture out on more shifting terrain. Chapter 6 makes the claim that Augustine's artistic practice, as exhibited in the *Confessions,* raises a number of questions to his theory of art. To several of these questions Augustine becomes explicitly sensitive, especially in his later writings—the burden of Chapter 7—so that an Augustinian thinker may feel himself entitled, without, one hopes, unseemly arrogance, to extend the development running through his later thought and trace the outlines of a "contemporary" Augustinian aesthetic theory: the work of Chapter 8.

If, in the first stage of my work, I have found Svoboda a trustier guide than Chapman, the reason is that Chapman too often seems to let the second stage of *Wiederholung* encroach upon the first. As to the character of this second stage, I am happier with Guitton's formulation in a related connection: that task is one of getting at what Augustine "was thinking, without knowing it, or better, what he wanted to think without being able to."[26] The years I have spent in critical appreciation of Augustine have been years of positive appreciation, too: years that brought me to marvel at the special power of this extraordinary thinker, to resonate with his *vera intentio*; this has prompted the desire that animates this work: of bringing to fresh expression, for today's minds, what I am persuaded Augustine most profoundly wanted to communicate. But that task involves a series of what I have termed retranslations: elaborating a new language, penetrated with a fresh mentality, and therefore incarnating a somewhat different (but, perhaps, rejuvenated) spirit. It means honestly admitting to the business of not simply uncovering but, at crucial junctures, of creatively reforming Augustine's thought. The agonies of writing, rewriting, of stepping back to reconceive and again rewrite so many items in this book, have convinced me that my original ambitions were more pretentious than once I knew. Let this work, then, especially its final three chapters, and most particularly its final one, be taken as a kind of *amende honorable*: one man's modest testimony to the greatness of Augustine; yet testimony, too, of how difficult it is, even after what one fondly thinks have been fifteen centuries of progress in human reflection, to hit upon the terms on which a fifth-century genius still remains vital to, still retains his unyielding grip upon our twentieth-century spirits. Let it be a testimony, then, but also an invitation, aimed at provoking some future *anima naturaliter Augustiniana* to articulate more cogently and compellingly what these pages only haltingly manage to stammer.

1

CASSICIACUM:

PROVIDENCE AND THE

LADDER OF BEAUTY

THE YEAR IS 386 A.D. The hills around Cassiciacum are touched with November as the small band of friends arrives at Vere- cundus' villa. Augustine, his mother, Monica, his brother Navigius, his son Adeodatus are accompanied by two cousins, Augustine's faithful friend and fellow convert Alypius, and two young students under his charge, Licentius and Trygetius.[1] The list of *dramatis personae* of the Cassiciacum Dialogues is com- plete. Much has been written about the question of why Augus- tine came to Cassiciacum, how he occupied his time, whether the image of the convert found in the works of this four-month period agrees with that drawn up by the Bishop of Hippo, some thirteen years later, in his *Confessions*.

It has been suggested that the English-speaking world was per- haps fortunate in being spared all but distant echoes of that controversy.[2] Augustine's conversion—was it to Neo-Platonism or to Christianity? The tumult and the shouting now are dying; it is clearer now that, badly posed, that question could not but be badly answered. And yet, the by-products of that twilight battle have immensely enriched our knowledge of Augustine, helped us frame certain questions more sharply, locate his development more exactly in terms of the thought-world of the fourth and fifth centuries, which to ignore is not to know Augustine. One of the side-effects of that false question, though, was that it masked the real intent of the Cassiciacum writings. They were made to represent a professor of rhetoric and grammar still plying his trade with Licentius and Trygetius, still dabbling in the study of literature, his interests and occupations essentially the same as they were before the conversion of which he speaks in tones so "different" from the fervid accents of the later bishop.

This effort to contrast Cassiciacum's works with the *Confessions* could not but obscure the profound continuity, the inner coherence of the two portraits of the convert set over against each other. Important for our purpose here is to grasp the fact that the Dialogues and their companion piece, the *Soliloquies,* embody the beginnings of that long meditation on God's work in his life which preoccupied Augustine till the end of his career. A certain reverence is needed to cross the lowly threshold of that villa, an ear attuned to the subtle overtones of what is spoken there. For the "fortune" that Augustine speaks of, the "Wisdom" that he symbolizes as bride of his soul, is no other than the *Verbum* of St. John; the substance of his meditations is the *Idipsum,* the "Self-same" of the fourth Psalm. So Augustine assures us in the *Confessions;* his assurance has been met with wide disbelief. But the penalty of that disbelief has been a blindness to the real import of his early works, to the structure and difficulties in his initial "understanding of the faith," to the exact lines of the problematic which is his from the outset to the end of his literary career.

It would be too much to ask that Augustine's aesthetic theory escape the damage. His aesthetic ideas gradually "spiritualize," we are told; the *De Musica* will register a strong reaction against the high evaluation of "art" implied in the Dialogues of Cassiciacum; the reason is obvious, the Augustine of 391 is a "convinced" Christian.[3] The implication is clear, it was undoubtedly encouraged by a number of conversion theories current when Svoboda wrote those lines: the Augustine of Cassiciacum must be regarded as not yet "convinced," his conversion at Milan in 386 was more to Neo-Platonism than to Christianity, the five-year period intervening must then have drawn him from his state of doubt to one of full Christian persuasion. More recent researches have stripped this theory of its last claims to credibility.[4] The question, therefore, of Augustine's evolution must be re-examined closely; one result of that scrutiny will call into question the very curve of spiritualization Svoboda has claimed to see in Augustine's estimate of art.

But initially at least, that curve of spiritualization furnishes a convenient focus for our question. It would only be fair, accordingly, to start with some fixed point for the study of Augustine's development, one which does not prejudice the issue. Svoboda's own summary of the *De Ordine* aesthetic will do nicely; that dialogue being far richer in aesthetic observations than either the *Contra Academicos* or the *De Beata Vita*, it furnishes Svoboda the occasion for presenting a first systematic picture of Augustine's early theory.[5]

Logically, if not chronologically, the *De Ordine* belongs after the *De Beata Vita* and the *Contra Academicos*. In those two Dialogues, Augustine had proven to his satisfaction that the soul's happiness required the assured possession of truth—Truth, that is, as a hypostatic, subsistent "reality," existing in an intelligible world beyond the reach of sense perception. Thus far the position would seem faithfully Neo-Platonic, and little more. Augustine's personal contribution to the understanding of that position, however, has been brought into prominence by a spate of more recent studies of the works he penned soon after his conversion. Two aspects, at least, of that contribution need underlining here.

First, he is persuaded—and in subtle fashion labors to show— that this Neo-Platonic conception is less a contradiction, much more the fulfillment of the logic and of the deepest aspirations of its apparent rival, Stoicism; as for its other apparent rival, the New Academy, he proposes the ingenious theory that Academic skepticism was a therapeutic maneuver, adopted to confound the complacent sensism of both Stoics and Epicureans, showing that the truth they seek is to be found not in this, but in the Platonic "other" world.[6]

His second contribution is specifically Christian; couched in a language of apologetic accommodation, it largely escaped a former generation of scholars who found these Dialogues betraying an Augustine essentially Neo-Platonist, only faintly tinged with Christianity. But closer study of his writings has ferreted out the decidedly Christian import of these two works. For the other-worldly Truth that Neo-Platonism reveals to the purified mind is none other than the *Logos* of St. John's Gospel, Second Hypostasis of a Divine Trinity in which, *pace* Neo-Platonists, no subordination of Son to Father can be found. And the Way to the beatific possession of that Truth is none other than Truth itself become Incarnate Way; now the many can hope to attain a goal which, until the Incarnation, might have seemed accessible only to a few superior souls. This Neo-Platonic understanding of the Christian mysteries, this bold Christianization of Neo-Platonism, Augustine proclaims as the *vera philosophia,* the true philosophy which the various schools of ancient thought had down the centuries been dimly striving to articulate.[7]

Truth, then, is the food our famished souls long for; the wise man will cultivate *Philosophia* in order to "possess" that Truth. Augustine's artistic imagination now swings into play: *Philosophia* he depicts (in a fable characterized as Aesopic)[8] as elder sister to *Philocalia,* the love of beauty that all too often results in our becoming enmired in the charms of sense-delights. It is *Philosophia's* task to liberate her younger sister, by drawing the soul's yearning upward to the beauty of that otherworldly truth.[9] But far from leaving *Philosophia* a rarified abstraction, Augustine depicts her as a bridal figure, radiant of visage; the merest glimpse of her beauty can fire an "incredible conflagration" in the soul,[10] sending it winging "an impassioned and holy lover, amazed and glowing with excitement," to embrace her, cling to her, leaving all other charms behind.[11] Here, as throughout his writings, the light of Truth is one with the radiance of Beauty.

The image of *Philosophia* is multivalent, however; not only bride, she is mother and nurse as well: the lover of true beauty longs to take refuge on her maternal lap, to be "nourished and cherished," to drink from those maternal breasts from which "no age can complain it is excluded."[12] Augustine's "conversion" to *Philosophia* is at bottom a "reversion" to the "religion" he drew in from the breasts of his mother, Monica, to Mother Church, to Christian Truth in all its feminine aspects, all its alluring charm, comforting security—and heaven-sent beauty.[13]

All that he had sought in womanly beauty, he is convinced that he has found at last in the supernal beauty of *Philosophia.* All the charms of poetry, too, despite their inferiority to those of philosophy,[14] have secretly functioned as so many Protean "pointers" to the Truth-Beauty that now holds him in thrall.[15] Indeed, philosophy's key function is to illuminate the entirety of the sense-world, to "make clear to her true lovers" that what may have seemed the chance results of "fortune" were really, all the while, the secret workings of a "hidden order", God's universal Providence.[16]

The intent of the *De Ordine* is to "make this clear". While the incarnate Christ is Proteus par excellence, the ultimate condescension of God's providential care for souls, it still remains true that, for those who can "see," the entire realm of sense-reality is a splendorous array of Protean "pointers" to the truth and beauty of the divine world. Making this "clear" will not be an easy task; the Manichaeism Augustine is implicitly battling forces him to entertain complexities he does not seem eager to confront as yet; his initial way of posing the question makes it extraordinarily difficult to resolve.[17] As a result, his meditation on the order the soul must pursue in its efforts to perceive Divine Order in and beyond the realm of sense-experience. Faith, moral purification, and the strengthening of the mind through "exercise" are all variously required.[18] But the soul, once properly ordered, will, Augustine is confident, be able to contemplate the world and all its workings as revealing God's providential designs. His confidence goes further: the soul so exercised will gain the strength required to glimpse the very source of the entire world order, to gaze upon the Divine Splendor in a rapture that is beatitude. Now Augustine becomes explicit on what was implicit all along: the quest for Truth and Wisdom is fundamentally identical with the quest for Divine Beauty,[19] source of all the multifarious beauties the world of sense discloses to the ordered soul. Hence the abundance of aesthetic observations studding the *De Ordine.*

What, then, is the aesthetic contained in the work? Svoboda summarizes it in eight points;[20] I shall do little more than present a résumé of his remarks, omitting for the moment his conjectures on the sources from which Augustine might have drawn the different features of his view. But I shall take the liberty of changing the order of his presentation.

Beauty, first of all, consists for Augustine in the relation (*ratio*) of the parts of the beautiful object to each other and to the whole. This relation Augustine variously designates as *aequalitas, parilitas, modus, concentus*: equality, measure, concord, and the like. True to a capital distinction forged in his early *De Pulchro et Apto,* however, Augustine stresses that this beauteous relationship causes pleasure to the beholder; the beautiful, *pulchrum,* must not be confused with the fitting, *aptum*: with that arrangement of part to part, or being with fellow being, which results in profit or utility. In fact, and the importance of this I shall have to stress later on, the delighted beholding of beauty seems to require a kind of detachment, a temporary suspension of concern with profit, advantage, a peculiar objectivity. Beauty of the sort Augustine is referring to can be perceived only by the two highest senses, hearing (which is more properly said to perceive the *suave*) and sight (which perceives the *pulchrum*).

What is the ontological basis for the beauteous "relation"? "Number" is Augustine's answer: the symmetrical arrangement of architectural elements, the rhythmic movements of the dance, the measures and harmonies of musical sounds, all reveal mathematical and geometrical proportions. In doing so, they reflect the intelligible order of pure number—the higher, unchanging world of numerical relations penetrates, as it were, into the world of sense, and the eternal quality of the relations, perceived by eye and ear, provide so many stepping-stones for rising to the Eternal Source of all beauty. The epistemological corollary is clear; the Augustine of the *De Ordine* makes it explicit: he accords to the higher senses the power to "judge" on the existence of sensible beauty.

Thus far three of the eight points in Svoboda's summary. He is not slow to point out several inconsistencies in Augustine's aesthetic views. Instead of calling attention to them, I have chosen to present his summary-exposé in two phases: for there are, at least on the face of it, not one but two families of aesthetic theory represented in the *De Ordine*.

Despite his assertion that beauty consists in the harmonious arrangement of parts, Augustine also affirms that beauty can be found in pure colors, in simple, uncomposed sounds, where no relation of part-to-part can be said to exist in the object beheld. Second, Augustine does not seem at all confident in according the power of "judging" beauty to the senses, even to the two higher senses: both poetry and dance, he claims, work not only on our senses, but also on our minds. Both convey a meaning (*significatio*), in the one case by words, in the other by movements, and this meaning can be judged upon only by the mind.

This tendency to make the perception of beauty the exclusive province of mind or reason becomes even more pronounced when Augustine assures us that true art (*ars*) consists, not in acting, moving, or singing harmoniously, "numerically," but in "knowing" the numerical relationships responsible for such harmonious activity. The regularity of the beehive, the chant of the nightingale, are products of nature rather than of art: the knowledge of numerical relationships is the exclusive province of man, endowed as he is with reason. Indeed, it seems to be the province of the educated few: the singing, or flute-playing of men who do not "know music"—who do not perceive and understand the pure numerical relationships that govern their performance—are also more properly viewed as productions of "nature," not of art.[21]

The grounds for Marrou's complaint, and its justice, are becoming clearer: whatever must be said of Augustine the artist—and we shall eventually have to ask whether his "practice" of art is not a telling refutation of his theory—his aesthetic plainly tends toward the thorough rationalization of art, toward making the artist *par excellence* a species of mathematical theoretician. That tendency has not escaped Svoboda's notice: the ancients, he reminds us, did not make the sharp distinction between art and science, which to us, particularly since Romanticism, seems so obvious.[22] But there is more to it than that. Svoboda has not entirely missed it, but I cannot think he attributes enough importance to the fact that when speaking of "art," Augustine regularly uses the term *artes* in the plural; when doing so, he is invariably referring to what the ancient world designated indifferently as the liberal arts or "disciplines"—grammar, logic, rhetoric, music, poetry, geometry, and astronomy. These he looks upon not as an accidental collection, but as a graded series of studies designed to train the mind in the ways of abstract, and ultimately mathematical, thought. This is the standpoint from which *musica* is enumerated among the *disciplinae*;[23] the end of the *De Ordine* has Augustine openly avowing his dependence on Varro's classic effort to interpret the traditional school disciplines in the light of Neo-Pythagorean mathematical categories.[24]

What did this graduated training of the mind promise? Augustine's answer goes back, through Neo-Pythagoreanism straight to Plato's *Republic*: the Platonic tradition generally equates the mind's growing power to deal with (what a modern would call) abstractions[25] with the ability to move among "intelligible realities," the archetypal realities beyond the world of sense. The "exercise" of the mind Augustine will regularly associate with its "strengthening," its "purification"; and this in turn will imply the mind's capacity to glimpse intelligible realities without the aid of sensual imagery. "Purified"—the final point in Svoboda's summary—the soul can arise to contemplation of the Supreme Beauty itself, dispense finally with all sense-intermediaries, and gaze directly upon the Archetypal Beauty of which the sense-world is only pale imitation.

But the ultimate source of beauty must be utterly simple, Unity without flaw; the beauties of pure color and uncomposed sound are witness, even in the normally multiple world of sense, that such "simple" intelligible beauty is far from inconceivable. This was the reason for Plotinus' stressing the existence of uncomposed beauty even in the sense-world. Svoboda is very likely correct in suggesting *Ennead* I, 6, *On Beauty,* as Augustine's source for this notion;[26] we know he read this treatise, was strongly impressed by it, and its traces can be found throughout the Dialogues of this period.[27] But what is significant is Plotinus' insistence on the notion, his anxiety to refute the rival Stoic thesis that beauty requires a multiplicity of parts in harmonious relation.[28] Significant, too, is the relative insouciance with which Augustine proposes these two rival notions, side by side, without any evident bother about their mutual inconsistency. And yet, for the aesthetician of the ancient world, the difference was an important one, pregnant with consequences anthropological, cosmological, and ultimately, theological.

Nor is this the only inconsistency in Augustine's theory; why does he glide over them so airily? Svoboda's preoccupation with ferreting out his sources in the various families of ancient thought suggests the reply that Augustine's relatively unprofessional background in philosophy may have blinded him to the incompatibilities that obtained between contending positions. There may be something in that: even where a touch of skepticism may be appropriate concerning this or that particular source attribution, Svoboda is surely right in highlighting the fact that Augustine's aesthetic notions are the result of a wide sampling; they originate with almost every philosophic tendency of the ancient world. Stoic and Neo-Platonist, Pythagorean and Peripatetic consort at Cassiciacum in uneasy truce, despite centuries of squabbling. Still, the coals of possible controversy smolder; Augustine does not seem to mind, does not even seem to notice.

Part of the reason for his relative complacency may have been the purpose of irenic synthesis he set himself: he is convinced, perhaps a bit too easily, that all these seemingly rival schools were really striving to articulate the fullness of the *Vera Philosophia* represented by his brand of Christian Neo-Platonism. Academics were really crypto-Platonists;[29] the Stoic theory of happiness through wisdom as "measure" found its needed complement in the transcendent Measure that is really God the Father;[30] and reliable writers have assured us that, at bottom, even Aristotle and Plato fundamentally agreed.[31]

That irenicism, it must be said, could have found encouragement in Plotinus himself. One must be wary of exaggerating about Plotinus' development; but as his career proceeds, there is, in Hans Rudolf Schwyzer's phrase, a notable "shift of accent."[32] Among other things, the near-ferocious anti-Stoicism of his early treatise *On Beauty* is perceptibly tempered as he moves into his middle and later periods of production; his mighty double treatise *On Providence, Ennead* III, 2–3, shows him unashamedly applying the Stoic notion of the *Logos,* ordering the world-process into a work of antithetical beauty; his anti-gnostic treatise *On the Intelligible Beauty, Ennead* V, 8, takes a far more, almost Stoically optimistic view of the sensible universe and of the soul's positive function in it; *Ennead* I, 4, *On Happiness,* draws liberally from their diatribic tradition and betrays his later readiness to propose his views less as a direct refutation, more as the logical fulfillment of Stoic positions on the question.[33] The evidence that Augustine was strongly influenced by the treatise *On Providence* is beyond serious question[34]— Svoboda is correct in pointing to features, phrases, and illustrations from it which Augustine has incorporated into the aesthetic of the *De Ordine.*[35] The evidence that the early Augustine drew inspiration from *Ennead* V, 8, *On the Intelligible Beauty,* is quite strong:[36] its shift of accent from the earlier treatise *On Beauty* could account for some of the inconsistencies we must later probe more deeply. And though the influence of *Ennead* I, 4, *On Happiness,* reposes on shakier evidence than the other two, it is more than possible it partially inspired Augustine's effort, in the *De Beata Vita,* to bring Stoic and Neo-Platonic theories of happiness into rhyme.[37]

But there is another reason for Augustine's insouciance: the inconsistencies in his aesthetic analysis fail to bother him overmuch, since his interest is by no means confined to aesthetics. The same would have to be said of virtually any thinker in the ancient world. The elaboration of an aesthetic theory in and for itself is a peculiarly modern preoccupation. Instructive in this regard is Porphyry's classification of Plotinus' *Ennead* I, 6, *On Beauty*: he includes it among the "ethical" treatises. *Ennead* V, 8, *On the Intelligible Beauty* he classes as treating of the Intellectual Principle, or *Noûs.*[38] And in neither case has serious injustice been done, for Plotinus' dominant interest in the first case is clearly ethical (or perhaps, in a more modern term, "anthropological"); in the second, his purpose is cosmological. If, on the other hand, one seeks to classify the *De Ordine,* the term "anthropological" comes easily to mind: for starting with the theological task of showing the universality of divine order, Augustine veers to prescribing a process of "self-ordering" for

the disordered soul; he is outlining a "way of salvation." Along
this way, the soul is counseled on the salutary "use" of beauty,
whether in art or in nature; on another level, Augustine himself is "using" aesthetic theory in the interests of his anthropological prescription.

One must beware of leveling anachronistic strictures on this
tendency to subordinate beauty, art, and aesthetic theory to
wider philosophic concerns, on this inclination of the pre-
modern world to "press them into service," so to speak. The
ancients showed a healthy refusal to divorce their views of art
from the wider human concerns they dealt with; modern ad-
vances in aesthetic theory have not seldom been bought at the
price of just such a divorce. And yet, that very divorce has is-
sued in a more sharpened awareness of what is properly "aesthetic," and of the distortions that can affect an aesthetic theory
when it is grown primarily from alien soil: when it is developed
as a kind of semi-casual corollary of a nonaesthetic theoretical
construction, whether ethical or anthropological, epistemological or theological.

This, it must be said, is effectively what Augustine has done.
His thesis that number is the basis of all beauty is plainly a
corollary of the Neo-Pythagorean view of liberal disciplines he
had found so attractive in Varro's encyclopedic presentation of
them. There are at least two instances where he almost yields
to the invitation to explore the art phenomenon on its own
peculiar terms; in both cases, his numerical bias is momentarily
shaken: both poetry and dance, he sees, must be understood as
conveying some sort of "meaning."[39] But even there, he ac-
quiesces in the prevailing assumption that the meaning of a
work of art can be classified in much the same way as the meaning
attached to the words of ordinary discourse.[40] Again, one can
understand this; he is anxious to get on with his primary, anthropological task. But his haste may exact an ironic revenge: we
shall, in time, have to ask whether the anthropological purpose
he set himself might not have been better served if he had taken
the pains to explore more conscientiously what his sensitive artistic perceptions might have revealed to him.

Fleshing out that suggestion must wait, however. Our business
at the moment is still that of understanding Augustine, of uncovering the roots of the tensions in his aesthetic. Another of
those roots is cosmological: man has never asked the question
about his own reality, destiny, and hopes, without that question's
swiftly turning into another—about his place in the cosmos and

about the readiness of the cosmos to respond to man's hopes. Man's central hope is for happiness, the Augustine of the *De Beata Vita* is persuaded; and happiness, he is further persuaded, is to be found in that "kingdom not of this world" of which both Christ and Platonists spoke.[41]

But if happiness is to be found only in that other world, how and why do we find ourselves in this world of misery? The problem of happiness is the other face of the problem of human misery, the problem of misery, the cutting edge of the problem of evil—and "whence comes evil?"

The question is familiar to any reader of the *Confessions;*[42] it was the persistent taunt of the Manichee objecting to the Catholic: if God created this visible world, this human body, sluggish and rebellious by turns, if He created the insect, the scorpion, and the welter of beings which do harm to man, if God's Providence extends to each smallest item of our lives, if, indeed, we do nothing except in virtue of God's power extended to us, then God Himself must be responsible for evil.[43] Precisely to avoid this impiety, the Manichee argument went on, a dualistic image of the world is necessary. Our misery here derives from a primordial invasion of Light by the jealous hordes of Darkness; our lives testify to the continuing struggle on the part of Light to liberate those particles of itself, men's souls and the souls of everything that lives, from the imprisonment in matter which resulted from that original catastrophe. Whatever semblance of order there is in the material, sensible reality about us has been instituted in the interests of this cosmic process of salvaging the particles of the Divine Light.[44]

Augustine's prescription for the soul's happiness cannot be complete without discussion of this problem of misery, anthropological focus of the wider problem of evil. The opening paragraph of the *De Ordine* shows him going straight to the heart of the issue: two positions seem at first sight possible, he writes to his friend Zenobius; we must admit either that divine Providence does not extend to the "last and lowest" beings in the scale of reality, or, on the counter-assumption that Providence is, in fact, universal, that "all evils are certainly committed by God's Will" (*Dei voluntate*).[45]

Before confronting the problem in this, its most acute form, Augustine invokes two principles common to the classic theodicies of the ancient world: they are intimately related to each other, and both draw their support from frankly aesthetic illustrations. The first we may term the principle of antithesis: the existence of evils is justified insofar as they bring the good into higher relief.[46] Like the color black in a painting, evil is indispensably necessary to highlight the bright spots in the universal world order. In the same way as rhetorical antitheses provoke delight or as dashes of the salt of common speech set off the more elevated portions of an eloquent discourse, so the mangled ugliness of the vanquished, the fearfulness of the executioner, even the prostitute, all contribute to the harmonies of the universal concert.[47]

The second principle might be termed the principle of totality: it requires us to take the total view of things instead of fastening our attention on this or that painful (or apparently ugly) part. See the whole painting, not just the black; hearken to the concert of the whole world order, not just its isolated parts; then those separate parts, however discordant when listened to in isolation, will be heard as contributing to the beauteous chant of the entire cosmic process.[48]

But Augustine is aware that such replies merely attenuate the problem of evil; they do not get to the heart of it. For the universality of Providence, as he has framed his question, must imply that each and every individual *part,* including the folly of the foolish, the sins of the sinner, must exist or occur by God's Will.[49] Twice he moves upon the question he has formulated in these demanding terms,[50] and twice seems to find it beyond the forces of his interlocutors and, as his later works suggest, beyond his own powers as well. In both instances, he turns to consider how the soul might be ordered to the point of dealing adequately with the problem of cosmic order in its acutest form.[51]

In this context, his aesthetic observations take on a different cast, one dictated by the needs of this new problem. He appeals, as we have already seen, to the power of the *artes,* the "liberal disciplines," to promote the soul's ascent from the partial, fragmentary beauties of the sense-world to the glimpse, and eventual contemplative vision, of the Intelligible Beauty transcending the entire order of evils he has been attempting to justify. It is far less a question now of situating particular evils in a total view of the sensible and temporal world in which we encounter them, of reconciling our hearts to this antithetical human "arena of struggle and flight"; the "ascent" holds out the promise of escape from that arena; it invites us to rise from the entire realm of the corporeal, whatever be the total harmony of its antitheses, to pass from its beauties as well as from its ugliness, to the unflawed "other world" of incorporeal beauty. This is the region of the soul's true happiness; however successfully we strive to survey the whole of it, the realm of time and of the sensible is, comparatively, a land of misery. The sense-world is only an image of the true world; and the beauty of the latter is perceptible not even by the higher senses but only by the purified "eye of the soul."

This brings us closer to the root of the inconsistency in Augustine's epistemology of beauty: the aesthetic of antithetical totality can conceivably survive by according the higher senses the power to "judge"—the beauty involved is, after all, the beauty of the sensible *universitas*. But once the ascensional aesthetic is made to involve another, trans-sensible world, Augustine feels naturally obliged to emphasize the power of the mind alone to catch sight of genuine beauty.

But there is something more to be noted about these two accents: they represent markedly divergent attitudes toward the sense-world, and as ancient thought would put it, toward the soul's involvement in the sense-world. The aesthetic of antithesis is designed to reconcile the soul to the apparent evils of that world, prodding it to see that its complaints arise essentially from an error in perspective. The sense-world *as a whole* is beautiful, and (at least presumably) "truly" beautiful. The ascensional aesthetic, on the other hand, would tend to relativize, even devaluate sense-beauty; it would incite the soul to flee that world as essentially a "mendacious" image, would present it with a ladder for mounting to a higher world where alone "true" beauty dwells.

Put in terms of the sources available to him in ancient thought, the amalgam of these two aesthetic accents represents another instance of Augustine's resolute effort at irenic synthesis. Nothing was more common in Stoic writings than the principle of antithesis, than the optimistic determination to reconcile the soul to the sense-world—which was, to the Stoic monist, the only world that existed. And with that conviction went the Stoic insistence that sense was penetrated with reason and capable of judging on sensible beauties. But just as characteristic of the Platonic tradition were its counteremphases: its dualism, its insistence on the discontinuity between sense and intellect, its nostalgia for the "other" true world. How could Augustine have been so sanguine as to think two such divergent accents could be brought into harmony?

Here, again, he needed only to look to Plotinus to find considerable encouragement for his task. The ascensional aesthetic, with its stress on rising to the Intelligible Beauty and on the

need for turning away from all sense-images in order to arrive
at this vision for the inner, spiritual eye, runs through Plotinus'
writings from first to last. But once again, his disaffection with
Gnosticism's hatred of the sense-world grows in tandem with his
more sympathetic attitude toward Stoicism, until his double
treatise *On Providence* dips unembarassedly into the aesthetics
of antithesis, unashamedly borrows illustration after illustration
from Stoic literature—many of which, again, find their way into
Augustine's *De Ordine*.[52]

On the soul's involvement in the sense-world, Augustine
would have found Plotinus similarly ambivalent. His early
treatise *On Beauty* (*Ennead*, I, 6) represents a powerful articulation of his acute sense of alienation from, his aching nostalgia
for the beauty of the higher, intelligible world. For the world
of sense and body, on the other hand, Plotinus here reserves an
array of the fiercest ephithets—not a few of which find startlingly
strong analogues in Augustine's writings at Cassiciacum.[53] But
even in the writings of his earliest period, Plotinus cannot rest
easy with so unilateral a position: when brought to face the
problem of *The Descent of the Soul,* he avows that there are two
sides to the question, even in the writings of his master, Plato.
The *Phaedo* and *Phaedrus* would intimate the relatively pessi-
mistic conclusion that the soul's presence in the body was due
to a "fall," was a kind of "emprisonment"; and yet, the *Timaeus*
speaks in more optimistic tones of the soul's having been "sent"
into the corporeal world with the mission of imparting to it the
beauty of the intelligible world: the mission of forming it, indeed, into a cosmos meriting the title of a "blessed god."[54]
Plotinus does not feel entitled, as others had before him, to
choose one of these solutions over the other: even his earliest expressed treatment of the question shows his resolve that they
must somehow be reconciled, brought into synthesis, however
uneasy and paradoxical that synthesis may turn out to be. It
must be true that the soul is fallen into a world alien to its ideal
station, a world that is essentially one of misery; and still, that
fall, however much due to some pre-existent "fault" on the soul's
own part, must coincide in depth with the inexorable workings of
cosmic law that sends souls into bodies fitted for them, into a
world that is, conceded, a sort of prison house, yet beautiful with
a beauty entirely worthy of divinity's work.[55]

Again, Plotinus' steady shift of accent shows him more and
more accenting the second, more optimistic view of the soul's
presence in the body: the series of treatises aimed against the

Gnostics[56]—of which his work *On the Intelligible Beauty* is one —crackle with righteous indignation at their unrelieved contempt of the sense-world: an indignation that Augustine could easily transfer to his own gnostic adversaries, the Manichees. But that indignation would be fed from another source as well; Augustine's early synthesis aims at being not simply Neo-Platonist, but Christian; and *Genesis* was unambiguous on the point, the God of the Bible was "creator of things both visible and invisible," and "all that He made was very good." Does it follow, then, that the soul's presence in the visible world was not to be construed as consequence of a fall from pre-existence? We might think he *ought* to have drawn that conclusion; but Augustine does not see it that way. His brave attempt to explore, in the *De Ordine,* how even the sins of sinners can occur *Dei voluntate* is only one way of reflecting Plotinus' efforts at showing the fallen soul's fault as coincident, in depth, with the workings of universal law, of the providential *Logos*.[57] That brave attempt will be succeeded by others in a similar vein: in not too many months, Augustine will set himself to showing his Manichee adversaries that a slightly modified Plotinian view of man furnishes an excellent key for unlocking the secrets and laying out a proper "understanding" of *Genesis!*[58]

Only then do all the pieces fall into place; looking back from his interpretation of *Genesis,* the eye detects beneath the relatively fumbling efforts at Cassiciacum the lines of a synthesis already taking shape. We are at the inmost secret of Augustine's early theory of art: he is elaborating an aesthetic for the fallen soul.

The dominant thrust of that aesthetic becomes clearest in the *Soliloquies.* Augustine is engaged in a dialogue with "Reason": but is it a dialogue after all? Or is "Reason" simply his inmost self? The latter answer is clearly the favored one:[59] and suddenly the reader is prompted to re-examine a number of tantalizing obscurities in the *De Ordine.* There, as Svoboda points out, the work of creating the ascending hierarchy of the liberal *artes* was attributed to "Reason."[60] Our modern eyes quite readily understand that affirmation to mean that the minds of individual men, in the course of human history, have succeeded in inventing these intellectual disciplines; but, apart from the absence of any historical reference whatever, there are too many difficulties in what Augustine positively says on the matter for this interpretation to stand. Closer examination of the texts strongly suggests that our individual souls either have, or quite possibly are, reason—but that our individual reason may be mysteriously identical with the overarching Reason that presides over the beauteous ordering of the entire sensible universe.[61] Not only does Reason impregnate nature with numerical proportions, it works in and through the reason of individual men to erect the ladder of those liberal disciplines whereon the reasoning soul can mount upward to reunification with universal Reason. Again, the firmness of Augustine's synthesis is obscured by the refractoriness of the various materials he is trying to synthesize: the "Supreme Reason," the *Summa Ratio Rerum,* of Stoicism refuses to fit perfectly with the antithetical *Logos* Plotinus puts to work in his treatise *On Providence,* and yet, the ostensible coincidence between them solicits him to toy with their possible identity with one another, as well as with the Christian *Logos* of St. John's Gospel.[62] And the hesitant framework he is tempted to throw about that synthesis is one Plotinus suggests when working in a slightly different register: in *Ennead* V, 1, for example (another treatise we know the Augustine of this early period had read and pondered)[63] Plotinus suggests that the soul may arrive at the necessary knowledge of its lofty station by recognizing that the grades of beauteous order in the sense-world are all its own production, acting in concert with the All-Soul, with which, despite the fall, each soul remains (in some obscure fashion) radically identical.[64] Our individual reasons then, are truly one with "Reason," and the ladder of the arts is designed by "Reason" precisely to entice fallen souls to reintegrate themselves into the sublime unity with, and "in," the All-Soul, which the fall has in some mysterious sense partially sundered.

There were thornier problems bristling about this aspect of his synthesis than the Augustine of Cassiciacum first realized; one by one he will deal with them in turn, discarding in the process features that he finds offensive to his Christian faith. One of the first of such features to go will be the underlying Plotinian assumption that the human soul was truly, in some real though subordinationist sense, divine.[65] The hesitancy of Augustine's formulations occasionally betrays his dim perception, even now, of the problems lowering on his horizon; but it will take him some time to abandon several central features of the view that he is provisionally convinced of now: that our individual souls are somehow one with each other and with All-Soul; that in that obscure one-ness they are responsible for the beauteous ordering of the sense-world, as well as for the ladder of the liberal *artes*; and that the function of beauty, both in nature and in art, is to operate as "admonition" for the soul, reminding it of the higher world of beauty from which it has fallen and to which, in its deepest core, it yearns to return.

Again, it must be stressed that he finds this a convincing "understanding of the faith": a synthesis no less Christian than Neo-Platonist. Eloquent testimony to this can be found in the *Soliloquies*. It begins, whether Plotinus would have approved or no, with a lengthy prayer that calls for aid on a God that is unquestionably the Christian Trinity vested in occasional Neo-Platonic phraseology.[66] It presents us with Augustine's questing impatience for vision of the divine splendor,[67] for that "embrace" —the erotic imagery of *Philosophia* re-enters strongly[68]—he burns for. But, Reason warns him, before that vision is granted him, certain dispositions have to be assured. A moral purification is required, to guarantee that his love for this beauty is single; meanwhile—what could be more Christian?—he must have faith, and hope, and love.[69] Faith he has, Augustine protests; he hopes for that vision, loves and longs for nothing else except as means to its attainment.[70]

But now the Neo-Platonic cast of his "understanding of the faith" becomes more evident: he passes to the anthropological conditions his view of the human quest implies. The soul must be immortal, capable of grasping eternal truth.[71] The sense-world in which it finds itself must be acknowledged as only a "mendacious" image of that higher world of Truth.[72] And— entry of the "reminiscence" theory so intimately connected with Plotinus' conviction of the soul's pre-existence—the liberal disciplines and the process of learning they represent imply the recovery of truth from "oblivion"; all such learning is literally "remembering," rekindling in the soul those residues of the vision it possessed before its fall into the body—vision of the eternal Beauty we once enjoyed, have not entirely forgotten, and to which we still obscurely long to return, to gaze upon in the unabating rapture of beatitude.[73]

Now it becomes plain what Augustine is proposing as the ultimate function of beauty, whether in the visible world or in the *artes*. The term he reverts to, again and again in the Cassiciacum writings, is *admonitio*. Whether it be the fright of a field mouse, the murmur of a running stream in the night, the contrast of victor and vanquished in a cock fight,[74] or any other of the multifarious reflections of Reason's ordering of nature and of the *artes,* they all incite the soul to search for "beauteous

Reason" itself; in all these things Reason is "signaling something," attracting her followers to seek her.[75] The evidence of the *Soliloquies* entitles us to gather all the stray hints scattered throughout the Cassiciacum works into a single, consistent translation for that troubling term. An *admonitio* is, in Augustine's lexicon, quite literally a "reminder"; beauties wherever found are providentially intended to remind us of that beauty we once beheld, beyond all sensible embodiment. Admonishing us, sensible beauties stir our restless hearts, set them musing, remembering—and longing; for escape from this sense-world, which, however beautifully divine Reason has ordered it, forever remains essentially a place of misery for the fallen soul, a ladder providentially designed for its return.[76]

One may feel entitled to question the overall cogency of this "understanding of the faith" but not the fact that it was proposed by a sincere and, in Svoboda's term, "convinced" Christian. And one may seriously wonder how such a view of art—and of the entire human condition—could conceivably become more spiritualized.

2

ART, THE ARTS,

AND ETERNAL ART

THIS IS SCARCELY the occasion for expounding more at length on Augustine's sincerity, nor on the firmness of his Christian convictions. Nor is it my theme to underline the many risks he ran in attempting to elaborate so bold a synthesis of Christian beliefs and the multiform philosophic tendencies of his time. But the *Soliloquies* highlight a feature of his aesthetic that calls for closer attention.

The final portion of that work is grappling with some of the difficulties involved in Plotinus' theory of memory; how can it be said to persist, even in souls apparently incapable of dealing with time-transcending truths?[1] The voice of Reason answers Augustine's query with a set of distinctions on the various types of forgetfulness and recall: the ability to recognize eternal truths, it is suggested, points to a memory "intermediate between forgetfulness and remembering" in the ordinary acceptation of those terms. The truth in question may seem to have been entirely forgotten, yet once the needed reminder comes, "the whole thing suddenly comes back to memory as if a light had been kindled."[2] "Such are those," Reason goes on to say, "who are well educated in the liberal arts. Doubtless in learning them they draw them out from the oblivion that has overwhelmed them, or dig them out, as it were. They are not content until they fully behold the face of Truth, whose splendor glimmers now even in those liberal arts."[3]

The splendorous face of Truth: the expression reminds us once again that for Augustine, Truth is fundamentally identical with Beauty.[4] But we are warned, as well, of a possible danger in Augustine's approach: whatever one may think of the ancients' unshakeable conviction that truth, goodness, and beauty were fundamentally identical—a conviction that Augustine obviously shares—the slow labor of the centuries brought the mediaevals to see that goodness, truth, and beauty were at least formally distinct. The same reality can be both true, good, and beautiful in the ontological sense—food for both the questing understanding, the desire for happiness, and the aesthetic sense of wonder—but the approaches to it as true and good may be distinct in important ways from the approach to it as beautiful.

There are hints of such a distinction in Augustine, particularly when it is question of the good and the beautiful; they are seeds rich with potentiality for later development. The distinction between the *pulchrum* and *aptum,* the beautiful and the fitting, the aesthetic attitude he requires for reconciliation to the evils of our world, imply acknowledgment, however dim, that goodness and beauty are somehow distinct. The same distinction is implied in Augustine's restricting the aesthetic senses to eye and ear: the "lower" senses are too geared to pleasure, too oriented toward the *aptum,* to stand off from their objects with the kind of detachment requisite for aesthetic contemplation. But the text before us, like so many others Svoboda has pointed to, suggests that the insight that went into those hints was at best an unsteady one. To propose, as Augustine does elsewhere, that the liberal arts—in the quasi-scientific sense of that term—provide a favored propaedeutic for the soul bent on glimpsing other-worldly beauty, is tantamount to proposing that the approach to beauty is subject to the same demands as the approach to truth. This, in turn, runs the risk of intellectualizing beauty or, at the worst, rationalizing it entirely.

Marrou's complaint on Augustine's tendency in this direction brought me to probe into the nagging ambiguity that haunts Svoboda's treatment of the term *artes.* Yet Sr. Joseph Arthur would defend Augustine precisely on this score: he was rightly anxious to place art in the service of truth. To gain any insight into the perennial value of Augustine's aesthetic—indeed, even to appreciate it within the terms of his own philosophic view and evaluate its power to render the anthropological service he exacts from it—this sensitive relation between the quest for truth and the delight in beauty requires fuller clarification. Augustine's varied uses of the terms *ars* and *artes* need fuller exploration.

Svoboda is surely right in warning us away from the anachronism of demanding a man of Augustine's time to hold rigidly to distinctions that would come naturally to a modern: between the practical or useful arts, concerned with the "good," and what contemporary terminology would classify as the "fine" arts;[5] between such *artes* as poetry or dance and those *artes* which turn out upon investigation to be far more akin to "sciences," the school disciplines like geometry and grammar.[6] Whether Svoboda has accurately drawn out the implications of Augustine's usage remains doubtful. One of those implications has already become obvious: the twentieth-century reader must beware of thinking that each time the terms *ars* or *artes* appear, they serve to designate what current usage would refer to as the (fine) arts. But the matter hardly ends there.

Augustine uses the term in at least three ways. First, in line with common usage, the term could be used in the singular, a singular normally followed by a term specifying the particular *ars* in question: so, for instance, the *ars bene loquendi,* the *ars gubernandi,* the arts of speech and governance. In such cases the meaning of the term was as often as not practical, useful: it referred to any skill, however common or distinguished, skill in eloquence, or skill in governing. The accent is on technique, "know-how"; its background was the Greek *technê* that threads its way so frequently through Socratic and Platonic discussions of art; the temptation it encouraged was that of judging the "success" of a painting or a poem in terms which apply first and foremost to the accomplishments of the useful or practical arts. In Augustine's terminology, the "beautiful" is in danger of sliding over into an identity with the "fitting."

Augustine's second use of the term occurs more regularly in the plural: here he speaks most commonly of the *artes,* meaning by that the liberal arts or disciplines which formed the backbone of the educational system of his day.[7] The modern's instinctive temptation is to consider poetry, music, and perhaps rhetoric, as strangely out of place in this enumeration of what we would more comfortably call "sciences"; the quest for truth seems to be getting mixed up with the taste for beauty. That instinct receives a slight jolt, however, when Augustine insists not only that numbers and numerical laws govern each one of these *artes* but that the student—even of poetry and music—should be brought to focus his attention on those numerical laws.[8] The implication is, as we shall shortly see, that he takes a far more "scientific" view of poetry, music, and rhetoric than our habit of mind might have led us to expect. A phrase in the *De Immortalitate Animae,* which Augustine blocked out as a sketch for the third book of the *Soliloquies,* is symptomatic in this regard: Augustine speaks of the *ars musica* as present in the *eruditus.* A French translator, working on an understandable assumption, renders that *eruditus* by the term *artiste.*[9] What more natural? Shouldn't "art" be the interior equipment of the "artist"? Yet however odd it may strike us, Augustine would have us query that natural assumption: he meant exactly what he wrote. For "art," in his quasi-scientific understanding of the term, requires a conscious theoretical "knowledge" (*scientia*) of the "numbers" presiding over all beautiful making or doing. And we are back to that danger Marrou alluded to: art is running the risk of being thoroughly rationalized.

But that same text in the *De Immortalitate Animae* brings us to a third way Augustine uses the term *ars.* In this usage, however, the term is much better capitalized: I shall consistently write it as *Ars.* For it refers to that divine world of archetypes which Augustine's Christian Neo-Platonism identifies with the creative Logos of St. John's Gospel: the art in question is the *Ars Divina,* the creative divine "artistry" and the Divine Beauty considered as normative upon all human judgments of beauty. To explain briefly, the stock example from Plato's *Republic* will serve: when a skilled carpenter decides to make a bed, he must have some idea of what makes a "good" bed, a bed that is all a bed *should be.* Where, however, does he derive this idea of bed? A Platonist like Plotinus or Augustine argues that the form or archetypal model—in the Platonic sense, the Idea or Eidos—is more than an idea in the craftsman's mind or creative imagination: it must exist in a purely intelligible world whose structures and relations are normative of the structures and relations which ought to hold in this "image-world" of sense-realities. The genuine artist, then, begins with an intuitive knowledge of the appropriate ideal Form and proceeds to embody that form, as far as can be, in matter.

That world of forms the orthodox Platonist insists is quite literally that: another, higher world, a system of subsistent realities interrelated to form a perfect, intelligible pattern. It con-

stitutes the normative model of all artistic activity here below
and hence governs the rightness of the knowledge from which
all such activity is held to proceed, whenever it is truly authentic.[10] Again, the view of art is frankly intellectualistic. But
it is more: it claims to require at its crucial incipient stage an
intuitive insight that is thoroughly disincarnate. For Plotinus
and Augustine, the contemplative insight into this intelligible
Beauty implies that the viewer has turned entirely away from
sense and all sense-images and has fixed the inner, higher eye
of the soul upon an eternal *Ars* that utterly transcends the world
of sensible realities.

The Latin *ars,* then, was already a multivalent term; this may
have had something to do with the way it slides about in Augustine's use of it. But there is more to it than that. He would surely
have consciously intended a distinction between *Ars* as transcendent model and the skill whereby an accomplished craftsman
goes about his work. We can hardly expect him consciously to
have distinguished the skill of a carpenter from the skill of a
flutist, singer, or painter: not only did the ancients fail to distinguish between useful and fine arts, but the intellectual insight
a Platonist would require for elegant accomplishment in both
types of performance would argue for blurring any such distinction. Nor would our modern distinction between art and science
have appealed to him as crucial: the first, and critical moment
of any art production, the ultimate and indispensable operation
in any act of art appreciation, was an act of "knowing" (*scientia*).

On this point, surely, Svoboda is correct in stressing the "constancy" of Augustine's aesthetic thinking. There are some minor
differences between the aesthetic of the *De Ordine* and the later
aesthetic of the *De Musica,* but this particular accent remains
firm: the very first move he makes in the *De Musica* aims to show
that "music," in his understanding of it, is quite properly a
"science" (*scientia*). Any nightingale can sing and not know what
the song is all about. The most uncultivated of flutists can hear
a melody and play it: but he does so, Augustine would claim,
by mere unthinking "imitation."[11] Neither of them, then, is a
musicus in the proper sense. For song, melody, poetic meter all
embody numerical sequences and relationships; what qualifies a
man as a *musicus* in the authentic sense is his capacity to rise
to an understanding, an intuitive vision of the laws of numerical
relationship in their pure, disembodied form. The true *musicus*
is the *eruditus*; the man characterized "not by numerical performance but by numerical knowledge": *non numerosa faciendo,*

as the *De Ordine* puts it, but *numeros cognoscendo.*[12] The *ars* Augustine denominates as *musica* is, therefore, quite correctly classed among the liberal *artes,* that graduated series of *disciplinae,* "exercises" for the mind, designed to remind the soul of the transcendent world of *Ars* it once beheld and still in its mute depths desires to behold again.

A modern would instinctively translate Augustine's ladder of the *artes* into a graduated series of steps to train the mind in dealing with abstractions, and no more than that. He would find himself baffled by the contention that this ladder of abstraction could lead to anything else than higher and higher, more and more generalized abstractions: the world of pure numerical relationships appears to be no more than a purely mental world, product of the mind's activity. Augustine's claim, however, is the contrary: with orthodox Platonism he would contend that the Ideas, or Forms, which the mind succeeds in intuiting at the term of this ascent is a world of "truths," not merely propositional truths, but Beings, *onta,* and indeed, True Beings, *ontôs onta.*[13] The difficulties inherent in this claim have been discussed, starting with Aristotle, all down the history of philosophy; so paradoxical does the claim appear that more than one commentator on Plato has been led to propose that Plato never meant to make it or, having made it, never meant it to be taken literally. But Augustine clearly makes that claim and faces us anew with the paradoxes involved in it: for his ladder of the *artes* is identifiably a ladder (in our modern term) of numerical abstractions become increasingly general and comprehensive.[14] How then can such a process lead the mind to an intuition of true "beings," boasting all the existential richness our minds attach to the individual concrete existent? And how can we accept the further assurances that all these truths are "in" the single unchanging Truth, the eternal Word[15] and not as separated off from one another but, on the contrary, each of them, as "parts" of the intelligible world, mysteriously coextensive with the whole of that world?[16]

Socrates, when leading his hearers' minds up a similar ladder of beauties in the *Symposium,* makes a similar claim; the education of the guardians in the *Republic* likewise claims to fit them for the "vision" of the intelligible sun of Goodness. In more than one instance, it should be remarked, something very like a mystical tone presides over Plato's descriptions of that final "vision."[17] And mystical Augustine's tone becomes, as well: there is no doubt that we are here at one of the strongest reasons for Plato's, and

Augustine's, perennial fascination for the human spirit. But does the mystical tone quite fit? Does an aesthetic of numerical abstractions really earn it? Is there a genuine continuity between the increased power of mathematical reasoning and the power to achieve—or be accorded—the quasi-mystical vision of transcendent Beauty? One may seriously doubt it; and to doubt it means to question not only the value of Augustine's entire aesthetic theory but, more crucially, its power to furnish the "service" his religious anthropology exacts from it.

One of the roots of Augustine's position is the conviction this chapter started with: that Truth is Beauty. This has led him to assume, a trifle too easily perhaps, that the approach to beauty is fundamentally akin to the approach to truth. And at this stage in his career, he is quite serious: the approach to truth is along the road of mathematics. The *Confessions* informs us that shortly before this point in his career, in the face of his academic temptation, he set one fundamental requirement for the approach to truth; he demanded that the reality of the spiritual should be as manifest to him as the truth of the proposition "seven plus three is ten."[18] The torment of his doubt was real; his desire for the rest, security of certainty must not be underestimated. But the mathematical flavor of that ideal of certainty entails important consequences. His refutation of the universal skepticism generally attributed to the Academics shows him still faithful to that ideal. Zeno's famous "definition" he artfully proves to be, ironically, a very model of intelligible transparency: much like "seven plus three is ten," it turns out to be an analytic statement whose unquestionable truth flashes on the intuitive mind the moment it is properly understood.[19] Indeed, all the certainties he claims in the *Contra Academicos* turn out, on examination, to be attempts at framing an indubitable set of just such enduring, unshakable analytic propositions.[20] Only in such "other-worldly" objects can the mind, embattled by doubt, find the restful, peaceful certainty it quests for. History supports what Augustine's own performance instantiates, that the human mind is repeatedly tempted to consider, as the most perfect examples of such intuitively clear propositions, the propositions of mathematics and geometry. Svoboda points up the fact that Augustine's numerical aesthetic rests largely on his confidence that embodied relationships of the mathematical type are reflections of the eternal, unchanging nature of Truth itself;[21] it is significant that the *disciplina* most prominently invoked in the *Soliloquies'* discussion of the ascent to Truth-Beauty is geometry[22] and that throughout his early career, the attempts at *exercitatio animi,* the "exercising of the mind, show Augustine's repeated preference for following geometric or mathematical pathways to the higher world.[23]

The persistent attraction of mathematics is, of course, a permanent feature of Platonism. In Plato's own case, historians attribute accentuation of the mathematical tendency in his thinking to his growing receptivity to Pythagorean influences: the "Forms" of his middle period appear to take on more and more the properties of intelligible numbers, whence the endless discussions on whether or where the *mathematika* "belong" in his world of Forms. We know that the doxographies of Augustine's period abounded with Neo-Pythagorean speculations; more to the point, Varro, whose work on the "disciplines" Augustine pillaged for his *De Ordine,* was a storehouse of Neo-Pythagoreanism. Augustine experiences no embarrassment in admitting this: when Alypius, at the end of the Dialogue, congratulates him for having presented them afresh the "venerable and divine teachings" of Pythagoras, he immediately pays homage to Varro.[24]

Faithful, again, to Platonism, Augustine will stress the mysteriousness of the mind's surprising confidence in its grasp of such "eternal and unchanging" truths: we cannot, he argues, have derived them from the contingent and changing perceptions, or images, of sensation; we must, therefore, possess them in the deep places of memory.[25] The solution is Platonism's answer to the still live problem of the mind's *a priori* workings: whence—in a slight adjustment of Augustine's way of putting the question—do we derive the normative ideals in terms of which we "judge" how the entities of our world ought to be? The ideals that concern Augustine are various: he will tend to assume that the cognitive ideals of the *Contra Academicos* are similar in nature and requirements to the moral ideals he will turn to in the *De Libero Arbitrio*[26] or to the aesthetic ideals he focuses upon in the *De Ordine.*[27] One conclusion from his examination of cognitive ideals he will then apply to the others: they must be objects of an intuition entirely beyond and free from dependence on the realm of sense. But since his models for such intuition are heavily mathematical in flavor, he is led half-consciously to assume a quasi-mathematical cast as present in all such intuitions.

This transfusion of Neo-Pythagoreanism only serves to accentuate a trait Augustine inherited from his training as a grammarian and rhetorician; without unkindness or injustice, it could be called a rationalistic streak. Marrou has shown how much the liberal arts training of Augustine's time was a child of rationalism. The treatment of poetry will serve as an example: far from concentrating on poetry as what we would call an art form, the educator of Augustine's time more often treated it as an object of dessicating grammatical analysis. The poem was chopped up into lines and words, then each dismembered atom subjected to the driest word-by-word examination.[28] The *De Magistro* shows Augustine selecting a line of Vergil and leading his son through something very like this process, though there the situation is complicated by the "point" of religious epistemology to which he intends the analysis to lead. Despite that complication, however, this much is clear: such treatment of poetry was scarcely designed to bring the student to appreciate the "long reaches and the peaks of song," to resonate with the great movement of Vergil's vision, to sense, much less reflectively to grasp, the peculiarities of a medium in which perception, sensibility, imagination, and mind all fuse in the creative incandescence that makes the genuine poem an approach to the world of human experience, peculiar and quite incomparable to other approaches. When first we hear Macbeth's "Tomorrow and tomorrow and tomorrow," all the preceding action, indeed, all the pathetic grandeur of human striving is gathered into the line. Were the importunate voice of the schoolmaster then to interject the question: "What part of speech is 'tomorrow'?" a spell would snap, we would feel a moment had been desecrated. Such desecrations the grammarian of Augustine's time quite regularly perpetrated, and Augustine himself seems persuaded they were justified. He never seems reflectively to have valued the subtle attunement, the deepening of sensibility that came with such experiences as his youthful sorrow over Dido's sorrow: far better, far more "useful," the learning of words and the meanings they denote in the pragmatic banality of everyday speech.

In fairness, it must be said that Augustine's treatment of poetry is not entirely of a piece: his "numerical" perspective will lead him, in the *De Musica,* to stress the formal beauties of metrical proportions. But poetry, he also suggests, uses words to express a *significatio*[29]—a *significatio* which he seems to assume can be explained on much the same lines as the ancients followed in explaining "meaning" in ordinary linguistic discourse.[30] Somewhat like the man who claimed to translate Keats into purely designative speech and thereby catch the meaning without all the unnecessary frills, Augustine tacitly assumes that whether they occur in prose or poetry, words are words and there is the end of it. No wonder, then, the *De Ordine* accords to grammar the ruling function over poetry.[31]

But whichever one chooses as the content of the intelligible insight to which poetry ministers—whether the formal numerical beauty of meter, or some transsensual *significatio*—the question recurs: what is to be said of all the sensible, imaginative, and emotional resonances that accrue to words when they become the medium of poetry? Augustine's solution is radical: earlier he flirted with the Stoic position that the higher senses, at least, penetrated with rationality, could judge on the presence of sensible beauty. That position, put in modern terms, would claim that the total human subject, sensitive as well as intellectual, is the percipient of poetic beauty. That flirtation soon breaks off, however; Augustine soon comes to reduce that judgment of sense to a reaction of pleasure or displeasure, thereby sapping the force of his original distinction between the "higher" and the "lower" senses, between those capable and those incapable of a proper aesthetic response.[32] The "beautiful," *pulchrum*, in the sensible world at least, is subtly fusing with the "fitting" or *aptum*: Augustine's suspicion of sense pleasures will result in repeated warnings that the reader, or hearer, attend to the formal beauty, or to the intelligible meaning, rather than be caught up in the web of sensual appeal.[33] And, he is obstinately convinced, that grasp of intelligible meaning, of numerical form, is the work of mind alone; sensual imagery can, in the last analysis, only distract from that grasp—the true appreciation of beauty comes only when sense and imagination have resolutely been left behind. The *De Musica* will test this dichotomized version of art's strange alchemy; the *Confessions* will show Augustine wondering over the peculiar force the Ambrosian hymns derive from their combining heights of meaning with the allures of sound. But the antitheses on which he has constructed his aesthetic leave him disarmed before the problem.

His rhetorical background does not help this situation:[34] one of the devices Augustine seems fondest of is antithesis, and his use of it is often of a somewhat facile sort. How frequently his philosophizing runs along the rather effortless lines of stark contrast: flesh *versus* spirit, visible *versus* invisible, temporal *versus* eternal, action *versus* contemplation—disjunctions like these leap all too readily to his mind and pen. That there could possibly be a paradoxical ingredient of spirit in flesh, of the eternal in the temporal, of the contemplative in the active; that this

ingredience might test, and testing, reform the original antithesis, is something that does not naturally occur to him. It did
occur to the later Plato, and to the later Plotinus; but, in his
earlier years at least, Augustine's typical performance is that of
the man sublimely confident in reason's forthright, "clear and
distinct" analyses, definitions, divisions.

A grammarian, a rhetorician in the twilight of ancient culture,
and now armed with the sanction of Neo-Pythagoreanism: one
could hope for equipment better designed for the refinement of
observation, the sensitivity of analysis required in the aesthetic
domain, so stubbornly refractory to rationalism. But it is hardly
a novelty to suggest that rationalism provides flawed equipment
for elaborating a satisfactory aesthetic; it is more to the point of
this study that it furnishes Augustine a seriously questionable
aesthetic for the service his religious anthropology demands of
it. I have been enlarging upon the difficulty of passing upward
along a ladder of abstractions, suddenly to arrive at the fullness
of true Being; but for Augustine's purposes, that difficulty is
immediately compounded by another: how will practice in en-
tertaining numerical, geometrical forms—impersonal as they
are and ever threatening to congeal into lifeless rigidity—truly
exercise the mind to glimpse a *Logos* that is living and personal?

Augustine is not entirely insensitive to these difficulties. Reason asks him in the *Soliloquies* what kind of knowledge he requires of the God he yearns to "see": would it be the kind of
clear and certain knowledge he claims to have of geometric
figures? No, Augustine answers, for the knowledge of geometry
does not fill him with delight (*gaudium*) he expects to receive
from the vision of God.[35] Significantly, the conclusion forces
him to revert to the classic Platonic image, with all its overtones
of the concrete: God is the intelligible Sun, illumining all such
intelligible realities, to make them knowable; the difference
between the vision of God and the certain knowledge of geometry
is as wide as the difference between the bodily eye's pleasure in
contemplating the beauty of earth and its delight in the superior
beauty of the serene heavens.[36] The resort, once again, is to
imagery and comparison; Augustine has been compelled to shift
into another thought register, quite foreign to the sharp uni-
vocities of rationalism.

The second book of the *De Libero Arbitrio* furnishes another
instance of his uneasiness. The Book of *Wisdom* confirms his
conviction that God created all in accordance with number;
numbers remain the source of all beauties whether of nature or

of art.[37] The rules of moral wisdom are, he submits, like the
rules of number, both unchangeable and evident to the mind
upon inspection. The route toward moral ideals is essentially
the same, therefore, as the route toward epistemological certainty. How is it, then, Evodius inquires, that good arithmeticians
are many, while the morally wise are so relatively few? Perhaps
the kind of knowledge involved in true wisdom is, after all, "far
more venerable" than mental agility in dealing with number?

Augustine strives to meet the difficulty: both wisdom and
number require, for their just appreciation, that the beholder
transcend body and sense; once that purification has been ef-
fected, their fundamental kinship will become evident. Then
number and wisdom will be seen as like light and warmth, respectively, both emanating from the same divine source.[38]

The parallel between the warmth of moral wisdom and the
colder light of numerical knowledge is suggestive of another of
the difficulties with which Augustine's antithesis between sense
and intellect faces him. In the *Soliloquies,* Reason asks if the
knowledge Augustine has of his dearest friend, Alypius, might
serve as a model for the knowledge he seeks of God. The lead is
a promising one; it might conceivably compel recognition of the
peculiarities involved in our knowledge of other persons—a type
of knowledge bearing striking analogies with aesthetic insight.
But we are disappointed: no, replies Augustine firmly, he does
not know Alypius enough (*satis*) for his senses may present him
with their questionable reports on his friend's body, but the
knowledge of his soul is a task for understanding (*intellectus*).
On the quest for such knowledge of the soul Augustine has only
recently embarked.[39] The conclusion has something desperately
unreal about it, but it follows straight from the logic of his
epistemology.

There is, however, a deep common bond between these three
instances: the knowledge of God, of another person's interiority,
even of such moral ideals as prudence, justice, and the rest, all
three involve a type of grasp which, like aesthetic intuition, func-
tions symbolically. There are, admittedly, important differences
between these four symbolic modes of thought, but for the moment it is suggestive that in all of them one may speak of a
warmth in the process quite unlike the relative coolness of geometric knowledge; they all require subjective dispositions of the
knower to place him in sympathetic resonance with the known;
and all of them imply a passage of what we can for the present
vaguely term mediation—the grasp of the symbolized must pass

through mediating symbols, whether those symbols be images like the Sun, the gestures and expressions of a friend, or the concrete embodiment of ideals, like justice, or courage, in another person.[40]

What is frequently referred to as aesthetic intuition is, I submit, one of the richest loci for exploring the peculiarities of such symbolic knowledge. It is far from clear that Augustine ever explored this phenomenon on its own terms: too often, he treats it as a corollary drawn from his epistemological conception that sets up an antithetic relationship between the operations of sense and intellect. Sense, he tends to think, apprehends the visible, sensible symbol; only the mind can attain to vision of the invisible reality that is symbolized. The visible sun may furnish a symbolic image of the divine intelligible Sun; the audible word or visible gesture may function as an exterior sign conveying—more or less trustily—knowledge of some inner personal conception, intention, or attitude. But the divine world, like the interior reality of the person speaking or gesturing, remains inaccessible to sense—it can be seen only by the inner, higher eye of the mind. And Augustine is impatient for direct, immediate vision, whether of the inner personal, or higher divine, realities in question; his impatience leads him to think of images, signs, symbols generally, as merely images, signs, symbols; and so he is inclined to rank all modes of indirect, mediated "knowledge by signs" as deficient *pis-allers* in contrast to the immediate knowledge he has implicitly supposed as his ideal of true knowledge.[41]

Instead, therefore, of considering the symbolic presentation as both revealing and concealing the intelligible reality it conveys to understanding, Augustine regularly stresses the "opacity" of the symbol: one of his favorite metaphors is that of the "veil" which conceals the reality that lies behind it; it must be removed before we can see the splendor it presently obscures from our spiritual gaze.[42]

This view of symbolic knowledge is exacerbated by the working of an allied principle in his aesthetic: he thinks of the embodiment of thought into words, of interior attitude into sign and gesture, of artistic meaning into sensible forms, as necessarily accompanied by a degeneration, somewhat as though the limpid purity of the higher—thought or meaning—were inevitably soiled, deformed, debased by its descent into the inferior realm of materiality.

A view of sense and intellect as antithetic and a conviction that the intelligible, spiritual, "higher" must suffer some degeneration through its entry into the sensible, bodily, "lower" realm: these two principles explain (in large part, at least), Augustine's repeated injunctions that in order to see what the beauties of the sense-world would admonish us to see, we must turn away from the admonitions themselves—away from all signs, symbols, Protean pointers—and consult the higher, spiritual Light that floods the soul "interiorly," enabling it to achieve direct, immediate vision of the true, unchanging realities above it—realities of which the world of sense presents only shifting, "mendacious" images.

It is initially tempting to write this whole matter off as simply evidence of Augustine's fidelity to the Platonic tradition. And surely Plato and Plotinus never weary of issuing warnings of the sort: for the pure, direct grasp of the true, other world, the reader is repeatedly urged to turn away from the images and appeals of sense. Yet closer examination of their actual thinking processes casts serious doubt on their own fidelity to that principle. Plato's real "place of the Forms," it has been suggested, is in fact the historical person of Socrates himself: in and through Socrates' concrete self-revelation, it has been strongly argued, Plato caught sight of those moral ideals, the *Eidoi of* justice, wisdom, bravery, and *sophrosunê,* that he dimly strove to relate to the highest cosmic *Eidoi,* the Good and the Beautiful.[43] The ladder method of the *Republic* and (though less obviously so) of the *Symposium* initially manifests all the characteristics of abstract thinking, but the mystical air that presides over the final upthrust to vision points to another mode of thought that has secretly been functioning all along: the Forms are in crucial respects the distillation of something very akin to an aesthetic experience that runs as a powerful undercurrent in Plato's thought from start to finish.[44] Despite all his manifold strictures on poetry and art, despite all the seductive appeal of Pythagorean mathematicism, it was much less Plato the strictly scientific thinker, much more the incomparable literary artist and seer, who succeeded in bestowing on Western thought the alluring heritage of the world of Forms. And it could be strongly argued that his success can be attributed to the way he joined, in a superb effort of symbolic thinking, the interpersonal experience of Socrates' interior, his quest for moral ideals, and his aspiration toward ideal Beauty. But in order to achieve this synthesis, he had to violate nearly every canon his outspoken aesthetic laid down.

A similar irony greets us when we study Plotinus' thought processes. The warnings are there—we must turn away from sense, image, all trafficking with the corporeal world that imprisons the soul: but the attractions of mathematical rationalism have been severely exorcised. Plotinus' treatise *On Numbers* (*Ennead* VI, 6) can hardly have functioned as strong encouragement for Augustine's Neo-Pythagoreanism in the *De Ordine;* there is an ironic thrill in watching Plotinus' mind move from speculation on those relatively lifeless numerical forms, to his rhapsodic finale, where the "measure" that presides over his intelligible world slides over to mean both beauty and life.[45] To Augustine's unrelieved instance that the Divine must be absolutely immutable, Plotinus brings a balancing accent: the unchangeable must also teem with superabundant life, primal, bright, and radiant, "here dimly seen, there purely." One thinks of the explosive rhetorical question in the *Sophist,* where Plato intimates that the congealed immutability of an overworld conceived on the model of mathematics and geometry will no longer do: it must not stand "immutable in solemn aloofness" but shimmer with "movement, life, intelligence."[46] That conviction seems to have penetrated Plotinus' way of envisaging the true world: despite his professed suspicion of imagery and imagination, his descriptions of the intelligible glitter with some of the most poetic imagery in philosophic literature, and the outstanding feature of them all is their "living" quality.[47]

Hence, too, his stress on the artist's obligation to penetrate his works, not so much with the frozen symmetries of number and geometry, as with "life."[48] The ladder of beauties becomes an ascending hierarchy of living forms; there is no discontinuity, no shock of mind, when they catapult our vision into a living world above. Nor are we overly surprised when his accent shifts to limning beauties here below, whether of nature or of art, as so many *agalmata,* so many concrete "embodiments," not opaque, but transparent with the beauty "there" that shines out from them.[49]

Finally, again despite his professed avowals, Plotinus' efforts to lead our minds to the higher world do not discard but employ sensual images in a uniquely powerful way. Bréhier describes the process with the phrase "dynamic image";[50] the treatise *On the Intelligible Beauty* provides an excellent example of it. Plotinus is trying to help us surmount our resistance to admitting of an intelligible world with the paradoxical property whereby "each member" remains itself, in distinction from all others, while at the same time all members together form a single unity. He asks us to imagine a transparent globe or sphere, "holding all the things of the universe." Keeping this image in mind, we are then asked to correct it: imagine another sphere, this one "stripped of magnitude and spatial differences." Now our minds are urged to make a final leap, toward contemplating an intelligible world wherein "each is all," one undivided "divine power," but a power "of many facets"; each shares the "one existence" and at the same time remains distinct from all the others, in a divine world so far beyond our usual conceptions that its "very members are infinites."[51]

The paradoxical conclusion defies our ordinary ways of thinking; it is, as we have seen, the same paradoxical conclusion Augustine would have us grasp.[52] But Plotinus has coached us into approaching it by the same route as he had used to such stunning effect in *Ennead* VI, 4–5, *On the Integral Omnipresence of the Authentic Existent*: to correct the conclusions we might draw from the first-level image, he asks us not to abandon imagery entirely but to "imagine another . . . sphere," one whose properties run directly counter to the first. The deficiencies of image-thinking are corrected by bringing the initial image to a second stage, then urging our metaphysical imaginations to leap beyond that stage as well, to the desired insight into the intelligible realm. Despite Plotinus' many disclaimers in other places, the process is not one of abandoning, of turning away from sensible image, but of using imagery to the point of strain and shatter: at the instant of shatter, he trusts, intelligible insight will occur.[53]

And despite his own disclaimers, I submit, this is a close analogue to the very process Augustine follows in vaulting past all the discontinuities his abstract rationalism sets up for him. We saw him speaking of God as the intelligible sun, irradiating the realm of geometric truths he prefers to think of as among the clearest reflections of eternal Truth: he must shift into an imaginative key in order to make that leap. Both treatises in which Plotinus most vividly illustrates this method have left their mark on Augustine's thinking and writing; when finally, in the *Confessions*, he coaches our minds to see the intelligible light the *platonici* helped him see at Milan in 386, the steps he takes are startlingly reminiscent of those Plotinus outlines in his treatise on omnipresence.[54] Like Plato, like Plotinus, he employs a method that his express theory of art would persuade him to deprecate; a method that, had he made it the object of conscious reflection, might have furnished him with a far different aesthetic, capable of describing the work of his own artistic imagination—and more adequate to the anthropological service he exacts from it.

But it would, as well, have tested the stark antitheses on which his anthropology is built; compelled him to query the numerical and geometric rationalism of his early prescriptions for the mind's "exercise"; and considerably modified the spiritualization of the arts whose rigidities were only further hardened by the Neo-Pythagorean enthusiasm of this early period.

That rationalization of the arts has not, I repeat, entirely escaped Svoboda's notice; it remains to be seen, however, whether he fully took its measure when insisting on his curve of spiritualization. The irony is that the rationalized view he has of the liberal disciplines persuades Augustine to devaluate art—in the modern sense of that term—precisely in proportion to the high value he sets on the *artes*: for it is something more like science that he values, the disembodied insight into pure number; his high regard for the disciplines is based on the service he expects them to render toward exercising the mind, strengthening it to turn away from sense and the world of bodies, to make a leap toward a disincarnate vision beyond all sensible embodiments. In a word, he asks the *artes* to help us leave behind the entire incarnate world of art. The rationalization of which Marrou complained is meant to subserve a Neo-Pythagoreanized version of Plotinian spiritualism, one become so radical that it constitutes a quiet but firm imperative for art to sign its own death warrant. Again, it is difficult to imagine how such an evaluation could genuinely become even more spiritual.

The nice irony is that, despite his firm and sincere intention of presenting an "understanding" of Christian faith, Augustine's view at Cassiciacum is more spiritual than Christianity would require, indeed, far more spiritual than it will allow. Symptomatic of this is Augustine's frustrated attempt to inveigle Monica into his "way of the disciplines"; she was, even counting all her limitations, the most unquestionably Catholic Christian figure at Cassiciacum; a theory that does not fit her way of living the Christian life becomes immediately suspect, as Augustine seems uncomfortably aware. But he manifestly fails in all his attempts to persuade her that the rationalized intellectualism of his "order of disciplines" is for her as well as for himself and his disciples.[55]

He is, of course, tempted to agree with Licentius that this reluctance is due to Monica's "superstitious" preference for remaining at the liminal, "cradle" stage of unreflective faith in the word of authority; hence her refusal to pass onward to the divinely ordered understanding of the faith, as a way to eventual vision.[56] Later he will be of another mind: the experience they share at Ostia will make him wonder if it was not rather he who had not understood her life, the Christian life of faith.[57] Part of the reason lies in the way the early Augustine tends to conceive of faith: it is, as Magnus Löhrer accurately describes it, an act *ohne innere Einsicht,* a kind of blind adhesion without any glimmer of insight.[58] In the *Soliloquies* Augustine protests the firmness of his faith but protests just as strongly his impatient desire to "see." Faith is depicted as grounding, motivating the task of self-purification that will eventually enable "reason," the *aspectus animae,* to "see"; it assures the novice that the unseen object of beatifying vision is truly there, turns the eye of reason in the proper direction.[59] But, in a return to the familiar image, Augustine desires to gaze upon the beauteous "Wisdom" *nullo interposito velamento,* stripped of the veil which, by implication, presently hides her from his sight.[60] The opacity that operates throughout his view of symbolic mediation operates here as well. Faith, in the title of a slightly later work, is "of things that are unseen" (*Fides rerum quae non videntur*); it is regularly described as according the soul no inchoation of that longed-for vision, however filtered or prismatized.

The object of faith's adhesion is, moreover, the invisibile intelligible world of divine splendor: the Truth-Beauty which Augustine identifies with the Second Person of the Christian Trinity. This eternal Christ in his timeless radiance is what the Christian soul longs to see in an ecstasy of vision. This eternal Christ became incarnate: yes, but all his human, historic words Augustine thinks of as sensible "outward admonitions" (*foris admonet*). They perform essentially the same function as any other admonition: they elicit our belief in his unique authority, but in doing so, they turn our glance "inward" to where He "teaches" us (*intus docet*) to aspire to the vision of the intelligible Light, to the vision of the supernal splendor the term "Christ" designates when referring to the divine component of His theandric reality.[61] It is not in and through the humanity of Christ that faith's eye gains access to His divinity; the believer must heed Christ's outward admonitions, but then, as with all admonitions, turn "inward" and *away* from them, in order to ascend the disincarnate steps toward that light.

Garriebam quasi peritus, Augustine later says of his Christological views at this time: "I gabbled on like one who knew,"[62] but the *sacramentum* contained in "The Word was made Flesh," "I could not conceive."[63] It would be expecting much of a recent convert, in the quite possibly confused state of Milanese Christology some sixty-five years before the Council of Chalcedon, to require of him a fully adequate grasp of how humanity and divinity are related in this *sacramentum*; but it must be added that Augustine's stark and rather facile contrasts between visible and invisible, temporal and eternal, bodily and spiritual and instruments a shade too blunt for dealing with the mystery.

Part of the irony of Augustine's failure is the fact that Plotinus, especially in his later writings, provides fertile suggestions for thinking out some of the very aspects of the Christian life where the new convert's thought is weakest. The treatise on omnipresence, *Ennead* VI, 4–5 is only one example of where Plotinus finds himself forced to pay far more attention than in some of his earlier works to what I shall, for the present, call the "ingredience" of the higher in the lower world. *Ennead* V, 8 develops a provocative line of speculation on how Egyptian hieroglyphics suggest, much as an art work might, the lack of discursiveness in the intelligible world, showing forth how the Ideas are not propositional truths, but Beings (*onta*). That rich suggestion is followed by another, that Ideas may be envisaged as *agalmata*, each bodying forth in a species of translucence the inner wealth of its ontic truth and beauty. He goes on to say that man who has "seen" this world of beauty will—and the suggestion is echoed but left unexploited by the early Augustine[64]—become himself, even in this sensible, corporeal world, an *agalma*, a concrete embodiment, in and through which others may catch glimmerings of the splendor which, once glimpsed, penetrates the seer through and through.[65]

The theme is strongly reminiscent of the Platonic Socrates, that Silenus figure which, once "opened," was seen to contain the images of the gods inside him. Plato returns again and again to that mysterious experience of his youth, to that encounter with the beloved which is at the same time encounter with a transcendent world of value embodied in, yet stretching infinitely "beyond," the concrete person involved in the immediate encounter. The *agalma* theme as he develops it in the *Laws*—where household shrines, the venerable aged, and the starry heavens are variously proposed as *agalmata* of the divine[66]—might even represent a conscious development of the paradoxical insight of the *Phaedrus,* in which, unlike the other Forms, Beauty alone can make itself manifest to the sensuous perceiver.[67]

It has frequently been said that the attempt by Augustine and others in the early Church to express the Christian mystery in the categories of Hellenic thought ranged from the heroically quixotic to something in the neighborhood of the perversely catastrophic. Even the few instances singled out above intimate that the matter may not have been all that simple; they tempt the mind to think that even the Platonic tradition—for I have said nothing about Aristotle and little about the Stoics—possessed richer resources than the early Augustine ever succeeded in tapping. They might well have furnished him with a far more delicate set of instruments than he actually employs, for unfolding the wealth contained in the personal encounter with the incarnate Christ that lies at the heart of Christianity; for unfolding what surely lay, without his having the terms to express it, at the heart of his own religious experience. Probing the close analogies that bind aesthetic, moral, and interpersonal experience, he might have broken through some of his more facile antitheses and groped toward more adequate ways of understanding the faith experience whereby the Christian comes to detect, embodied in Christ, incarnate and risen, what Paul terms the "fullness of the Godhead."[68]

There is, however, one remarkable passage in the *Contra Academicos* where Augustine comes very close to making this breakthrough. He is describing to Romanianus the propaedeutic for vision that, to him, the Cassiciacum experience represents. He is, as always, eager for the vision of the very face (*facies*) of the Truth, Wisdom, Beauty to which he refers by the single name, *Philosophia.* "A hidden Providence," he suggests to his former patron,

has decreed to arouse that divine faculty of yours, which has been benumbed, as it were, by some kind of sleep or lethargy (*somno sopitum*) of this life . . . Awake, I pray you, awake (*Evigila, evigila*) . . . [*Philosophia*] nourishes and cares for me (*nutrit et fovet*) . . . . [and] promises to give a lucid demonstration of the most true and distinct God; and even now she deigns to furnish a glimpse of Him, as it were, through luminous clouds (*quasi per lucidas nubes ostentare dignatur*).[69]

It is suggestive that the numb drowsiness, the wakening, the vision of the shining visage of Truth, and the further glimpse of the divine splendor through those luminous clouds, all these features strongly recall the Apostles' experience on the Mount of the Transfiguration.[70] Significant for our purposes, though, is the fact that Augustine's more habitual mode of relating the visible and the invisible has here given way to a far more positive kind of relation. Saying nothing for the moment of Christ's own glory directly seen, the "luminous clouds," *sacramentum* of the Father's glory, are for once not thought of as perfectly opaque; they are translucent. The light from the "other side" is caught, however filtered, shining both in and through the visible medium. Strongly, though momentarily suggested, is another way of conceiving the relation of symbol to symbolized, a way infinitely more germane to understanding the interpersonal experience residing at the heart of Christian faith: the experience of Christ precisely as incarnate embodiment of the "splendor of the Father's glory." As with the Socratic experience, one need not turn away from the sensible embodiment; one need but plumb its depth to find it the place of a universe of value "in" it and at the same time stretching infinitely "beyond."

All of this suggests another, though for the moment a merely possible, reason for the *De Musica's* later deprecation of the *disciplinae liberales*—the *artes* in Augustine's meaning of the term —and his rejection of the high evaluation the Cassiciacum dialogues put upon them. That rejection, the modern reader is tempted to think, could conceivably have stemmed from Augustine's dawning realization that Christianity is, in fact, far less spiritual than his earlier version of Christian Neo-Platonism would have it. For Christ has come to the humble, even to the much abused flutist; He draws the Christian to Himself, far less by some intellectualist leap into the incorporeal realm, far more by the *clair-obscur* discernment of faith, by the sacramental touch of His body, by a grace that works not only in the rarefied air of a contemplative Plotinopolis but also, if not especially, in the humdrum, everyday encounter with the neighbor. *Garriebam quasi peritus,* Augustine says of his first Neo-Platonic fervor: "I gabbled on like one who knew." But in those "Platonic books" there was nothing of the fact of Incarnation.

And yet, paradoxical as it may seem, there was much more than he saw to help him come to grips with the *Sacramentum* hidden in those words *Verbum caro factum,* "the Word made flesh." For the incarnate condition is above all a school of patience, and the very mystery of transfiguration was, one may think, a momentary concession to the understandable impatience of the Apostles, eager to see the kingdom established, not in parable or sign, nor subject to the slow working of time but here, now, and with blinding clarity; with the blinding clarity Augustine sought as quietus to his mind's agonized quest for unchanging truth, certainly possessed; with the ultimacy that made him restless with all intermediary goods, in his striving for the highest Good, enduring and unfading, that alone, he was convinced, could put his heart at rest. It may be that the heart's quest for the highest Good sanctions such a holy impatience as Augustine's was. It is less certain that impatience for the clarities and certainties— mathematical, analytic, intelligible, whatever—of a pythagore-anized Neo-Platonism, is a trusty formula for attaining to truth in all its sinuous complexities.

But beauty, as Augustine himself was brought, however unsteadily, to see, enlists us in a school of patience, very much as Incarnation does. It exacts a regard for its intermediaries far less hurried than Augustine's was for intermediary "goods," a contemplation of its sensual embodiments more lingering, more reverent, even, than his eagerness for the vision of intelligible truth would tolerate. Though God may be Truth, Goodness, and Beauty, all intertwined in ineffable unity, we must consent to His mediating His richness to us in a variety of ways. Augustine sensed, vaguely at least, that the attitude demanded of us in our approach to beauty differed from that required for our approach to the sure possession of truth. More clearly, he saw and said that the conditions for recognizing beauty differed from those required for glimpsing and pursuing the path to our heart's highest good. But neither of these insights came to dominate his early aesthetic as, given a little patience, they might have. Yet time, and further exposure to the conditions of incarnation, will slowly work their changes in his thinking.[71] Not only will he come to glimpse more lucidly the *sacramentum* both revealed and concealed in the Word made flesh; he will come to understand the forms of incarnate insight implied in those other words, so applicable to Monica, *beata quae credidisti*: "Blessed are you, for you have believed."[72]

3

GROUNDWORK FOR THE

De MUSICA

WHAT, THEN, does the *De Musica's* lowered evaluation of the arts imply about Augustine's developing thought? So far, it should be plain, first what that term "art" does and does not mean for the early Augustine; and second, how untenable the assumption is that the Augustine of Cassiciacum is to be considered as not yet a "convinced" Christian. For even in his earliest writings, his evaluation of the arts is really an evaluation of the liberal disciplines, and it is tightly interwoven with the religious anthropology, the "understanding of the faith," he is elaborating: he requires that the *artes* assist in the task of promoting the fallen soul's return to the bright beauty of the intelligible world.

But the lines of this fallen soul theory are, in his early Dialogues, at points confused and hesitant: there were more problems involved in a semi-Plotinian synthesis of Christian and pagan philosophic currents than he had at first envisaged. The Augustine of the next five years will, I suggest, be coming to closer grips with one after another of these problems. Only when he achieves greater clarity on them, will he feel ready to launch his only formally aesthetic treatise, the *De Musica*. To understand that book, a survey of his progress from 386 to 391 is indispensable.

The first work Augustine projects on returning to Milan is the *De Immortalitate Animae;* and "project" is the only way to describe it. It stands, even now, as a mere outline for a third book of the *Soliloquies,* one that Augustine himself later found nearly unintelligible.[1] But several features emerge with clarity: among them, his dependence on Plotinus' own treatise of the same title (*Ennead* IV, 7), his acceptance of the "two world" view encased in that treatise, and the (for modern ears) odd insistence on the soul as immovable "place" or subject for the immutable truth of the higher world.[2] The soul's immortality is proven from the premise that such an essentially immovable subject is required for the truth(s) of the intelligible world to inhere in.[3] Augustine's conclusion regarding aesthetics flows from this provisionally entertained conviction: not only is the "art idea" from which the artist works unchangeable, but the soul of the working artist himself is in some respect unchangeable as well.[4]

That seeming oddity makes sense, I suggest, if reset in the framework of Plotinus' theory of the fallen soul: one of the paradoxical features of that theory involves the affirmation that the soul is never entirely fallen; that even in its fallen state, its topmost point remains "still there," immovably in the intelligible realm.[5] It will take Augustine time to ferret out the difficulty this affirmation presents to the Christian thinker: for it leaves the soul in some sense untouched by the fault that resulted in its fall; it puts the soul essentially beyond need for salvation.

This becomes one of the problems Augustine grapples with in his *De Quantitate Animae*. The series of questions introducing the work and the brief allusions at the end hint broadly that Augustine had intended a more comprehensive treatment of the soul: indeed, a complete *De Anima* in the classic Neo-Platonic tradition.[6] But the point of the soul's *quantitas* received such extended treatment that other issues never received the attention his original scheme envisaged for them.[7] In treating of the soul's "quantity," however, Augustine shows his continuing fondness for "exercising the mind" through the use of geometrical considerations. The triangle, the square, the circle are presented as successive approaches to the perfect "equality" that he still finds at the base of beauty and of ontological excellence more generally. From consideration of the circle, the mind then moves toward acknowledging the excellence of the perfectly inextended point, the center of the circle: such exercise aids the mind to grasp in turn the superiority of the inextended over the spatially extended, to experience its own power to deal with inextended, incorporeal realities, and hence to recognize its own essential inextension.[8]

Augustine's friend Evodius is electrified by the realization: "What else am I but a soul?" he exclaims,[9] a soul whose relations to the body and to all things bodily have been shown to be so loose and remote as to fade into near-irrelevance. That realization achieved, Augustine is soon ready to shift the meaning of his title word: the soul's true *quantitas* consists, not in any spatial quantity, but in its greatness. Its greatness, in turn, can be judged from its power (*virtus*), a power manifested in the seven ascending grades of its achievement.[10] The first three of those grades imply involvement with the body: animating it, empowering it with sensation, and at the properly human level, producing the multiform variety of creations that Augustine designates, quite singularly, for him, by the term *ars*.[11] But the point of all this is to urge the soul upward, above and beyond the body, beyond all implication with things corporeal, to the secure and undisturbed "mansion" where it gazes contemplatively upon the divine Beauty itself.[12]

Augustine could hardly have been more outspoken on the soul's essentially alienated condition in the world of body; the "angelism" of the *De Quantitate Animae* is hardly preparation for the first book of the *De Libero Arbitrio*. For here, perhaps once again in pursuit of synthesis, he launches forth strongly in a Stoic key.[13] His aim is to find a definition of sin; the instruments he applies are, for the bulk of the first book, the categories of Stoicism. The "happy life" (*beate vivere*), must coincide in depth with the "righteous life" (*recte vivere*).[14] Moral evil, then, must consist in desiring those goods of which one can be deprived against one's will: the single indispensable good must be entirely within one's power to possess—it must be one's own good will taking itself as its purely autarchic object.[15] Were the equation to hold, the soul's sense of alienation would have to vanish, as the world-affirming Stoics determinedly tried to make it vanish. But the equation eventually breaks down: the righteous life becomes the *condition* for happiness, its eternally ordained "accompaniment";[16] the object of the soul's love becomes, in turn, that eternal Law which ordains the union of these two.[17] A moment later, that eternal Law has become once more Wisdom,

Truth, Logos, object of the soul's contemplative quest for disembodied vision.[18]

The second book of the *De Libero Arbitrio* continues in this
key: Augustine opens with a spirited defense of his determination not to remain a simple believer, but to seek an understanding of his Christian faith: the Gospel of St. John is quoted to
support the legitimacy of his effort.[19] The remainder of the work
makes clear what Augustine sees as involved in such a quest: the
mind must be "exercised" to entertain the conviction of a Truth-
Beauty above the mind, source of all truth and beauty in the
universe and norm for all the mind's evaluative judgments on
the world's graded levels of beauty.[20] That Truth-Beauty he
shows to be the "common" object of the mind's delighted contemplation and hence of our souls' shared beatitude;[21] our fallen
condition he now traces to our having voluntarily sought—out
of pride, concupiscence, and curiosity—to possess lower, temporal realities as sources of beatitude "proper" to ourselves, that
is, as exclusively "ours."[22] Conversion from that fallen state
implies, again, our souls' being led from faith, through understanding, upward along the ladder of truth and beauty, to recovery of the vision of which our fall deprived us.[23]

That understanding of the human condition may be very well
for a Plotinian; but is it truly an understanding of the Christian's
faith? At this juncture, Augustine boldly faces the most critical
challenge of his early career: he sets himself to showing that
essentially the same evaluation of the soul's situation can be
elicited from the ancient world's classic locus for the Christian
anthropology, the book of *Genesis*. In the *De Genesi contra
Manichaeos*, he confronts the Manichee's "carnal" interpretations with the tools of "spiritual exegesis" he could feel he had
inherited from Ambrose.[24] As a result, *Genesis* correctly understood presents us with a vision of man in his pristine state, a soul
directly illumined by the light of the Word, flooded with delight
by that divine fountain of bliss.[25] Here Augustine enters an
important qualification: man's soul in this ideal, unfallen state
was embodied but with a "celestial" body, different in quality
from the mortal body of our post-lapsary experience. Luminous
and perfectly transparent, it allowed for direct, immediate intuition of soul by companion soul.[26] Only when the soul had
turned away from the radiant divine source of its bliss and fallen
—through pride, concupiscence, and curiosity[27]—did it lose,
along with that beatifying vision, its transparent celestial body.[28]

Along with the fullness of immediate vision of God, it has lost, as well, the immediate soul-to-soul perception it once enjoyed. Now it is consigned to the realm of symbolic mediation, condemned to "labor" through the thorny foliage of sensation, language, and symbolic communication of all sorts[29] not only to regain the vision of divine Truth[30] but to receive as well the "renewal," the "change into angelic form" that will make each soul again transparent to every other.[31]

With the *De Genesi contra Manichaeos*, Augustine has put finally into place the lines of his early understanding of what he feels Christianity's faith reveals on the soul, on man, and on the condition we presently experience as human. That understanding is basically Plotinian: neither more nor less Plotinian—or Christian, at least in intent—than the understanding prevailing in the Dialogues of Cassiciacum. It is firmer, clearer, more outspoken. But it constitutes, on at least two vital points, a definite step forward from the Cassiciacum view. First, Augustine is no longer tempted to treat the soul as in any sense divine; its responsibility for ordering and beautifying the ascending levels of the sense-world is vindicated[32] and yet no longer remotely confused with the ordering work of Providence; for the soul is not immutable; its progress from unwisdom to wisdom and conversely its fall from wisdom into folly prove this beyond doubt.[33] Highest of all creatures, equal to the angel in nature while inferior to the angel only as a result of its having sinned and fallen,[34] its changeableness in time (though not in space) demonstrates its radical inferiority to the immutable God Who created it.

The second sign of Augustine's progress as a Christian thinker is his explicit reference to the soul's embodiment in its pre-fallen state. He seems here to have exploited a hint from Plotinus' writings;[35] but its effect is paradoxical: it will, as time goes on, permit Augustine to integrate into his understanding that central Christian tenet, the resurrection of the body—with consequences for his aesthetic we shall eventually have to weigh. But one potential consequence suggests itself immediately: the radical "spiritualism" of Cassiciacum may, in time, have to be considerably softened.

This is not the place for showing in detail that the anthropology outlined above was, in fact, Augustine's view of man during this period of his creativity: that effort has been made elsewhere. The task before us now is to see what light that anthropology may cast on the nature, position, and function of art, and of the *artes,* as Augustine conceives of them. Here, once again, Svoboda's indications, substantially seconded by Tscholl's, remain essentially unexceptionable.

For beauty remains, during this period, essentially what it was in the Cassiciacum Dialogues: it is the mark of "form,"[36] form that can be found in varying degrees at every level of creation, bringing the multiplicity of matter into ascending levels of increasing unity, disposing parts numerically[37] into higher and higher grades of "equality,"[38] thereby showing forth traces of the divine source of all unity, the Wisdom that "disposed of all in [accord with] measure, number, and weight" (*mensura et numero et pondere*).[39]

The beauties of the sense-world, then, are all derived beauties: derived from the highest Beauty, whose imprint arranges them in successive orders—the beauty of earth being inferior to that of the visible heavens, and all visible beauty inferior in turn to the beauty of the invisible world above it.[40] Not only source, that highest Beauty is the norm in accordance with which the mind judges on all beauties inferior to it.[41]

As before, that judgment of appreciation is exactly the converse of the intellectual process of artistic creativity: the artist's idea is drawn from his contemplation of the immutable world of Beauty, a world still considered as one with the world of Truth, Wisdom, and Number:[42] the artist, whether man or God, must first know the ideal form he wishes to embody, then work until he judges that the enmattered reproduction has reached the stage where form has been embodied as perfectly as can be.[43] But he must accept the inevitable: embodiment necessarily involves deterioration; the art product will always be inferior to the ideal form captured in the artist's idea.[44]

There are several crucial differences between human and divine artistry, however: only God can create out of nothing (*ex nihilo*) the very "inform" matter to be formed by His creative power;[45] and, consequence of the anthropological development noted above, only God's mind remains utterly immutable throughout the process of creation.[46] The immutability, with which Augustine was once tempted to credit the soul of the human artist, has now become the exclusive property of God.

The inevitable inferiority of embodiment to ideal is connected with Augustine's constant emphasis on Wisdom's lofty superiority to all its created images.[47] Coordinate with that evaluation come two others: intellectual insight is superior to all sense perception,[48] just as the delights accompanying the purely intellectual vision of Truth-Beauty are essentially loftier than those arising from sensual perception of bodily beauties.[49]

The double function performed by the *De Ordine* aesthetic is still, therefore, assured by this interim theory: against the Manichee complaints about the evils of the bodily world, Augustine opposes a relatively Stoic, world-affirming view; true to his distinction between the beautiful and the fitting, he requires that we change our attitude to one of relative detachment, disinterestedness: we must prescind from the evil this or that "part" of the sense-universe may inflict upon us and focus on the beauty of each part—even of the annoying insect, the poisonous scorpion—but then, more crucially, he counsels us to expand our view to take in the marvelous providential arrangement of these various parts whereby they each contribute to the beauteous concert of the whole.[50]

But the other side of his *De Ordine* aesthetic seems, if anything, to have gathered strength: the function of beauties, whether artistic or natural, is more than ever that of leading the mind upward, beyond the world of mortal bodies, phantasms, and sensations, beyond the realm of mediate, symbolic communication with God and with fellow men, to the longed-for vision of beauty's divine source, vision direct and unmediated of the divine Beauty itself.[51]

Certain hints dropped in the *De Ordine* have now become unequivocal indications: that vision is accessible to the purified, the "exercised" soul, even during this life in the body. This is the *mansio,* the dwelling-place, to which the ladder of the *De Quantitate* mounts;[52] saintly men have attained this vision,[53] a vision prefigured by the ecstatic vision granted Adam in his slumber before the birth of Eve,[54] the vision Christ promises to grant his faithful, "all veils removed."[55]

Throughout this period, however, Augustine becomes increasingly sensitized to one important difference between Platonic intellectualism and Christianity: the central demand of the latter is charity. We shall shortly examine some results of this process of sensitization, but for the moment this much should be said: he bridges the gap between philosophic intellectualism and Christianity by putting into play one of Platonism's outstanding features, source of its perennial hold upon the human spirit— the "erotic" character of its intellectualism. As for Augustine, so also for Plato and Plotinus, Truth in the last analysis is one with Beauty and Goodness—the beatifying vision of that Truth-Beauty answers to the deepest, consubstantial longing of the

soul. This ultimate coincidence of truth, beauty, and good occasionally leads him to lose track of his own vital distinction between the beautiful and the fitting; for the moment, it permits
him to speak of the love of divine Beauty and Truth as one with
our "appetite for happiness" (*beatitatis appetitus*).[56] That same
coincidence grounds another somewhat forced identification: the
angel set to guard the gates of paradise symbolizes the "fullness
of knowledge" required for our return thither; and yet, since
knowledge in its fullness is the privilege of the few, the angel
also symbolizes charity.[57] All the subsequent battles concerning
Augustine's central accent—was he intellectualist or voluntarist,
the patron of knowledge or of love?—emerge from such roots;
roots bared with singular clarity when one traces out the importance of aesthetics in his thinking. For Augustine's intellectualism is at bottom "erotic," his eroticism profoundly penetrated with intellectualism. The Truth he longs to see is never
merely propositional, never a dry or antiseptic reality; it shim-
mers with all the grace and charm of beauty. The *Philosophia*
he trusts to lead him to that vision, like the Lady Continence
who inspired the surrender of his conversion, invites him, en-
tices with all the allures of femininity. And he must limn the
God to whose fondling care he surrenders in similar terms.[58]

Augustine is understandably impatient to arrive at a vision of
this beauteous divinity; to this end he constructs the various ladders—in the *De Quantitate Animae,* in the *De Libero Arbitrio,*
and later, in the *De Musica*—designed to permit the soul's ascent
to that vision. The numerical and geometric cast of his mental
exercises (*exercitationes animi*), betrays his lingering confidence
that the way of reason is fundamentally coherent with the way
toward vision. He is still convinced that the body's contribution
to all this is chiefly negative: it can do little more than impede
the mind in its quest for understanding and vision[59] or, at most,
mediate that understanding and vision through symbols more
or less deceptive.[60] He has, moreover, found a term for man's
tendency to linger over sensual experience and dismisses it as
curiositas: the temptation to inquire into spiritual realities with
the "earthy eye."[61] Now, even more peremptorily than before,
the images of sense must be banished, turned away from by the
mind in its ascent toward vision.[62] Paintings, which on his view
produce only sensible images of the mortal body, scarcely interest Augustine; his remarks on this art are so infrequent and
parenthetical as to leave us only with hints and guesses.[63]

We are, again, dealing with Augustine's view of symbols and

their working: the mortal bodies of post-lapsary man are like "tunics of skin" that hide the interior from view;[64] the vision will be attained only when Christ removes the veil;[65] the symbol, in Augustine's view of it, still remains opaque, more hiding than revealing the truth that shines bright behind it. The celestial body of man before the fall[66] is an exception, of course, one easily accounted for: such transparency is proper to the other world, not to be found among the symbols of our present human experience. All the "labor" of erecting and interpreting this forest of symbolism, of wrestling with language, with images of sense and phantasms of imagination—including the entire realm we would designate as art—is punishment and by-product of man's fall. Admonitions, all of them, they remind us effectively only if we promptly turn away from them and inward;[67] only there do the remaining rays of the divine Light shine, memory-become-illumination, still piercing our world of darkness. The soul's return is to the unmediated vision that belongs to mind alone.

What of the creative imagination vaunted by so many later aesthetic theories? The most Augustine will accord it is the power to combine the various images drawn from past sensation, augmenting or diminishing them at will.[68] Such images are proper to the world of shadows and darkness; one eager for the vision must resist them.[69]

The power of judgment once provisionally accorded to the higher senses of eye and ear undergoes a similar reduction: the senses react with pleasure or pain to objects sensually fair or ugly;[70] their reactions serve, at best, as admonitions; the judgment on beauty is now the exclusive province of the incorporeal reason, uniquely endowed with knowledge of the intelligible numbers ruling all the world of sensual beauties.[71]

To judge the adequacy of Augustine's aesthetic to the Christian task he exacts from it, it must be noticed that his theory of symbolic intermediaries is made to fit the entire realm of faith on the guarantee of religious authority.[72] Even the "clouds" that for one exceptional moment shone with radiant translucency at Cassiciacum have now become opaque after Adam's fall: they stand for the entire "sacramental" economy of Scripture, prophecy, apostolic preaching, and even Incarnation.[73] Fallen man, to all appearances, must wrestle with the words and images of Scripture, with its parables and allegories, on the same terms as with any other symbols.[74] Even Christ's human words to us, spoken during his temporal existence in the flesh, are admonitions, reminding us to turn within ourselves to glimpse the light of Truth still streaming from the timeless, spiritual realm we deserted in our fall.[75]

Consistent with this view of authority's symbolic intermediaries, the Augustine of Cassiciacum was boldly willing to entertain the prospect of discarding all such "vehicles" toward truth as Daedalus would his wings, or a sea traveler would the boat that brought him to the land he sought across the sea;[76] similarly, now, arrival at the *mansio* of vision seems to dispense the seer from need of the maternal "milk" of faith he once required.[77] But a novel note is creeping into his thinking, a note surely not unconnected with his experience as a Catholic Christian: even the adult seer must never despise the milk of authority others may still require.[78] There is a greater reverence for religious authority here; it will wax as Augustine grows older. One would expect it to force a thorough review of his theory of symbol; yet to my knowledge it never does. In any case Augustine's view of authority's working is generally, at this period of his life, commanded by the theory of symbol firmly embedded in his aesthetic.

There can be no doubt that he wants this aesthetic to be Christian; yet one may be forgiven for thinking that it still remains— particularly in the *De Quantitate Animae*—far too spiritual for Christianity. The soul, the mind it is, not the incarnate man, that climbs the ladder of *exercitatio* by dealing with the incorporeal entities of number and geometry.[79] Conversely, it is the soul that endows the body with whatever beauty it possesses;[80] and finally, it is the soul that brings with it, from a pre-existent life—disembodied? or, more likely, clothed with a spiritual and celestial body?—the persistent "memory" of the world of divine number.[81] Hence, Augustine suggests, the soul brings with it into this life all the *artes* flowing from its original acquaintance with that world of number.[82] For this reason, the soul's progress in the *artes* is only apparently a sign of growth; all its learning, after all, is only remembering.[83] Its true progress must be measured on another scale.

That scale will give us the first clear measurement of the value Augustine attaches to art: art, not in the sense of the quasi-scientific *artes* he hopes will exercise the mind toward spiritual vision; nor in the wider, diffuse sense of skills, techniques of whatever variety; but art as man's effort to embody the beauty of the spiritual world, in the medium of words, rhythms, harmonies, pictorial forms, bodily motion, and gesture, in short, in whatever sensual, corporeal medium one can think of. Never, until writing his *De Quantitate Animae,* did Augustine use the term *ars,* unqualified, to designate this entire array of activities. But there, quite singularly, he does so. And for the first time, too, he pronounces himself squarely on the value of such activity.

All such production, he assures us, occurs on the third level of the soul's activity—a level above the activities of simple animation and sensation which the human soul shares in common with souls of plants and animals; a level he qualifies as "peculiarly human" (*homini proprius*).[84] With an enthusiasm that surprises, he bids us cast an admiring glance over all the *multimoda miracula,* the various marvels, that witness to the wonder of man's inventiveness: the various crafts, or useful arts come first; but then we are asked to marvel at "the invention of so many symbols" (*signa*). At first that symbolic world confines itself to writing, language, gesture; but then we pass to symbolic expression "in sounds of various kinds, in paintings, and in statues." The variety of human languages, books, the ordered forms and institutions of societal relationships parade before our gaze, until once again our admiration is directed toward "the power of reason and of thought, the floods of eloquence, the varieties of poetry . . . imitation . . . the art of music." The world man's reason has created is indeed a luxuriant forest of multileveled art forms.[85]

The sentence reads very well; Augustine has taken pains to see that everything concurs in sustaining an elevation of spirit recalling Cicero at his most rhythmic, eloquent, sonorous. We are temporarily thrown off our guard: there is little here to prepare us for the austere judgment that follows. *Magna haec,* Augustine proclaims, *et omnino humana*: there is grandeur in all this, and a grandeur entirely befitting man's estate. And yet,

all these achievements (*ista*) are shared by learned and unlearned alike, they are the common heritage of good men and bad. Look higher, therefore, and leap to that fourth stage, where goodness and all genuine praiseworthiness begins.[86]

Suspice . . . insili: Augustine's impatience has penned those terms; for no true *bonitas,* no *vera laudatio* is to be found on this level of *ars;* "properly human" though it be, it is proper to a humanity precisely as "fallen." This is why all authentic value begins only when the soul takes its distance from the mortal body and its defilement, learns to hold body and bodily creation in contempt and to reserve its love for its own true, incorporeal self (*sese abstrahere a sordibus, totamque emaculare ac mundissimam reddere et comptissimam*).[87] A low evaluation of art, indeed, but perfectly consistent with his Cassiciacum view—and with its vaunting of the *artes* providing the ladder the soul may mount to escape from all such involvement with body, sense, and symbolic intermediaries.

There is something all the more disconcerting in that evaluation of the multifarious wonders, the *multimoda miracula* man's creativity has fashioned, given Augustine's obvious spontaneous appreciation of their grandeur. Again, we are faced with the gap between the artist and his theory of art. But it is only fair to acknowledge that we have been warned: the soul's true progress, we have been told, has nothing to do with advance in dexterity, skills, even in those skills we should call arts.[88] Playing the flute is as valuable to the soul as outsize teeth are to the body;[89] the virtue that measures the soul's true growth is marked by contempt for mortal, sensible realities,[90] renunciation of the entire corporeal realm, as the Christian mysteries teach,[91] the readiness to cast off all bodily habits[92] in order to reconquer that spiritual status which alone constitutes our likeness to God.[93] The entire Dialogue is calculated to make us share in Evodius' arrival at wondering self-recognition: we are souls; and the initial duty consequent on self-recognition is that of purification, a purification tending (much as the Socrates of the *Phaedo* claimed) toward the flight, escape, the *fuga, elapsio* from the body which is eventually completed at death.[94]

"Stop!" the reader is tempted to cry: "We are, after all, humans!" But what are humans, after all, the Augustine of the *De Moribus Ecclesiae* coolly replies, but "souls using bodies"[95] and condemned by their fall to the relation with bodies we now experience. For it still remains true that by nature we are the equal of the angels, and our present inferiority to them is due only to our having sinned.[96]

That "angelistic" view of humanity is what roots Augustine's ardent longing for the vision he claims the soul once enjoyed; it helps us understand his impatience with all the bodily, sensual intermediaries of artistic creativity, an impatience that prompts him to construct an aesthetic designed to persuade the soul to transcend, to rise above the realm of art and leave it all behind in its upward ascent.

The *De Quantitate Animae* represents a high-water mark in Augustine's spiritual view of humanity and of art. Its teaching, he is convinced, is the message not only of the *platonici* but of the Christian mysteries as well. Yet even here a number of Christian tenets are at work to soften the bleak judgment on the visible world and the soul's involvement in it: a softening action that soon becomes even more perceptible. The visible world is God's creation, a world that the God of *Genesis* found "good, very good": though a world of "vanity" (*vanitas*), from which the exiled soul must escape in order to re-enter the higher world of truth (*veritas*), it boasts nonetheless an order which makes all these things both "wonderful" and "beautiful."[97] Even the punishment of our fallen souls contributes to the beauty of that order, even our sins are integrated into the divine plan which works insuperably toward achievement of the highest beauty possible to such a bodily universe, an *ordo perfectus*.[98]

On the other hand, Augustine's way of dealing with the Incarnation is far from reassuring;[99] it does, in any event, little or nothing to modify his evaluation of the flesh. He mentions the resurrection, to be sure—"Even the resurrection of the flesh," he advises us, "in which some believe only haltingly, others not at all," will become as clearly a future reality to us as tomorrow's rising of today's setting sun, when once we have attained the highest level of the soul's contemplative activity.[100] One wonders if the Augustine of the *De Quantitate* knew quite what to make of that mystery; Plotinus' discreet suggestions about a spiritual, heavenly body "there" present him with leads that he will soon begin to exploit; but they fail up to this point seriously to challenge the radical angelism of his anthropology.

The most decisive challenge comes from another, somewhat unexpected, but identifiably Christian quarter. We noticed earlier that the Augustine of this period is beginning to wrestle with the centrality of charity in the Christian message. The first commandment, that we love God with our whole heart, is one that Augustine can more easily deal with within the framework of his erotic intellectualism: he translates it into a desire for the vision of God, one that engages the entire strength of our interior being. Understanding the second law, the love of neighbor, is another matter, however; it is not so easily, nor so neatly dealt with in the categories he has chosen for understanding the faith. And yet, however awkward one may deem his efforts to integrate the love of neighbor into his scheme, the evidence is clear that it strongly affects his values, his thinking, and eventually, his aesthetic.

Twice in the *De Quantitate Animae* he is brought to qualify his stress on the soul's ascending purification; this must be done, he warns us, in the measure that is permitted in this life.[101] We have seen a similar second thought affect his attitude toward religious authority.[102] Despite his confidence that the soul can attain the summit of vision, dwelling in it as a kind of *mansio* even during "this life," it has been suggested that Augustine is already beginning to have some doubts: perhaps embodiment, and the persistent refractoriness of the body in the face of such angelistic aspirations, is an irreducible feature of human existence, one that must be accepted. Perhaps, instead of an ascent upward through levels of reality, timelessly hierarchized, a better image for human life would be that of a journey, long, patient, and slow, a journey through time and history.[103]

But more plainly at work in such reservations is another motivation. To dispense the "milk" of faith, as religious authority does, is a "most praiseworthy work of charity";[104] and, right within the context of his deprecatory judgment on the human estate and all its artistic achievements, Augustine exhorts us to preserve a lofty regard for human society (*societatem humanam magni pendere*),[105] a counsel immediately followed by the injunction to wish nothing on another which one would not have happen to oneself. We ought to bring help to wandering, laboring souls akin to our own, thus in some sense mediating God's own providential work on their behalf, in the measure in which that aid is both permitted and commanded.[106] There is, then, a limit to the single-mindedness with which the Christian Neo-Platonist may pursue the upward way of disengagement from the body and from bodily activity; and the limit is set precisely by the golden rule, by the law of charity, and the needs of fellow souls.

One factor compelling Augustine to explore the central Christian emphasis on charity was his anti-Manichaean focus: their repeated claim to superiority over Catholics was based partially on the contention that Manichees were urged to a far more ascetic attitude toward the sexual, toward the bodily and temporal more generally, than Catholics plainly taught and practiced. In the *De Moribus—The Morals of the Church and of the Manichees*—Augustine takes up the challenge implicit in their claim. The second book of that work contains a trenchant, sometimes pungent criticism of the Manichee morality, in both its practice and theoretical formulation. Against the "materiality" of a moral scheme erected mainly on the dualistic flight from the evils of enmattered existence (one which presented all too many parallels with Augustine's own stress on purification from the body), he finds himself driven to develop a morality of "intention." The intention embodied in all good action must, as St. Paul taught the Corinthians, be charity.[107] Charity with respect to God comes down to a clearly erotic desire for God as object of a beatifying vision;[108] interpreting it this way, Augustine finds it somewhat difficult to show how the second commandment of charity is like the first, but he strives to overcome the difficulty.[109] Charity toward the neighbor then becomes a desire that he arrive at the same beatitude one desires for oneself and calls for aiding him in that journey toward arrival. That aid must take the double form of "medicine" and "discipline" which minister respectively to body and to soul.[110] But even the desire for God above all things permits the right "use" of bodily and temporal goods inasmuch as that use serves the necessities of human life, the life of "souls using bodies."[111] The *De Moribus* shows Augustine experimenting for the first time with terms which will eventually emerge as his classic *uti-frui* distinction between goods to be used and the supreme divine Good which alone must be enjoyed.[112] The result will be a relativization of all created goods and activities—they are accorded merely instrumental value in our soul's quest for possession of that Wisdom and Truth to which we "cleave" in charity.

But even such relative, instrumental value involves a more benign judgment on the bodily and temporal than the unrelieved stress on purification and ascent would have accorded. The Plotinian matrix of his view of man remains substantially firm; and yet, we have noticed some fissures running through it. Those fissures will bear close watching as we come to the only formally aesthetic work Augustine wrote, the *De Musica*.

4

THE *De MUSICA*

The best evidence for Augustine's continued high regard for the *artes*—the liberal disciplines—is the simple fact that he wrote the *De Musica* at all, and wrote it when and as he did. In six books, the work represents the only substantial result issuing from an ambitious project conceived of during the period following his return from Cassiciacum. Penetrated with his conviction that the liberal disciplines could provide an excellent ladder for the soul's ascent, he intended to take those *artes* in turn, presenting each of them in such a fashion as to lead the reader's mind upward, "through the corporeal to the incorporeal."[1] Something of what he had in mind may be guessed from the *De Magistro,* where a dialogic meditation on corporeal words and signs issues in just such an ascent to the world of timeless Truth, to acknowledgement of the inner "Master" whose light still illumines the soul.[2] As for the other works projected, they seem, with the exception of the *De Musica,* to have gotten little beyond the outline stage.[3] But the persistence of his intention can be judged from the fact that, having no more than begun the *De Musica* at Milan, he takes it up again after his return to Africa in 388, writing the bulk of the work, therefore, between then and 391.[4]

That chronology, despite its being plainly stated not once but twice in the *Retractations*, has been thrown into doubt by Heinz Edelstein in his study of Augustine's views on music.[5] Those doubts have been shared by Svoboda, who follows Edelstein in the matter.[6]

The substance of their joint view comes to this: the Augustine who wrote the Sixth Book of the *De Musica*, unlike the enthusiast for the liberal arts who wrote the first five books—far more kindred in spirit to the earlier *De Ordine*—begins by leveling a decidedly "skeptical judgment on the metrical exposé presented in the [five] books which preceded"; "child's play," he calls them, no more than "preparation for knowledge in the true sense of the term," a knowledge apparently embodied in the Sixth Book where he means to cull the fruit of the preceding five. This lowered esteem "for the liberal arts he so vaunted in the *De Ordine*"—along with allied considerations, to be sure—betrays, in Svoboda's term, a "purely Christian character," showing that during the intervening five years Augustine has developed into a "convinced Christian." Hence his approval of Edelstein's proposal that the Sixth Book "was not written immediately after the ones that precede it."[7]

We have seen how untenable Edelstein's view of Augustine's conversion has, in the light of subsequent scholarship, turned out to be. It takes a surface view of the Cassiciacum writings to miss their Christian point. But further, a slightly closer inspection of the reasons given for inserting a time gap between the sixth and its preceding books actually retorts that view; it only sharpens the sense of profound continuity linking the *De Ordine* and the *De Musica*: essential to any preliminary "exercise of the mind" is that it be just such a preparation for true knowledge, and that the fruit of that preparation be culled only at the end of the process.[8]

Why, then, the apparently uncompromising tone of Augustine's deprecation of those first five books? That difficulty can be removed, again, partially by a closer inspection that discloses just how much value Augustine still concedes to this "way of the disciplines."[9] But more decisively, the difficulty vanishes when one takes into account that these expressions of deprecation occur in only two places—in the opening and closing paragraphs of Book Six: the very paragraphs that Marrou convincingly identifies as constituting an "emendation" inserted by Augustine the Bishop, in 408 or 409, nearly twenty years after the original composition of the work.[10]

There is, then, a time gap after all; Augustine's mood has undergone something of a change; but we can be confident that his change of mood occurred a considerable time after 491, and that—the two paragraphs of emendation excepted—all six books of the *De Musica* will, on examination, manifest a view that is in substantial continuity with one outlined in the preceding chapter.

Musica *a science*

The opening paragraphs of the work already bring us back to the atmosphere of Cassiciacum. Augustine means to focus only on that part of *musica* which deals with the beauties of poetic meter.[11] But *musica,* more generally, he makes clear, is no more an art in our sense of that term than it was in the *De Ordine*: Augustine initiates his work with a determined effort to show that music is a science (*scientia*), a knowledge of the numerical relations which govern the production of harmonious sounds; a knowledge which is, therefore, accessible only to the eye of reason.[12] Immediately this classes both flutist and nightingale in a lower order; they go about their performances "acting numerically" (*numerose faciendo*) but not *numeros cognoscendo*: they lack the crucial insight into the pure laws of number which would make them *musici* in the authentic sense.[13] Having established this connection between music and the knowledge of numerical progressions, Augustine goes on to present his disciple with a compact Neo-Pythagorean manual of numerological aesthetics. Number is what imposes form and order on the indeterminate and is, accordingly, the mark of reason, the hallmark of beauty in the things of sense.[14]

Faith, Reason, and the Numerical Universe

This numerical view of music is preparation for the real task Augustine had set himself: in the Sixth Book, he traces out the grades of the various numbers involved in poetic meters. Even the limited focus on meter brings the mind to realize that the universe entire is at every level formed into beauty by the pervasive power of number. He establishes a hierarchy leading from the lowest numbers accessible to sense observation, upward through six higher levels—the familiar septenary scheme remains intact—terminating at the very seat of intelligibility and beauty, the divine.[15] The implication is that the sound-embodied numbers, which delight us in measures of verse as they strike our ear, proceed in downward cascade from the "eternal numbers,"[16] which themselves proceed from God.[17] This cosmic backdrop for the mind's ascent from lowest to highest numbers and to God, the fount of numerical beauty, is precisely what Augustine had in mind when he conceived of his ambitious project on the disciplines: the mind must be led "through corporeal to incorporeal realities" *per corporalia ad incorporalia*. But implied in all this, ostensibly at least, is a somewhat more positive correlation than his Cassiciacum works exhibit between the order of supernal numbers and traces (*vestigia*) they have left in the sense order.[18] The sensible and intelligible orders are now on speaking terms. Connected with this is the supposition that our senses in their activity reflect some dim vestige of rationality: Augustine speaks of the judgment of sense (*judicium sensus*) often enough, equating it with a pleasure-pain reaction;[19] but he attributes to it at times a higher value than heretofore; the pleasure-pain reaction is now considered as herald (*nuntius*) of the truth to which reason "points" as *index veritatis*.[20] *Per corporalia ad incorporalia*. It is hard to guess how fully the *per* in that motto was intended; the Dialogues of Cassiciacum tend more to stress the dualistic contrast of sense *versus* reason, the need for "leaving sense behind" and moving *from* corporeal reality, rather than (as here) *through* it, to the world of spirit.[21] Here, however, Augustine is systematically working out of a more amicable relation between the worlds of sense and reason. The shift in accent recalls much more Plotinus' later treatise *On The Intelligible Beauty* (*Ennead* V, 8) than his earlier work *On Beauty* (*Ennead* I, 6). It is no more than a shift of accent; but it will ground, nonetheless, a more kindly attitude toward sensible creation.

Sense judgment, Authority, and Reason

That relatively closer continuity between the higher and lower worlds allows for a maneuver Augustine puts into play repeatedly throughout the *De Musica*: the passage from sensual to rational judgment. His attempt to initiate his disciple into the secrets of musical science regularly begins with consideration of a concrete foot, or verse, of poetry; he first asks his disciple whether it *sounds* right to the ear; then he sends him searching for the infallible and unchangeable numerical law which is manifested in the judgment-by-ear of one who like his disciple,

is "learned" and "practiced" (*doctus, exercitatus*) and consequently equipped with good judgment in these matters.[22] Sound
"judgment of sense" and the laws of numbers will, he is convinced, invariably agree.[23]

Augustine comes very close, then, to implying that rationality
can penetrate the judgment of sense. This would situate the total
human composite, as unified subject, at the very center of the
art experience. Yet, despite his broad concession to continuity,
"reason" remains the ultimate judge of what is beautiful in the
numerical progressions of metrical science.[24] It is, in fact, a
judge more ultimate and trustworthy than even the most ancient
and revered authorities on the subject.[25] Augustine is adamant
on this: again and again he refuses to allow the disciple to rest
with acceptance of authority's judgment in the matter; he must
pass on to apply his reasoned insight into the numerical laws
the vision of which is "common" both to him and to those authorities, indeed, common to all.[26] In two instances at least he
approves his disciple's insight as right, even though it question
or go against the word of authorities;[27] reason, he would lead him
to discover, is superior to any man.[28] Not only in the Sixth Book,
therefore, but throughout the earlier books as well, the presiding
thrust of the work is this ascent from the realm of sense and authority to the higher world directly accessible to the eye of
reason.

And yet, there is a realm in which authority is omnicompetent.
That realm is exactly what the *De Genesi* and other works of this
period would lead us to suspect; it embraces the post-lapsary,
conventional establishment of language and its laws, a work of
human "custom" which has to do with names (*nomina*) rather
than with realities (*res*).[29] For these are purely temporal and historical matters, wherein no genuine knowledge (*scientia*) is accessible; only that faith (*fides*) which relies upon the transmissions of authority is possible on this level of the life of opinion
(*opinabilis vita*).[30] In our acceptance of such reports, what semblance of knowledge (*cognitio*) we gain is passed down by history,
it is not subject to the authenticating insight proper to art as
Augustine understands that term; "therefore, it is believed rather
than known . . . we cannot know it, but only believe it by hearing and reading" (*creditur potius quam cognoscitur . . . neque
scire hoc possumus, sed tantummodo credere audiendo et
legendo*).[31]

This view follows neatly from the classic Platonic division between the higher world of unchangeable, ahistorical intelligi-

bility, and the lower, temporal world where only opinion (*doxa*) is possible: here, as the *De Vera Religione*[32] makes abundantly clear, is where faith and authority have their exclusive domain. Where the teaching of authority bears upon intelligible matters, however, its function is limited to the semi-occasionalistic operation of "admonishing" the soul to turn inward and upward to contemplate the eternal truth.[33] This holds for the words which history assures us Christ spoke "outwardly";[34] it holds for Scripture's utterances for the same reason: though highest among "authorities," it must still yield to the superiority of reason's direct contact with the upper world.[35] The *De Musica's* reminder of Scripture's importance is, significantly, encased in a development which is frankly a "way of reason."[36] This passage from faith to reason is illustrated in the Sixth Book when the master asks his disciple:

M: From where, then, are we to believe (*credendum*) that what is eternal and unchangeable is communicated to the soul if not from the eternal and unchangeable God?

D: I don't see how we are to believe otherwise (*credi oporteat*).

M: Well, then, isn't it *evident* (*nonne manifestum*) that he who under another's questioning moves himself to the God within in order to understand (*intelligat*) the unchangeable truth, cannot be reminded (*revocari*) by any outside admonition (*nullo extrinsecus admonente*) to gaze on (*intuendum*) that truth, unless that movement [to his own interior] be contained in memory?

D: It's evident: *manifestum*.[37]

It is still the power of reminiscence, then, which links our souls with the world of eternal truth. Once interrogated we can turn within and recover the insight latent in memory; subsequently, we may not even need the "admonition from without" we may have required at first. As with the other works of this period, therefore, the movement involved in the *De Musica* would induce us to pass from authority to reason, from what is believed to what becomes evident to the mind's gaze, from the copy world of sense to the true world of intelligibility, from corporeal to incorporeal, from temporal to eternal.

Music and the Soul's "Fall" into Time

The deeper implication in all this is that the intelligible is, quite literally, a "remembered" world, one of which the soul is literally reminded, to which it needs to be recalled (*revocari*). The upward way is in the strictest sense of the term a return to that contemplative delight from which the soul is fallen.

Edelstein attempts to buttress his claim that the Sixth Book manifests a specifically Christian character, by noting that Augustine shifts abruptly there[38] from metrical examples drawn from worldly letters to the opening lines of Ambrose's hymn, *Deus creator omnium*.[39] But a perfectly analogous shift to the very same hymn occurred at the climax of the *De Beata Vita*.[40] There, as here, it accords with the task imposed by Augustine's Christian Neo-Platonism: what is best in the world of culture, when examined in depth and purified, coheres with the Christian message, properly understood. Nor is the shift so abrupt as Edelstein makes it out to be: he fails to notice that repeatedly throughout the early books[41] the master intersperses metrical models largely of his own composition, and that all of these turn out, on examination, to be little morality verses, subtly hinting at the revelation to be uncovered in the Sixth Book: that the soul's involvement in the world of words and authority, of time and its measures, is the result of a fall. The point of the *De Musica*, from start to finish, is to bring the soul to a recognition of its fallen state and thereby promote its return. The reader's mind is being carefully attuned to a soul-flight from its toil amid books (*labor . . . in chartis*) to the upper regions (*per auras*);[42] to lay aside the love of fragile temporal realities for secure love of that stable, satisfying good that in the end—"happier thought" than all which has preceded—is identified with God.[43] Unhappy the man, and never sated, who seeks his good outside himself; but happy the man who desires the vision, the enjoyment of God,[44] the delight in that Truth, "Art of the God most high," whence all sensible beauties proceed.[45] "Blest and best the man beyond the reach of toil" (*procul negotio*).[46] For he has left behind the world of time and action for the blissful peace of contemplating forever that *Deus creator omnium* Whose entry in the Sixth Book has been artfully prepared by all the verses of Augustine's own composition which preceded.

But *procul negotio*: the key term taken from the last of Augustine's own verses gives a clue to the precise aspect under which the *De Musica* depicts the soul's situation: as fallen from a state of timeless contemplation, into a world of time and action. For *otium* (leisure) to the Plotinian, is the characteristic of eternal contemplation; *negotium* (busyness) is the curse of time.

The entire work concentrates on the temporal "measures"

which govern the composition of poetry: Jean Guitton entitles his consideration of this work appropriately, for it is a meditation on "le temps poétique" in its relation to eternity.[47] From this point in his career until the *Confessions*, Augustine invariably begins his discussion of time by taking the example of a line of poetry, preferably as here, the *Deus creator omnium,* inquiring how we "measure" the timing of it, then passing to a more generalized speculation on the nature of time when compared with God's eternity. The conclusion is always the same: the experience of time indicates that the soul is "distended," fallen from the *otium,* the restful contemplation of eternal truth, into the busy *negotium* of temporal activity.[48]

The ponderous numerical accent, the septenary scheme are both Augustine's own: they represent, again, a somewhat intrusive insertion of Neo-Pythagorean elements into a basically Plotinian matrix. But, as analysis of Book Six will show, the atmosphere, central intuition, and method are all drawn principally from Plotinus' treatise, *Ennead* III, 7, "On Eternity and Time." And the origin of artistic activity, indeed of all man's symbolic activity, is to be found exactly where Augustine placed it in the *De Genesi contra Manichaeos*: it emerges from the soul's "fallen" state.

The doctrine of the fall, discreetly insinuated in Augustine's morality verses, enters the picture more overtly in *De Musica* VI, 7. Augustine is bringing his disciple to see that the various operations involved in the investigation of metrics suppose the existence, first, of "sounding numbers," numerical proportions embodied in spoken verse; then "reacting" numbers embodied in the ear's rhythmic reaction to the sounding numbers it hears. Another grade, of "advancing" numbers, is required to explain the soul's capacity to produce numerically proportioned sounds. Still another grade is needed: the soul must harbor a store of sensible "memorial" numbers, equipping it to recognize meters it has become familiar with. Finally, but still on the sense-level, a fifth set of "judicial" numbers must account for the natural, prerational "judgments of sense" whereby sounds are found either pleasant or painful.[49]

Augustine now sets out to rank these various grades of number hierarchically. The question swiftly arises whether "sounding" or "reacting" numbers are superior. Initially, the answer is entertained that the former seem to act toward production of the latter, and therefore, as causes to effects, must be of a higher order. But this would imply that the body is superior to soul, since the "sounding" numbers are evidently bodily, whereas the "reacting" numbers are present in the soul.[50] This power of the body to act upon the soul Augustine concedes to be subject of amazement: things would not be so, he suggests, if the body which the soul used to animate and govern without trouble and with the greatest ease were not changed for the worse by the first sin and [rendered thereby] subject to death and corruption.[51]

This apparent reversal of the law that cause must be superior to effect has something monstrous about it. Augustine wants, at first, to explain this anomaly in terms of our fall. It was by pride that we "most justly fell" into a condition where such reversals could take place; into a condition condescendingly shared by the Incarnate Word, who "took upon Himself man," chose to be "humanly born, to suffer, and to die" to atone for our primal sin. It is not surprising, in view of the radical inversion of values implied in our fall, that "a soul operating in mortal flesh experiences the passion of bodies." Augustine goes on to explain that the "sounding" numbers are "true" in their lower, bodily order, and for this reason superior to the reacting numbers whose existence in the soul is really "improper" to it and therefore "false"; the soul is improved by "turning away" from such carnal numbers; their presence in it may seem appropriate to its actual, but hardly befits its ideal, situation.[52]

At this point in the argument it would seem Augustine has conceded the power of body to affect the soul, attributing that "amazing" inversion to a fall. That fall seems to have changed the original body (presumably a "heavenly" body which the *De Genesi contra Manichaeos* describes the soul as possessing in its unfallen state) from an immortal to the mortal body of our human experience; it also deprived the soul of the untroubled ease with which it formerly governed that heavenly body, and so inverted the ideal soul-body relation that the body now has power to act upon the soul.

But, in the very next paragraph, he withdraws that apparent concession and sets about elaborating a theory of sensation whereby the soul alone is truly active: its "attention" to the body permits it to become aware of various affections of the body which, in its turn, is now shorn of any power directly to act upon the soul.[53] I have tried elsewhere[54] to show that this entire section derives from the *Enneads* and embodies among other features Plotinus' contention that bodily consciousness becomes attenuated in the very measure that the contemplative soul recovers its "healthy" relationship with the entire sensible order, a relationship enjoyed in its former, unfallen state. So too, absorbed in contemplation, the soul's "active" command of the body and of the bodily universe does not require its attention but issues as the undistracting overflow, the spontaneous by-product, of its contemplation. The reader intent on what he is reading does not attend to his act of reading; when walking, steeped in thought, we lose almost entirely our consciousness of walking.

Exploiting this view of the ideal body-soul relation, Augustine can now propose that if the soul were to turn away from the body, its "servant," and back to its master, God, it would furnish even its body "a life of utmost ease, no longer, as now, laborious and full of busyness." At the same time it would need to pay its body "no attention" in the "surpassing peace" which will attain fulfillment in the resurrection, when the body itself will be "re-established in its original stability".[55] Clearly Augustine is speaking here of a "return" to a condition of "security" and "rest," "interior freedom" and "peace," a condition it enjoyed before the fall plunged it into the "troubles," "unquiet," the tumult of "carnal busy-ness" and "disturbing memories" that followed on its being "borne off into things outside itself."[56] Significantly, though, the ideal, unfallen state is now explicitly limned as an "understanding" of the Christian's faith in the resurrection of the body.

The soul's fall, so recently ascribed to the sin of pride, is next connected with "carnal concupiscence" whereby the soul is "seduced" into directing its attention to the body to the "neglect" of its Lord.[57] In the De Genesi contra Manichaeos, Augustine had attributed the fall to a triadic sin; only two members of that triad would seem to have made their appearance here. But the effects of the fall have been so generously portrayed in the language of "care" and "unquiet" that the reader is already prepared for the introduction of the "curiosity" motif further on.

For the notion of "curiosity," as we shall see, is directly linked with the soul's fall as precisely into "time" and the "busy" temporal "action" of constructing an "imitation" of eternity. This central theme, already foreshadowed in the language which preceded, is soon to make its overt entry.

But first, Augustine must set the stage, raise the backdrop, that makes its entry intelligible. He must show that the "eternal" consists of a higher, unchanging order of "numbers." Those numbers preside over reason's judgment upon lower, sensible numbers.[58] It is reason's continuing insight into true and perfect

equality—into the "eternal" world—which grounds its power
to judge upon the lower, defective "imitations" of the temporal,
sensible world.[59]

The metaphysical setting is familiar. Reason's native world
is the unchanging, intelligible, eternal. How, then, account for
its activity and presence in the changing, sensible world of time?
Before addressing himself to this aetiological issue, Augustine
is eager to point his moral: from the enjoyment of the lower,
imitation world, the soul is urged to turn away. Though "beautiful in their kind and order," such imitation realities are inferior
to the soul, below its ideal station. Its proper place in reality is
the *mesê taxis* which Augustine perceives as central to Plotinus'
thought on the matter: the same "mid-rank" station, above the
sensible but below the purely intelligible worlds, which represents the soul's ideal condition in the *De Genesi contra Manichaeos*. "Let us," he counsels us accordingly, "order ourselves
between those things beneath us and those above, so that lower
things do not trouble us, and higher things alone afford us delight." That higher world is where the "most sublime and
changeless, undisturbed and eternal equality abides"—the timeless sanctuary of the world order which brings the circuits of all
the temporal into the "numbered succession" of the *carmen
universitatis,* the "poem of the universe."[60] The image, as I have
tried elsewhere to show,[61] is almost certainly drawn from the
Enneads: its function here is extended to show that we, having
become through the fall so many individual "words," each forming part of that universal poem of the temporal whole, are understandably unable to perceive the harmony and beauty of the
connected work, "cannot perceive or approve of the totality":
on account of our sin we have deservedly been "sewn (*assuti*)
into the order" of these inferior, spatio-temporal realities, thereby "losing the universe we possessed while obeying God's precepts." We have been "ordered as part" of the time tapestry into
which we fell.[62]

Once again, a theme familiar from Cassiciacum on: Augustine's earliest writings insisted on our regarding the beauty of
the whole despite what seems disorder and evil in the several
parts. But now, the specifically *temporal* character of both whole
and parts is more prominently displayed. In addition, the motive
underlying this justification of the cosmic beauty is more firmly
stated: the entire cosmic poem is God's work and must therefore
be beautiful. Now, too, our immersion as parts in the temporal
sequence is firmly traced to the fall of our souls from the mid-

rank station where the whole was subject to our purview, into
the series of temporal realities. In consequence, it seems no
longer possible for the soul, while fallen, to acquire a view of
the "whole" temporal series. The thrust of a basically Stoic
argument has been transformed: it is no longer a question of
complacently accepting the visible, temporal world as beautiful
and consequently good. The "ascensional" side of Cassiciacum's
aesthetic has decisively won the day: the soul is being urged to
escape the temporal order altogether. For only then, secure and
peaceful, can it dominate the entirety of that order. This more
decisive Plotinization of a Stoic argument could be looked upon
as making Augustine's view more "spiritual" than it was at
Cassiciacum. But, *pace* Svoboda, the influence working in this
direction can scarcely be called specifically Christian; nor does
this development imply any lowered esteem for the *artes;* quite
the contrary.

Memory, Reminding, and Fall

For the *artes* remain what they were for the Augustine of
Cassiciacum: the accomplishment of *ratio,* of soul incarnate, but
precisely inasmuch as it maintains, even in its incarnate condition, an enduring link with its previous, relatively disincarnate
condition: and with the vision it still "remembers." *Ars,* as we
have seen Augustine use the term in the *De Quantitate,* boasts
quite another lineage. It is the peculiarity of soul *precisely as
incarnate.* The poetic art discussed in the *De Musica,* for instance, is proper to the soul enmeshed in body and in time: in
this state, the poetic soul produces "advancing numbers," which,
through their influence on other bodies "produce the sensible
beauties of time." The danger of this involvement in *ars* is that,
through the memory that is based on the continuity of its self-
awareness, the soul takes all its own motions into itself, and
accordingly "multiplies, you might say, in itself," makes the
entire work of carnal memory a webwork beautiful enough to
entice the soul into its entrapping coils.[63] Is the world of temporal beauties, then, evil? Here again, Augustine strikes a typical
balance: God is not "envious" of the beauteous numbers of the
sensible world (as Manichees might contend), even though constructed by the soul's own proud and insubordinate activity,
even though it be a rival imitation of the divine, eternal world.
And yet He beholds the fallen soul entrapped in that lower
world, and so through His Providence He works constantly that

we may "turn back and be recalled" from such inferior delights. Reverting to his Plotinian interpretation of the soul's progress toward the resurrected condition, Augustine assures us that our contemplative growth will restore in us the ability to "delight" in the numbers of reason rather than in those of sense, so that "our entire life is converted to God." This absorption in God will allow the soul to confer on the body the "numbers of health" instead of the unhealthy numbers that now distract the soul away from contemplation into the dispersion of temporal action. The soul will confer those numbers accordingly, "without taking delight"—or being distracted—in that operation.[64] Augustine associates this "turning" from sensible to rational numbers with a higher sort of memory, one that records the mind's "spiritual motions"; a memory that indicates that the unchangeable equality which the mind seeks amid the numbers of time is an equality it could "never desire unless it were [already] known from somewhere" (*nisi alicubi nota esset*), a "somewhere" neither spatial nor bodily.[65] Subtending all of this, therefore, is the Cassiciacum conviction that all learning is, after all, "remembering." For the art in the artisan's mind is already a participation in the divine Art, the admonition of questioning serves merely to "recall" the mind, to turn it back to renewed contemplation of that higher world. The mind must, therefore already "know" what it is now summoned to remember, must have known it and forgotten it, so that now it needs another's recalling it to actual memory.[66] But what could possibly have incited the soul to turn away from its original blissful contemplation?

Augustine has arrived at the point where he gives the fullest account which the *De Musica* presents of the fall. His description starts from the classic division of the four civic virtues. This brings him to remark that the fallen condition involves an apparent paradox: the soul, though fallen, remains "prudent" enough to know that it should cleave to eternal realities, yet it does not in fact cleave to them. In all the beauties that delight and distract it, it seeks (and dimly knows it seeks) the divine, unchangeable equality which constitutes perfect beauty.[67] And yet it remains in a state of diversion, distraction from the beatifying contemplation of that perfect beauty. What causes this?

Augustine feels he can explain the soul's distracted state by the effects of the lower "numbers" which the previous investigation uncovered. The disquieting "care" (*cura*) for sense-pleasures prompts the soul to act, through "reacting numbers," upon the stream of sounding numbers impinging on its bodily senses; a "love of operating on bodies" through "advancing numbers" in turn makes it "restless," distracting it from contemplation; the network of "memorial numbers," comprised of the phantasies and phantasms generated in this activity, further confirms the soul's "turn" away from suprasensible Truth. But finally, those judicial "sensible numbers" which contain certain "rules, as it were, rejoicing in [their power to] imitate the [divine] Art," fill the soul with a "love of the most vain knowledge" of lower-order numbers and their operation. This whole complex of sensible numbers then, gives birth to "curiosity, incapable, in its vanity, of grasping truth, and enemy of security as the name itself [from *cura*, "care"] implies."[68] The psychology of "distraction" is, therefore, initially complex; its causes range from the desire for sensible pleasure and for acting on bodies, to the delight in "imitating" God's own Art and the disquieting love of "vain" knowledge that Augustine terms curiosity.

But the root of the matter lies in a "general love of action" (*amor generalis actionis*); this in turn arises from the vicious pride (*superbia*) which originally prompted the soul to "prefer imitating rather than serving God." *Initium omnis peccati superbia*: "Pride is the beginning of all sin." The scriptural image Augustine chooses for pride is taken from the then extant translation of *Ecclesiasticus* 10, 9–14, wherein the proud man is depicted as having "spilled forth his insides" (*projecit intima sua*). Once filled with the "inmost" riches of the divine presence to it, the soul turns away, literally "apo-statises" (*initium hominis superbiae apostatare a Deo*). It "puffs up" (*intumescit*) with pride and goes forth to the outermost (*extima*), to the ranks of inferior being furthest from the divine center, thereby becoming "less and less," "giving up [its] inmost things" by putting itself "far" from God.[69]

Superbia, pride, the restless, "curious" desire to be engaged in action, the arrogant will to construct a temporal imitation of the eternal world of beauty, the dissipation, literally, "spilling forth" of its interior riches in a flight further and further from the divine to the outermost reaches of "less and lesser" being— all the key elements of Plotinus' description in *Ennead* III, 7, of the fall from eternity into time are firmly in place.

Elsewhere I have tried to show the likelihood that Augustine understood this treatise in connection with the opening analysis of *Ennead* V, 1;[70] Plotinus there identifies the source or beginning (*archê*) of the souls' evils with the self-will or audacity (*tolma*) which prompted them to enter the sphere of becoming (*genesis*). Rejoicing in their self-propulsive power over themselves, they travel a great distance (*apostasis*) into forgetfulness of God and of their divine origin.[71]

But in the central portion of *Ennead* III, 7, Plotinus' meditation "On Eternity and Time," this analysis is both completed and subtly altered by the introduction of another image. The soul in its pre-fallen state, Plotinus tells us, was "at rest" in "real being"; it was not yet "in time"; it "kept quiet in the reality [of Noûs]." But even in this state of contemplative serenity, the soul contained a "restlessly active nature" (*phuseôs de polupragmonos*), an "unquiet power" prompting it on the one hand to "rule itself" and be "on its own," and on the other, to "seek for more than its present state." It "did not want the whole to be present to it all together," but at the prompting of the "unquiet power" (*dunamis ouch hêsuchos*) within it, goading it to pursue the bewitching variety of "what comes after and is not the same, but one thing after another," the soul sought to transfer what it saw as inbound unity in the intelligible world to "somewhere else"—to the lower, sensible world, a world spun out, dilated into the "one thing after another" of both spatial distention and temporal sequence: a world that, compared with the self-gathered richness of the intelligible, exhibited the deceptive appearance of "more."[72]

So did the soul, as Plotinus tells it, pass from its contemplative rest into active motion, and as it passed, "time moved with it." This "passage" he now illustrates with an image strikingly reminiscent of the one Augustine found in *Ecclesiasticus*: he compares the soul to a "seed" (*sperma*) whose "formative principle" (*logos*) "unfolds itself" in a movement of growth toward what it thinks of as "largeness" (*polu*). That largeness is, however, deceptive, since the soul can achieve it only at the price of self-division. "Instead of keeping its unity in itself," accordingly, "it squanders itself outside itself and so goes forward to a weaker greatness" (or "extension," *mekos*).[73]

There are other images and conceptual schemes operative in the *De Musica* besides those contained in this treatise; Augustine is becoming surer and stronger than at Cassiciacum in his ability to integrate elements from other *Enneads* along with Biblical imagery drawn from a variety of texts. But the commanding framework of his thinking here is, I submit, furnished by the Plotinian description of the soul's fall into time.

Both Plotinus in *Ennead* III, 7 and Augustine in the *De*

Musica are explicitly concerned with the soul's temporal condition, with its capacity to measure time and what that implies. Both throw the question back to the soul's original condition in eternity. For both of them, being in time is, for the soul, a fallen condition; that fall had its deepest root in a kind of pride. The soul's will to be "on its own" (*Ennead* III, 7) sends Augustine's mind quite naturally back to Plotinus' earlier account (*Ennead* V, 1) of *tolma* as the root of "genesis," or temporal becoming. But associated now with *tolma,* pride, is that "restlessness," that unquiet property of soul, a "careful" property that Augustine finds echoed in the *cura* of *"curiositas."* From a kind of sated weariness with the serene leisure (*otium*) of contemplation, the soul itches—through its "general love of action"—to plunge into the hectic, "busy" world of action and *"negotium."* In that plunge, its self-gathered, interior riches are dispersed, squandered, literally spilled forth to the exterior. From a blissful beholding of the "real," the soul sets itself to the construction of a rival, "imitation" world of becoming, passes "away" from the higher into this lower world, which, once the soul has created it on the model of the higher, becomes an entrapment for it, an "enslavement."

That strange and arresting image of "pride" in *Ecclesiasticus* encouraged Augustine, doubtless, to surmise once more that Plotinus' image of the seed uncoiling, spilling forth its interior riches, only underlined the fundamental concord between Bible and *Enneads*. Doubtless, but it suggests an answer to a question that, though seldom adverted to, needs answering. Why, of all the images of pride one might find in the biblical writings, did this one, this baroque *Vetus Latina* distortion of the original impress Augustine so forcefully as to become for him, at this period of his development, his central image of "pride," of its root, of its consequences? Is it not likely that, given Augustine's lively sensitivity to the compelling image, its very similarity with Plotinus' image in *Ennead* III, 7, triggered in him an attentiveness, prompted him to accord it the importance it assumes in his thought and imagination?

In any event, and given the evidence we have that Augustine read this treatise and was strongly influenced by it, the proposal I am making here allows us to understand a whole series of expressions that proliferate throughout the Sixth Book of the *De Musica*. Among them figure the recurrent allusions to the "toils," "difficulties," the "disquieting care" and "busy-ness" (*aerumnae, difficultates, cura, inquieta negotia*) involved in a life of temporal activity. The soul has abandoned its original *stabilitas, securitas* in the contemplative eternal world; it is *provecta in exteriora*: it finds itself chasing restlessly after the transient "outward" realities of time; its inner resources are spilled forth into "tumultuous remembrances" (*tumultuosae recordationes*); it has lost that *summa facilitas,* the splendid "ease" it once enjoyed, and is "busy," "toilsome" (*negotiosa, operosa, laboriosa*) among the "traces of numbers pertaining to spaces of time." The soul, in short, is literally *polupragmôn,* "busy about many things," torn everyway like Martha by the cares and disquiet of the active life, and quite the opposite of Mary, composed as she is, and restfully enjoying the leisure (*otium*) of contemplation.[74]

But Plotinus' term, *polupragmôn,* contains another sense as well. Besides referring to the "restlessness' and "unquiet" of a soul busy about many things, the meanings that have chiefly occupied us until now, it can and does mean "curious." Ambiguous notion; one is tempted to speculate on how Marius Victorinus translated it in his Latin version of the *Enneads.* In any case, that ambiguity is not only preserved in Augustine's account of the fall, the ambiguity is traced, however verbally, to its root. For *curiositas,* he reminds us, is derived from *cura,* "care." From this standpoint, the restless "general love of action" which plummeted the soul from its "most easeful life" (*facillima vita*) of contemplation continues to distract her, even now, from the sublime object of her contemplations, thus entangling her in the disquieting life of temporal "cares." But that same love of action, Augustine is encouraged to think, also accounts for the soul's "curious" thirst for sense-experience as such, for the "vain" imitation of true knowledge.[75]

Yet the pride (*superbia*) that is Augustine's counterpart of the Plotinian *tolma* has not, from the specifically Christian point of view, been adequately described. Augustine now goes on to complement Plotinus, by attributing to pride an intersubjective dimension. It amounts to the soul's appetite, not only for acting on bodies, but for subjugating other rational souls—its "neighbors, fellows, whose lot the soul shares under the same law" (*proximas suas, et sub eadem lege socias et consortes*). This action, made possible only by the state of sin (*peccatorum . . . conditione*) is exercised through the body, and more precisely, by "signifying" (*significando*), by communicating through body movements, looks, gestures, all of which are "natural" signs; or by conventional signs, like words. The aim of all this is to influence other souls by command, persuasion, or any other means available. Such sign-communication has its root, often enough, in a vainglorious desire to excel over other souls, to win "honor and praise" through manipulation of the entire panoply of "numbers and motions" with which the *De Musica* has been concerned.[76] Again, the whole array of symbolic operations has been traced to the soul's fallen state but as associated now with the proud desire to master other souls.

At last Augustine feels, the paradox of prudence which raised this entire issue has been resolved: he feels we can now understand why the soul's residual "knowledge" of where it ought to take up its abode is not tantamount to a "power" to do so. It is scarcely surprising, Augustine feels, that a soul so "entangled" in this welter of preoccupations is "turned away" from the beatifying contemplation of eternal Truth.[77]

Not only is it psychologically understandable, he thinks, it is also just (*jure secutum*) that such activities, particularly when motivated by pride, should turn souls away from the vision of that "pure and unmixed truth" which is God.[78] Not only is it imprudent in that eudaemonistic sense which all too easily comes down to meaning "foolish" or "ill-advised"; immersion in such activity has been related to the sin of pride whose referents are not only God but fellow men as well—or, more precisely, fellow souls.

And the activity in question clearly covers the whole domain of what the modern would call aesthetic activity: the world of words, signs, movements and gestures, rhythms and proportions, in short, the entire symbolic universe of human art and culture. All this, were we to stop with what has been said so far, is roundly condemned as natural consequent of the soul's original proud itch viciously to imitate rather than serve its God; symbolic activity has further been associated with the frequent desire to subjugate rather than love neighbor-souls in this fallen world. The deprecation of the "human" leveled in the *De Quantitate Animae,* even the linkage of symbol and fall in the *De Genesi contra Manichaeos,* were mild by comparison.

Again, it would seem, Svoboda's judgment, though for reasons he did not suspect, has been sustained: Augustine's view of art has become, if not precisely more spiritual, at least more reflectively, self-consciously so, than in his earlier works. But this has transpired through a play of influences traceable to *both* Plotinus *and* Christianity. For the task of bringing Plotinian *tolma* into closer harmony with biblical pride was one incumbent on Augustine from the moment he conceived the ambition of presenting a Plotinian understanding of the faith; nowhere has he acquitted himself of that task so boldly as here; and nowhere is the resultant judgment on art so austerely negative. At least, in principle.

Art and "Return"

For Augustine has not said his last word on the matter: he has situated artistic activity only from one direction, that it, as prolongation of the restless love of action which originally prompted the soul's fall; as such, art is little but a continuation through time of the Plotinian fall into time. The intersubjective dimension of Christian "pride" serves in this context to darken his view of such fallen activity, giving it a distinctly moral and religious flavor which it does not possess in Plotinus. But both of these dynamics are double-edged: art must be situated not only in its relation to the fall, but also in terms of the function it can perform in connection with the soul's "return"; and the intersubjective dimension raises the question of what positive service souls can perform for fellow souls through this medium of symbolic communication.

To this task Augustine now sets himself: he turns to consider another species of "action": the sort of activity God commands for the return of the soul. That action the authority of Scripture tells us is love: love for God and for our neighbor. It will be by "referring" all "movements and numbers" of our action as humans to the end of charity, that we shall be "purified" of their entangling quality.[79] The "reference" of charity can therefore immunize the soul, validate its engaging in activities which the foregoing analysis would seem unrelievedly to condemn. Instead of a "purification" which would peremptorily command us to "turn away" from all symbolic action, we are offered a way of engaging in that action and still becoming purified.

Augustine then proceeds to explain the working of this reference of charity. It involves turning our hearts from the "more laborious" love of this world of defective sensible imitations, and toward the perfect divine equality, constancy, and eternity we seek in loving passing and changeable things but never find there. "Do not love this world," St. John's Epistle rightly warns us, "because all things in the world are concupiscence of the flesh, concupiscence of the eyes, and secular ambition": the moral triad which Augustine found hinted at in various places in Plotinus' *Enneads,* he has finally succeeded in synthesizing.[80]

Once he has turned back his love from this to the other world, the Christian succeeds in neutralizing the effects of this triadic sin: he learns to refer all his activity amid sounding numbers not to "carnal pleasure," but solely to the "body's well-being"; to refer all activity of soul-to-soul communication not to his own "proud excellence" but to the "utility" of the fellow souls with whom he communicates; to indulge in all such activity not out of superfluous and dangerous "curiosity" but only to render indispensable "judgments of approval or disapproval" on the beauties of the sense-world. Choosing only to prevent hindrance to the body's health, and referring all these actions to the "profit of his neighbor" whom he has been commanded to love as himself, such a man can "act [amid] all these numbers and avoid their entrapments."[81]

The soul is still committed to an upward passage, to an ascent from lower to the highest, divine Beauty; and yet, the attitude toward that lower order is couched in more benign terms than formerly: the body is a "creature of God" (whatever the Manichee may say); though held in contempt in comparison with the soul's native dignity, it is like the "finest silver" when compared with gold.[82] The world of inferior numbers is the product of our "morality," the result of our having been punitively immersed in time and action; and yet, it constitutes by that very fact a divinely providential order and therefore is, in its own kind, beautiful.[83] That positive evaluation of the sensible order is only underlined when later Augustine proves the reasonability of its all having been created "from nothing"; not from the Plotinian *mê on* he toyed with as equivalent of "nothing" in the Cassiciacum Dialogues, but now, quite literally "nothing."[84] We must not "love" the beauties of sense-creation as though we could find our happiness in "enjoying" them (*eos perfruendo*). We are meant to free ourselves of them since they are "temporal," but this freedom we shall gain "by using them well" (*bene utendo*), as one would a plank in shipwreck; one neither throws it aside nor thinks of it as a stable anchorage.[85]

There is much in this milder evaluation of the sensible and of artistic activity which can be duplicated in Plotinus. His later accent treats of artistic effort in this same ascending, hence more optimistic context;[86] action, then, becomes the shadow image and hesitant initiation of contemplation for souls whose weakness suggests they begin that way.[87] His entire series of anti-gnostic writings justifies the existence and stresses the value of the sensible universe—a copy, but nonetheless a beautiful copy of the true archetypal world. Yet his own continued suspicion of that world has metaphysical grounds in a view of matter which Augustine has in principle abandoned once he admits a "creation from nothing" taken in full rigor of the terms.[88]

Augustine's attitude toward sensible creation is, therefore, much milder than heretofore; a similar mildness shows when he comes to describe the soul's final state. Here, as I noted earlier, he applies Plotinus' view that bodily consciousness diminishes, becomes less distracting to the soul, as it ascends. Now, for a final time, he speaks of the soul's relation to the resurrected body. When the body is separated from the soul by death and then given back to it, "reformed,"[89] when God has "vivified our mortal bodies, as the Apostle says, 'because of the spirit remaining in us,' " then whatever phantasms or temporal numbers of bodily movements may conceivably remain will "pass us by without being noticed" as they do now when the mind is absorbed in higher activities. Then, wrapt in the face-to-face contemplation of divine Truth, we shall experience no disquieting effects from the numbers by which we move our bodies, but only joy.[90] This represents a conscious, and conscientious effort to think out the resurrection of the body, a mystery whose place in a Plotinian understanding of the faith so recently seemed to puzzle him.[91] That mystery is still something "properly believed before it is understood"; it implies that the body will be "restored to its former stability," and more emphatic still, that the soul, "there," *must* be accompanied by its servant the body, in order to "excel" in a way befitting its dignity.[92] The earlier idea of death as the soul's escape from the body and flight from all relation to the sensible order has, at least in Augustine's alertest thinking on the question, been discarded. And by the same token, the soul's ideal mid-station—from which it fell and to which it seeks return—now unambiguously comports the "heavenly body" and the soul's intrinsic relation to the sensible order which it has in certain genial moments in Plotinus' thought.[93] The fact that this body is immortal and heavenly, that "there" the soul's relation to the sensible is radically different from what we experience "here," will permit Augustine even yet to speak in terms whose occasional looseness might suggest a "flight from the body and sense." But when brought to face the issue squarely, his thought from this point on is alert to the need of taking the body's resurrection into account. An identifiably Christian tenet, therefore, has forced him to focus more clearly on an element in Plotinus' system which had earlier, and notably at Cassiciacum, received but sidelong attention. Here, another Christian influence has worked toward making his initial aesthetic not more, but less "spiritual."

Tensions still remain; Augustine ends his *De Musica* with a very probably Plotinus-inspired attempt to show that all four of the classic "civic" or "political" virtues can be interpreted as serving the soul's return to contemplation,[94] and in such a fashion that they will survive, transformed, in the soul's life of final bliss.[95] Those virtues, in the original Platonic tradition, assured the possibility of men living with men in order, friendship, and peace; there is some irony in Augustine's insistence, now especially, on their contemplative character.

For if there is one piece he strains to tailor to his view of man as fallen soul, it is this central strand of the Christian moral view, this ineradicable regard for the human community, the *societas humana*. The dominant logic of the *De Musica* presents man as a fallen soul, whose central ethical preoccupation must be return from the temporal life of action to the heavenly bliss of contemplation. The most obvious way of that return is purification, not the mutual regard of man for man. Augustine has made a determined effort to connect the pride at the origin of the soul's fall with the desire to subjugate fellow souls through symbolic action; he may have felt that this entitled him to claim that the "most certain upward step" (*gradus*) in the soul's re-ascent toward "cleaving to God" in contemplative union is the love of neighbor commanded by the Gospel.[96] The affirmation is a brave one, but it leaves the reader with misgivings.

One is tempted to think Augustine was more lucid in the pages where he seemed to sense a certain irreducibility, if not opposition, between the ways of purification and of charity. The stress on purification in the *De Quantitate Animae* was qualified by a somewhat guilty "inasmuch as permitted"[97]—the Christian valuation for human society, Augustine seems to have seen, must operate as a limiting factor on the soul's enthusiastic flight from involvement in the human. The élan that moved the soul from authority through reasoned understanding to disincarnate vision broke, in the *De Utilitate Credendi,* on this same cornerstone of Christian morality: his Manichee friend, Honoratus is brought to a lower, slower route than his native gifts would seem to authorize, precisely out of regard for the *societas hu-*

mana.[98] One is reminded of Socrates' analogous difficulty in the *Republic*: once the philosopher has been educated to the glimpse of that intelligible sun, how is he to be brought down to minister to the city and its human concerns?[99] Little has changed since that difficulty first was posed: the view of man as fallen soul aspiring to regain contemplative happiness will always find regard for the city and its human community at least a limit, more likely a stumbling block, to the logical thrust of its ethic.

Noteworthy here is the fact that Plotinus' systematic thought has little if anything to contribute toward regard for the human community. His solicitude for Porphyry when a fit of depression drove him to the brink of suicide, his almost scrupulous conscientiousness in keeping the accounts of orphans placed in his care, these features of Plotinus the man are both well-known and endearing. But the man Porphyry depicts as refusing to let his portrait be done, the man who refused to speak of his parents or birthplace, and persistently discouraged all political involvement,[100] may well have been more faithful to a philosophy that has little or no enthusiasm for human relationships and attachments. Love for neighbor a "most certain *gradus*" for the soul's ascent? The "reference of charity" a guarantee that the soul may engage in these activities and not only not be "caught in them," but actually be "cleansed" from attachment to them? Again, brave affirmations; but Plotinus would likely have been the first to pose a mild, but merciless set of questions to anyone who made them.

All his life long Augustine will struggle with the problem of charity: how can the love of God, interpreted as the intellectual appetite for vision, be made to cohere with the love of neighbor? The neighbor, one is forced to think, must necessarily become (like any other creaturely good) an object of "use," a rung on the ladder upward to vision of God Who alone must be "enjoyed." But is this "love" of neighbor in the Gospel sense? And even if it were, why should it impose the active concern for him, the involvement in a life of apostolic action on his behalf, which validate the very activities which a theory of man as fallen soul would logically condemn?

Such questions are central to Augustine's evaluation of art. Every specifically Christian influence detectable in the *De Musica*—the doctrines of resurrection, creation from nothing, charity to the neighbor—argue that a more positive value be assigned to properly aesthetic activity than the Cassiciacum works, more single-mindedly intent on the way of the "disciplines" as a flight from body and sense, could logically assign to it. But among these specifically Christian themes, the reference of charity, the regard for human society, is uppermost in Augustine's mind and more powerfully operative than any other. It would be comforting to be able to report that its operation was destined to lead Augustine, in time, to a properly human estimate of this "properly human" sphere of activity.

Yet the promise latent in this central theme is never really fulfilled. And the reason why it could not be fulfilled is already evident from the *De Musica*: why indeed should the soul devote itself to "raising up vast monuments" in this visible world, when all they amount to in the end is an array of mud-huts, slapped together from the soul's own "ruins."[101] For the human domain is not the soul's native air; it was never object of the original creative design. Rather, it is God's condescending second thought, as it were, providential apparatus to promote the fallen soul's return to the other, spiritual dwelling from which it wandered. Even the incarnation fits into this same description; Augustine still expresses that "ineffable *sacramentum*" in the *logos-anthrôpos* terms he was later (and somewhat too severely) to condemn as "Photinian":[102] if God "assumed a man" *hominem suscepit*) it was principally that we might avoid the pride through which we merited our fall into these things," and following his example, calmly pay the debt of death we owe on account of that fall.[103] *Ista*: the entire sum of human achievements and their historic drama can be summed up in that semi-contemptuous pronoun, and then ticked off with the single word: "ruins."

For despite the brief flirtation we have seen him carry on with the concept, human society—precisely as human—must struggle fiercely to win favor in Augustine's eyes. The Adam whom God made to work the garden, to whom He gave commission to "subdue the earth," stamping it with his image, molding it to make an increasingly human world for human beings, that Adam regularly becomes, in Augustine's spiritual exegesis, contemplative inhabitant of another world than this: primordial man, or better, primordial soul. All his "labor" is a tenacious struggle to win his way back to the vision of Truth, to that "heavenly city" where society is true society: not human, but of soul with soul.[104] Only much later, when he has abandoned once and for all his theory of the soul's fall, will a distinctively new note enter his thinking.

However "properly human" he must concede it to be, the logic of Augustine's anthropology presently compels him to say of

art what he says, in the *De Vera Religione,* of the entire network
of relationships which make up human society. He is, significantly, explaining the "love of neighbor" which promised so
shortly before, in the *De Musica,* to temper his hard judgment
on man's symbolic activity. "Man is not to be loved by man," he
interprets that commandment, "as brothers after the flesh are
loved, or sons, or wives, or kinsfolk, or relatives, or fellow-citi-
zens. For such love is temporal."[105] "If we are ablaze with love
for eternity, we shall hate temporal relationships."[106] All such
relationships are traceable to the primal sin: "We should have
no such connections as are contingent on birth and death, if
our nature had remained in obedience to the commandment of
God and in the likeness of His image. It would not have been
relegated to its present corrupt state."[107] In calling us back to
that original and perfect state, of soul endued with an immortal,
heavenly body, soaring above the sensible world of our present
experience, "Truth Himself . . . bids us resist carnal custom"
and to hate "these carnal bonds" of fatherhood, motherhood,
brother-and-sisterhood which weave the texture of "human society."[108] The fundamental reason for all this is clear: "Our real
selves are not bodies"; hence "human nature is to be loved . . .
without any condition of carnal relationship."[109] Carnal, human,
temporal: those realms are coextensive; they are all the domain
of sinfulness, corruption; the ruined world of souls fallen from
eternity into time.[110]

Hence the *De Vera Religione* can present an ascending aesthetic;[111] of exactly the same type as the *De Musica,* but climax
it with Augustine's celebrated critique of all imaginative activity.
He has already warned against the image-maker's function,[112]
but (with typical ambivalence) qualified that warning by admitting the provisional, pedagogic value of such imagery.[113] Now,
however, he presents the ideal, the attitude toward images which
the fully matured soul is expected to adopt; "Give me such a
one," he cries,

as can see without any imagination of carnal things seen . . . Give me
one who resists his carnal senses and the blows they inflict upon the
soul; who resists the usages of men . . . and does not love vanities
exterior (to the soul) . . . who has learned to say: "if there be one
Rome, on the Tiber . . . then that Rome is false which my thought
imagines . . . If there be one sun, then that sun is false which my
thought imagines . . . " False, all such images; on falsities like these
no man can fix his understanding. When I contemplate such images,
therefore, and when I give them credence, I do not understand.[114]

Such disincarnate understanding is, Augustine would persuade us, threshold to the vision which the soul has lost, and strains to recover. The ladder of temporal, carnal beauties is there for it to mount; upward, by stages it must climb; from lower to higher to the highest Number which is God Himself; till everything carnal, temporal, symbolic, and imaginative, is left behind. Despite the momentary hesitations his determination to be Christian causes him—determination neither more nor less sincere and firm than at Cassiciacum—despite the crucial urgency he senses, in this period of his development, to take the web and work of human society more seriously than his Plotinian theory will permit him, Augustine here has signed the death warrant of all art. It is no small irony that the hand that signed was the one which wrote one of the Western world's greatest literary masterpieces, the *Confessions*. Incomparable triumph of human sensibility and imagination, its burden, when scrutinized in depth, is an uncompromising call for the utter annihilation of both.

5

ART IN THE

CONFESSIONS

Magnus es, Domine: "Great art Thou, Lord, and greatly to be praised"; from its opening notes the symphonic power of Augustine's *Confessions* leaps to life. For the work is quite literally a symphony. We moderns *read* the *Confessions,* usually in translations more or less adequate to the near impossible demands of the original. But Augustine plainly meant them to be read aloud, to be *heard*; meant their rich sonorities to swell, diminish, interweave, and echo to each other; intended his masterful play on the resources of the Latin tongue to fall upon the listening ear, fade, and return with ever-mounting vigor and suggestiveness, as theme announced becomes theme deferred, developed in subterranean forms, then finally unfurled in climax after climax of artistic orchestration. Much has been written concerning the unity, and the unitary meaning of the *Confessions*:[1] it has been averred that the book is badly integrated and that the scholar must simply face that fact. *Augustin compose mal,* once wrote one of the most sensitive students of his work: "Augustine composes badly," and there, H. I. Marrou was persuaded, is the despairing end of it.[2] Some years later, in his handsome *Retractatio,* he thought better of that judgment: the intervening years had brought him to realize that Augustine's style of composition is a "musical" one.[3] Alas, one does not demonstrate the validity of such a proposal in *wissenschaftlich* terms, any more than one could prove the unity of import that weaves the recurrent themes of the Eroica symphony into a single, rounded work of art. The only test is in successive hearings, and then our subsequent analyses fail to bring us very far in rendering an account of what we have heard.

All of which is to make the claim that the *Confessions* must be interpreted as one would any other superb work of poetic art. *Magnus es*: the opening note calls attention to the fact that the very title of the work is bewilderingly multivalent. Augustine's intention was to "praise God's justice and goodness for all the good and evil" that had befallen him along his road of life, and so "to excite men's minds and hearts" to equal praise and love of Him.[4] Confession of sinfulness, profession of faith, thankful wonder, loving, adoring praise, the term *Confessiones* throbs with all these connected motifs.

It is initially tempting to view Augustine's purpose as one of intentional edification. The rationalistic overtones of his theory of art, the *rhetor's* notorious adeptness at calculating his effects, would both conspire with his own avowal of pastoral purpose, inducing us to envisage the *Confessions* as a kind of academic set piece, as though Augustine started with a firm conception of the object in view, then chapter by chapter, line by line, lucidly selected incident and detail, tested term and phrase and sentence melody, with the *rhetor's* practiced eye and ear for creating a desired atmosphere, eliciting an intended response. Indeed, Augustine himself may well have thought this was his mode of procedure. There is reason to believe that the occasion that prompted him to write was of a proportionately pedestrian order. Paulinus of Nola wished to know him better.[5] The magical power of the finished masterpiece, however, betrays the fact that something happened along the way. Deeper places of his soul became engaged in the creative process, the *rhetor's* lucid purpose was transfused into that baffling catalyst, the genuinely "poetic idea"; what might have remained a merely occasional work took on the flesh of "all time and all existence"—what may have been meant as religious rhetoric suffered the sea-change into art.[6]

If this be true—and one can try only to illustrate, not to demonstrate its truth—then we must be prepared for certain surprises. Plato was wise: when the "divine madness" afflicts the poet, we must not expect him to be able to tell us in cool ex-

pository terms, what he is about. The same may well be true of
Augustine. Whatever the "conscious" purposes he may have
had for composing the *Confessions,* the forces generated in the
process of creation may have burst forth from their initially con-
fining channels; deeper levels of consciousness, obscurer levels
of intention may come into play; the result may be a work whose
import resonates with, but transcends, and even occasionally defies what was consciously intended.

Consequently, we may expect the *Confessions* to be, on occasion, even more revelatory than Augustine might have wished.
We may also find them a truer touchstone than anything else
he wrote, not only for querying the value of his theory of art
but for uncovering the value that art *de facto* held for him.

To that "unintended" theory of art, embodied in rather than
explicitly presented by the *Confessions,* we shall come in time.
First, however, what of the theory of art Augustine consciously
meant to communicate to his readers?

He wastes little time getting to it: the very first book of the
Confessions treats, in critical tones, of the education in the *artes*
he received as a young boy. The strictures he levels at that youthful exposure to Greek and Latin literature might lead the un-
wary reader to conclude that the Bishop of Hippo no longer
has any use for the *artes* so vaunted by the enthusiastic convert
of the *De Ordine.* But use for them he still has, as closer study
of subsequent books will demonstrate. Books X and XI, particularly, show that his views remain substantially identical
with those encased in the *De Musica.*

Books I–IX have dealt with Augustine's "autobiography":
with his memories of childhood, youth, manhood, his wandering away from, and pilgrimage back to the God of his heart. Augustine has found Him: but where did he find his God? The
theme announced in question form in the very first paragraph
of the *Confessions* has several times reappeared in varying regis-
ters throughout the work; it is now up for final resolution. How
can man even call upon God, seek to know Him, unless in some
mysterious sense he knows God already?[7] Meno's objection to
Socrates[8] may initially seem a clever sophism, but the Platonist
is committed to taking it with deadly seriousness. The classic
answer invariably takes the form of showing that all true "learning is remembering." That doctrine of Platonic memory we
have seen in close connection with Augustine's early enthusiasm
for the "mental exercise" of the liberal *artes*; despite all the
changes the years have wrought, the connection remains firm.

He must, though, lead our minds to acknowledge that, beyond the ordinary memory of past experiences with which his "biographical" books have dealt, there lies this other dimension of memory as well: a memory containing, not images of past temporal events and objects, but realities (*res ipsas*).[9] But what realities might these be? Augustine exemplifies them as all those things "learned from the liberal sciences," such as "what literature is, what the art of disputation is, how many types of questions there are": knowledge of such timeless, unchanging essences (or forms), he is convinced, the mind cannot have attained through the shifting, passing report of the bodily senses.[10] The same must be said of the principles and laws of number (*numerorum dimensionumque rationes et leges innumerabiles*).[11] These are not mere words, not the bodily realities we number and measure, nor images of the latter: they are the supernal archetypes we glimpse as norms for numbering, measuring—and judging upon—all the realities of the sense-world; as such, they must exist somewhere, indeed, they "truly exist" (*valde sunt*).[12]

Augustine is leading our minds, then, up the familiar ladder of the *artes*—the "arts" in the sense of school disciplines, hence arts envisaged, as always in this context, with an eye to their "scientific," mathematical component. The aesthetic at work is the rationalistic, Neo-Pythagoreanized aesthetic of his earliest writings. But he still firmly hopes that it can be pressed into service to aid the mind to "ascend": to recognition of the God Whose truth and beauty still discloses itself, half-forgotten, half-remembered, in the deep recesses of the soul's "memory."[13]

Book XI, another testimony to Augustine's persistent recourse to the liberal *artes,* shows that the insights and method recorded in the *De Musica* have not been forgotten over the years. He is meditating on the law that overarches all created reality: the eternal, unchanging word in and through which God made everything. His aim is to lead our minds to grasp the difference between the eternity of that Word and the temporal character of all our human words. As in the *De Musica,* he chooses as his illustration a line of verse: once again, his choice falls upon St. Ambrose's *Deus Creator Omnium.*[14] Its meter involves syllables both long and short, requires that the mind be able to "measure" such temporal intervals. But how can this be? Augustine multiplies, dilates upon the paradoxes implied, but always with the same purpose as in the *De Musica*—the ascensional aesthetic is being pressed into service once again, leading the mind to recognize that its "distension" into the multiplicity of numbered times has not entirely eclipsed its grasp of supernal Unity, the font of all such lower numbers.[15] Into that divine Unity, the soul is brought to see, it longs to have its fragmented being "flow together"; it is, indeed, the gift of God that "re-collects us" "brings us back to the One, from whom we flowed downward into the many" in a fall that would appear to have brought our souls from the peaceful bliss of contemplation into the frenzied, distracting world of temporal—and symbolic, artistic—action.[16]

There is a judgment on the value of art implied in that final phrase: only further examination will disclose how firmly Augustine still traces art to the soul's fall. But even at this point this much is clear: the use he makes of the liberal *artes* is substantially the one he made of them in his early works. The *exercitationes* of Books X and XI are both designed to lead the mind upward—from "corporeal to incorporeal realities"—to a recognition of its kinship with an eternal world transcending the sensible, temporal universe of man's embodied experience. The *De Disciplinis* project he had once intended to pursue may have been abandoned, but its ascensional, its art-annihilating spirit pervades his thinking.

The *exercitationes* of the *Confessions* are, however, by no means confined to the materials of the disciplines. Augustine has cast his net considerably wider than that. His pastoral endeavors, the meditation of Scripture that nourished his preaching activity, his growth in personal and prayer experience, have brought him to see that the whole fabric of life, of human struggles and strivings, longings and sorrows and joys, is matter for *exercitatio*. He looks on the stuff of his own life as food for probing reflection, and finds it not untypical of what the mass of mankind has known. So, he prods our minds to ponder a series of his own life experiences, of the sort, he is confident, that we will recognize as our own, or so very like our own as to spark in us the recognition he hopes will dawn. We have all learned our native language in childhood: how many of us have realized what a strange, mysterious process that was?[17] We have known something like the schoolboy's dread of being punished,[18] his zest in competing against his peers,[19] we have tasted the fearful joy of some forbidden escapade.[20] Surely we remember some early experience with death,[21] and the slow work of weeks and months thereafter that anesthetized the anxiety the jarring prospect of our own death brought with it.[22] There must have been a poem or a play that made us weep and wonder why that sorrow was sweet to us,[23] or some reunion we shared, whose happiness we vaguely sensed, was all the more intense because the pain of separation had been so keen.[24] *Grande profundum, homo*: a mighty abyss, mankind;[25] yet, how many of us have ever queried these features of our common humanity to the point of becoming an "immense question" to ourselves?[26] "Woe, thou torrent of human custom," Augustine means us to see, that bears us along so swiftly that, unthinkingly, we assume that the "customary" is the same as the authentically human.[27]

Augustine is persuaded that his understanding of the faith sheds light on all these features of human life; pierce beneath the surfaces of these seemingly banal experiences and one sees, he is convinced, that the human soul is a journeying thing, like Israel in the desert, a stranger in a strange land. We all begin as wanderers, estranged from the God of our bliss; but if, through growing docility to the welter of "admonitions" Providence scatters along our way, we come first to believe, then to understand the truth of our situation, we may convert our wandering into pilgrimage, into a return to the heavenly Jerusalem from which we have strayed.[28]

Among those multifarious admonitions belong all the features of our human life that interest the aesthetician. Central among these is man's common reliance on signs and symbols. Assuming, as always, that the symbolism of language and the symbolism of art are fundamentally parallel, Augustine invites us to focus on the infant's efforts to communicate.[29] As always, too, he thinks of the true, inner self as soul, a center of perceptions and desires. The wants of the infant soul, however, are "within," invisible to the perceptions of others "outside." The ideal counterpart would be that souls should lie open and transparent to each other's gaze: the strangeness of the human condition lies in our mutual opacity to one another. And so, to communicate its inner wants, the infant must resort to gestures and cries, must employ signs as similar as possible to the wishes being conveyed, similar but "not like the truth."[30] Toward the end of infancy, the child begins to look for more adequate signs, by which to make known its meanings to others.[31] Time passes, and eventually the infant has become a "chattering boy": Augustine asks us to reflect with him on how he—and we—learned to speak. Others did not teach him by presenting him with words in any sequential form, as his masters taught him letters later on: he himself; with his God-given mind, wished to express the inner feelings of his "heart," and employed the outward means of various cries, sounds, and limb movements to do so. Still, expression remains unsatisfactory. And so the child observes the connection between a word used by an adult, and a gesture toward an indicated object: he infers that the word is the name—conventionally established —for the object indicated. The inference is confirmed when adults employ those words, transcending local and temporal convention, those "natural" signs—gestures, nods, changes of countenance, and vocal sounds—to indicate their approval of the connection the infant has established. And so the child goes on to grasp that words are signs of things, masters the conventions of ordering words into sentences, and learns to express his inner wishes by means of these outward signs.

Like a younger version of Odysseus, the boy is now launched upon the "stormy society of human life."[32]

This entire infancy experience, Augustine repeatedly reminds us, we in time forget. With that forgetfulness we lose the sense of strangeness that reflection on this process suddenly renews: how strange that the "inner" self should be so straitened, jacketed, so barred from direct perception of the wishes and intentions of fellow souls, that it must resort to penetrating—or better, circumventing—that mutual opacity whether through natural signs or the conventional human "institution" that language represents.

Again and again Augustine leads us back to puzzle on, to come to increasingly sharpened recognition of the various facets of the battle with signs, symbols, and images; they invariably stand as a forest of "outward" media, more or less "like the truth"; the soul must struggle with, yet past, beyond them, in its unending quest for meanings, realities—for the Truth that alone can satisfy the wishes of its inner being.

One pivot of Augustine's thinking is this horizontal contrast between "inner" and "outer"; but the opacity of the flesh that impedes communication of soul to soul has a vertical counterpart: in the "blindness" which prevents the sinful wanderer from glimpsing the radiance of the Truth that enlightens its "interior" from on high.[33] Thus, the flames of his first conversion at nineteen were kindled by the *Hortensius* of Cicero, whom men revere more often for his tongue than for his heart; yet that work impressed Augustine less by the outward polish of its language than by the inward message of supernal Wisdom it conveyed to him.[34] The Gospels repelled him, on the other hand, by the lowliness of their style—he failed to penetrate to their inner meaning.[35] In his quest for Truth, he fell among the Manichees, whose radical failure in this regard was to encourage his

own penchant for thinking of the spiritual God in images and
phantasms drawn from the outer realities of the sense-world[36]—
the very tendency that Augustine thinks vitiated his own attempt to elaborate the early aesthetic of the *De Pulchro et Apto*.[37]
The diptych subtly drawn of those two bishops, the shallow
Faustus and Ambrose of Milan, pivots on the contrast between
glittering words[38]—outward vessels empty of truth—and the
soberer eloquence whose spell induces the soul to welcome the
realities, the nourishing truths expressed.[39]

The success of the admonition given him by those "Platonists'
books," the *libri platonicorum*[40] can be measured by the fact
that it brought him to transcend his inveterate habit of "image-
thinking" and glimpse the "invisible things of God" with the
inner eye of his "soul";[41] he marvels, now, that it is God he
loves, and not some imaginary phantom in His stead.[42] He has
learned that our judgments on the ascending ranges of sensible
beauties imply a mysterious precognition of the immutable
Beauty existing unchangeably as norm for judgment above the
changing mind; knowledge of this open secret delivers him finally from the "tyranny of habit," withdrawing his mind from
the "throngs of contradictory phantasms" that had blocked its
vision before. In a tantalizing parenthesis, he links that precognition with a "memory, loving and longing," and swiftly passes
on.[43]

The incarnate Christ he sketches as participating in the "coats
of skin" God conferred on Adam after his fall[44] but leaves us
momentarily to wonder if this had anything to do with His having like the rest of us, to communicate by words and gestures,
to "move his limbs" and "deliver wise sayings by means of
signs."[45]

His conversion progresses, his assimilation of the Catholic
faith deepens; the contemplative interlude of Cassiciacum is followed by the baptism at Milan; the entire process is crowned by
his, and Monica's, joint experience at Ostia.

It begins with both of them conversing tenderly together,[46]
until their discourse transcends the realm of sense and bodily
delights, ascends "higher yet, by inward thought" to a fleeting
glimpse of eternal wisdom; but then, they must turn back to the
"vocal expressions of [their] mouths," words that both begin and
end, unlike the immutable Word of the creative God.[47] For enjoyment of that Word requires that all else fall into silence: all
images of earth and of the heavens, all dreams and imagined
appearances, "every tongue, every sign," all creation's witness

to its Creator, until God alone speaks and we hearken to His Word, not uttered by any "fleshly tongue," not through any riddling comparisons—we must hear Him "Himself," without the aid of any created intermediary. Augustine's language turns abruptly into another register: now he describes that vision that is granted when all "inferior visions" have been withdrawn, the vision that will ravish, absorb, enfold the beholder into its profoundest joys: the "joy of the Lord."[48] The entire regime of signs, images, symbols and symbolic intermediaries must be left behind for this immediate vision of God to be attained.

Soon Augustine returns to the coordinate question of man's opacity to his fellow man: his confession to God can be made not with bodily "words and sounds," but with "words of the soul," with the "outcry of thought," with a silence of all sound, but with the interior sound of love.[49] But confessing to his fellow man is a different matter: here, he must use sounding words that leave them room to doubt whether he speaks truly what he knows "interiorly"; they cannot place their ears next to his "heart, where I am whatever I am"; to this hidden inner self "neither their eye nor ear nor mind can reach." Only their love for him will prompt them to "believe" him.[50] For like themselves, he is that strange amalgam, a man: "body and soul . . . one without, the other within," whose knowledge of the incorporeal God beyond all bodily reality has been achieved "by the inner man . . . through the ministry of the outer," by the true self, "I, the inner man . . . I, I, the mind, through my bodily senses." The message of the bodily world is "spoken" to all, but it can be understood only by those "who compare its voice received from without with the truth within them."[51] The dichotomy of "inner," spiritual and "outer" bodily man was never more stark; the perilous indirection of soul-to-soul communication, baffled by the obstacle of bodily covering, has seldom been more dramatically portrayed.

Now Augustine interweaves the theme of words and images with the ascent through memory: our ordinary memory of the temporal past involves our retention, not only of images but of words associated with them and with the bodily realities they image; images and words we take in with our senses, but neither of them can claim to be identical with the realities they image or denote,[52] nor with the "notions of the realities themselves" which we never received through any bodily avenue.[53] Augustine "labors" over the many paradoxes involved in this uncanny set of relationships between realities, conceptions, images, and words and admits he has become a "resistant earth, to be worked by the sweat of my brow"; the reader's memory of the curse laid upon Adam flashes briefly into view and is gone,[54] but the labor continues. How is it that Latins and Greeks, despite the conventional differences of their languages, both understand the same reality when queried about the meaning of happiness?[55] This reality all men must naturally know of, must remember somehow. They must, therefore, "somewhere" have experienced it.[56] There must, we are persuaded, be a root from which all these interweaving perplexities emerge; aside from a few rather broad hints, Augustine leaves us wondering for now, and passes on.

For a Christian understanding of man's mystery must be gleaned from Scripture, and particularly from that dense compendium of all Scripture, and classic locus of patristic anthropology, *Genesis'* account of the six days of creation, the *Hexaemeron*. "In the beginning God created": the opening words of Scripture prompt a fresh review of the differences between our human words that come to be and pass away, and the ever-abiding Word in which God created all things.[57] But a problem immediately confronts him; apparently only liminal, it will swiftly take on greater proportions: for the scriptural faith about creation is conveyed to us through the human words of Moses. As such, it faces us with essentially the same questions as does all human communication: how are we to be sure of the inner intention Moses had in speaking these words? And how, a distinct but related question, how would we know he spoke truly, except by comparing "what he said" by means of vocal "sounds" with the soundless, wordless Truth speaking within us?[58] This double question, raised allusively, Augustine drops for a time and enters on the *exercitatio* previously examined: the sounding temporal words of a poetic line are made to lead our minds upward to the timeless Word presiding over all measurements of time. Throughout, however, he keeps us constantly reminded of the problem he has raised; in the process of doing so, he situates the incarnate Word in terms of it. In the Gospel, Christ spoke "through the flesh," consequently, his word "sounded outwardly in the ears of men." But to what end? First, in order that it "might be believed." But is that all there is to it? No: once believed, Christ's divine reality as Word must be "sought inwardly, and found in the eternal truth, where the only good Master teaches all his disciples." For, as in his earlier works, Augustine is convinced that teaching in the truest sense is the work of that "stable truth" whose light still illumines us from within;

we can be no more than "admonished" by a changeable creature
—even, presumably, by the changeable human nature of the
incarnate Christ—and once admonished, we are led to the
changeless Truth—the eternal Word—from whose light we
truly learn.[59] Whether it applies to Augustine writing his *Confessions,* Moses writing the *Hexaemeron,* or Jesus of Nazareth
speaking the historical human words of his temporal life, the
problem of human communication, indeed, the entire problem
of symbolism, promises in the end to receive identically the
same solution. And the root of the problem may be the same in
all three cases: wisdom, Augustine now tells us, "Wisdom itself,
gleams through me, piercing my cloudiness which again covers
me over." He falls back because of his "darkness" which he immediately identifies as a "punishment":[60] the regime of symbolism is somehow connected with the "darkness" of those
"clouds" that bar us from immediate vision of the divine Light;
a darkness somehow equivalent to a fall beneath the weight of
punishment.

By now, Augustine has left a number of questions nagging at
his readers' minds: where is that place, beyond all words, images,
created intermediaries, which he and Monica so briefly touched
upon in their joint ascent? And where the place from which all
men, whatever the differences of their language, derive their
natural memory of the "life of happiness"? Where the "place
on high" from which we fell into this cloud-covered darkness?[61]
Book XII answers all those questions in a single pregnant phrase:
the "Heaven of Heaven," the heavenly Jerusalem. He defines it
as an "intellectual creature," partaking of God's eternity by reason of the "sweetness of its most happy contemplation" of Him.[62]
He goes on to describe this creature as a community of "holy
spirits," "citizens" of the heavenly Jerusalem, so harmonized
into serene and perfect union that they compose a single "pure
mind,"[63] rapt in blissful contemplation of the divine delights.
This community of spirits "clung fast" to God and consequently
remained immune to all the turnings and vicissitudes of time.[64]
Intelligence "there" knows everything at once, not, in Paul's
description of our knowledge here, "in part" only; knows not
"darkly, in a mirror" or by means of enigmatic figures [*in aenig-
mate*], but directly, immediately, "face to face."[65]

Augustine, I have suggested, conceived of his *Confessions* as
a single, extended *exercitatio,* composed in a musical mode: at
no point before the final book does he mean to resolve completely
all the tensions set up in our minds—and imaginations—by this

artful interweave of questions, hints, images, and suggestions, all
pointing toward the meaning of man's life that he unfolds fully
in Book XIII. At this juncture of his work, however, the reader
is in a position to bring those tensions into some partial resolution.

The interpretation he has given of the "Heaven of Heaven"
fills out some important elements in his view of the human situation. The world in which we live is twofold; first, there is the
"earth" of sensible reality, with its "heaven of earth"—sky, sun,
moon, and stars—open to the gaze of our fleshly eyes. But beyond that sensible world—in imaginative terms, "above" it—
there lies the "heaven" of spiritual reality. In that place, a community of unfallen spirits[66] dwells in unchanging bliss, contemplating "face to face" the Truth-Beauty that is God. They have
no need of words, for the fullness of the eternal Word is open
to their view; their vision is immediate, direct, they stand in no
need of "admonitions," either from language, sense-perception,
or imaginative phantasm. The world of meanings, so haltingly,
symbolically conveyed by language's conventions, is object of
their direct and effortless contemplation: in His Truth, they
see all the partial truths to which the ladder of the liberal arts
conducts our minds.

Man's soul, the real "I" of this strange amalgam of soul and
body, appears to have fallen from that world of immediate vision.
Our punishment has set us in the place adapted to us, a place of
relative darkness, where a layer of clouds blocks our direct vision
of the radiance of the higher, spiritual world. And yet, our darkness is not complete: we still dimly remember the eternal word
of truth we once directly beheld; we should not be able to make
judgments on beauty and value, grasp what happiness means,
measure intervals of time, understand the truths Scripture symbolically points to, unless that memory persisted in our inner
being, in the deep recesses of our true reality, the mind. Words,
images, all the trappings of symbolic communication, are meant
first to awaken our belief, then turn our gaze inward to where
that supernal light still illumines our spiritual interior. Then
we can grow in power to recapture, truth by partial truth, facets
of the Truth that once was totally open to our gaze.

Thus far the first main pivot of Augustine's thought on symbolic communication: our need for words, images, and symbols
generally stems from our having fallen from the higher world of
Truth into the cloud-covered darkness of this lower world. Our
punishment is that we must "labor," must "toil and sweat," like

Adam after his sin, to earn the bread of incorporeal truth which nourishes our spiritual being. Our inner reality is soul, mind; all meanings that we grasp are seen by this center of our being; the ministry of the bodily senses, the outward proddings of language and symbol, consist in their presenting us with admonitions, literally reminders, of what we dimly remember. Their function is to direct the eye of the soul back to that world of Truth which was once the object of our contemplation.

On the second pivotal dichotomy in presence, however, Augustine has, until now, been more discreet. How does our mutual opacity to one another fit into the picture? To this point, Augustine has replied with a series of hints: one of them insinuates that our inability to see each other's interior being has something to do with our having been clothed with the coats of skin God made for Adam and Eve after their fall. Having raised the question so sharply, however, Augustine cannot let the matter stand at that. He must return to it now.

For his interpretation of the "Heaven of Heaven" confronts him with this problem in acute form. He has taken the liberty of viewing *Genesis'* account of the creation of heaven and earth through the lens of Psalm 113 which speaks of the "heaven of heaven";[67] he has brought to bear the resources of Plotinus' account of spiritual matter;[68] and there are some loyal Catholic exegetes, who would claim that, however *true* his views on the higher, spiritual world may be, this was not what Moses *intended* in writing his account of creation.[69] Augustine underlines his assurance that their complaint does not bear on the truth of the views the text has suggested to his "interior ear" and "eye."[70] He then goes on to argue that there are many true views one might come to while pondering the terms of *Genesis'* creation account.[71] At this stage of the discussion he does not directly question the presumption that no more than one of them could correspond to Moses' *intended* meaning. But how can his adversaries be so sure that they, not he, have discovered Moses' intention? Augustine's argument is the familiar one: it is difficult, nay, impossible for any man to gain insight into the mind and heart, to perceive the intention of another human speaker or writer; here, we must all remain content with belief.[72] But we do, on the other hand, have direct, intelligible insight into the truth of the views that divine illumination has prompted Augustine to propound when reflecting on *Genesis'* account;[73] his critics, he contends, would have to admit that they are not only true, but spiritually fruitful as well. Furthermore, his views are not private or "proper" to him; they came to him from that light of truth that is "common" to all lovers of wisdom, including, he would fondly hope, his present adversaries.[74] Indeed, God may quite possibly inspire each of us to find different truths, each of them true, on the occasion of pondering the words of Scripture.[75] These truths we do not see, I in you or you in me; both of us see them by consulting the single same unchangeable Truth above our several minds. Disagreement about Moses' intended meaning is, consequently, a squabble about words, not about realities; it would have us dispute about truths seen "in Moses," as it were, distracting us from truths seen in the supernal Truth. Such squabbles arise, accordingly, from his adversaries' proud attachment to their own "private," "proper" view, and can only be harmful to the charity that should join them with Augustine in brotherly pursuit of the one "common" Truth.[76]

Now Augustine is about to take an even more drastic step. Already he has succeeded in slackening the bond between the sacred author's intended meaning and the various truths that (God inspiring) may "occur" to the ardent reader, not precisely to see "in" the text, nor "draw from" the text, but to see "when reading," "when" pondering, even prayerfully reflecting on the text.[77] The crucial move of the mind in the process Augustine is suggesting is *away* from the text, as it were, an inward and upward move to consult the light of eternal Truth still streaming downward into the soul. Now he assures us of what he has to this point only suggested: the admonition of a single phrase from *Genesis,* like "In the beginning God created heaven and earth," can indeed excite the mind to a variety of insights, all of them legitimate if all of them are true.[78] If generalized, this position would imply that any single symbolic item can point the mind to a multiplicity of referent truths in the eternal world of Truth. And Augustine is about to take a radical step toward that generalization. It does him credit, however, that he takes that step with a twinge of hesitation. He may have been disquieted that the intention of the sacred writer, Moses, is in danger of being reduced to an essentially secondary consideration: his adversaries' instinct would imply that the single legitimate truth to be drawn from the inspired text is the one that Moses intended when writing, and Augustine's theory does not do sufficient justice to that instinct. Now he will attempt to do it greater justice: he cannot believe, he avers, that the power of eloquence with which God equipped Moses was inferior to that for which Augustine himself, if in Moses' position, would have pleaded. And had he pleaded for it, surely God would have granted it: an eloquence equal to the task of so choosing his words as intentionally to give rise to a variety of interpretations, all of them true, depending on the lights that God then variously conferred on subsequent interpreters.[79]

This, he feels, would be perfectly in keeping with the richness of nourishment God would want Scripture to convey. For its words must feed neophyte Christians, still babes in the "nest" of the faith; their way of thinking, admittedly, is sensist, "animal"; but the everyday images and terms of Scripture speak a language they can understand; even if they interpret it in "carnal" terms, still, it provides them with a certain core of sound belief, to which they ought firmly to cling.[80] Others there are, however, more advanced, "fledgling" Christians; these are able to understand the truths insinuated by those everyday terms and images in a higher, more spiritual way.[81] It is obvious from the context that Augustine feels that this higher interpretation was in God's, and Moses', intention. But just as obviously, this higher mode of interpretation reasserts the possibility that any single phrase of Scripture may have more than one meaning. If any doubts linger, Augustine will shortly lay them to rest. The multiple strands he has teased our minds with all along, are soon to be brought together. Book XIII will fill in whatever gaps the reader still finds in his theory of words, meanings, and symbolism more generally.

Augustine begins this final book of the *Confessions* on a note that scarcely promises to touch on this question of signs and symbols: he starts by insisting[82] on God's utter lack of any need for creation, on the lack of any claim creatures can make upon His creative, or redemptive goodness. This he goes on to show, holds even for the "inchoate spiritual creation" which came into being when God said "Let there be light." He comes closer to our theme when he proposes that *Genesis'* account of the production of light and darkness suggests an array of corresponding images for describing the fortunes of that spiritual creation. By cleaving to God, the community of blessed spirits held fast to the light they drew directly from God's own light, and so became the "Heaven of Heaven"—enjoying unmediated contact with truth—elaborated on in Book XII. By cleaving to God, or in other terms, by preserving this immediate contact with Him, they avoided falling into the formless life of the "darksome deep." Our minds respond: what does this fall into the darksome deep imply? Augustine's manner of replying is to say that our fate has been a less happy one: "spiritual creatures when it comes to our souls", we "turned away" from the divine light; we became, in consequence, "darkness" in this life—read: the human life of our present experience—to be in "this" life is to be condemned to "labor amidst the relics of our darkness."[83] Once again, therefore, Augustine has connected our need to labor toward the light of truth with the "darkness" of the life into which we fell by reason of Adam's sin. We are expected to remember, even if only dimly, that Adam's labor committed him to fight his way through the thickets of symbol to the naked vision of Truth. Now Augustine pleads with God to dispel the darkness of his heart,[84] and, still in the same light-dark image register, sketches the Holy Spirit's work in bringing back the fallen. Lest we have any confusion on the identity of these fallen spirits, he groups them in a perfectly coordinate phrase: "The angel flowed downward, man's soul flowed downward," thereby showing forth the "miserable restlessness of fallen spirits . . . revealing their darkness" once they have been "stripped of the garments" of the divine light. Clothed in those heavenly garments, it would seem we were spiritually transparent to one another, as well as in immediate visual contact with the divine Splendor. Now God is at work to recall us to that pristine state: He will "illumine our darkness"—stripping us of the opaque earthly garments we now bear—and at the end confer upon us once again those transparent garments which will make our darkness to each other "as the noonday."[85] Glowing with the "inward fire" of charity, we shall mount in returning pilgrimage from this restless misery to the "peace of Jerusalem" we once deserted.[86] There, in God's own light, "we shall see Light,"[87] the immediacy of the vision will be restored.

Even more clearly now, the reader is again being asked to believe that our human souls once dwelt in the "Heaven of Heaven," all clothed in "garments of light" (veste luminis).[88] The question arises: does Augustine mean that in this state, where we were all lightsome and transparent to each other, we were (before our fall) purely spiritual beings? So that our fall into this world of darkness clothed us with the coats of skin that figure the opaque, mortal body? Or does he, by those radiant garments, wish us to understand the kind of spiritual body to which the Christian looks forward at the final resurrection?

We must wait for him to answer that question in his own terms. For now, he tells us, we must be content to journey by faith and not by sight; we should desire, in St. Paul's terms, to

be "clothed with [that] dwelling-place which is from heaven,"
a phrase whose ambiguity he partially clarifies by immediately
associating it with our need to "wait upon . . . the redemption of
[our] body." The terminus of our pilgrimage is, therefore, the
redemption of our body, a redemption figured as a clothing in
a heavenly dwelling.[89] Darkness before our Christian conversion,
we still carry the relics of that darkness "in our body, 'dead because of sin.' " The nocturnal character of our present existence
is, therefore, connected with the mortal character of our bodies;
but "in the morning," as the Psalm reminds us, when the "day
breaks, and the shadows fly away," we shall stand and we shall
see: see the God Who is the salvation of our countenance, who
will vivify our mortal bodies through the Spirit that dwells
within us.[90] His indirections exasperate; the pressure of our
questioning mounts: does that vivification really imply a return
to mutual transparency, such that all our "labor" with words
and symbols will come to an end?

Augustine is preparing us for an unambiguous answer to that;
but first he takes pains to make clear how this transformation of
our mortal bodies will be achieved. It requires that we be "reformed by the renewing of [our] mind," become "perfect in our
minds," keep our minds from being "corrupted away from
chastity."[91] The Holy Spirit, he insists, dwells "within" us;[92] and
we remember Augustine's customary equation of interior man
and mind. The transformation is to effect a crucial renovation
in our power to attain to direct knowledge of God: only on its
completion shall we be able to gaze upon that "light of Beauty"
in which we shall see God "as He is."[93] That renovation, as we
are about to see, involves our transcending the essentially indirect knowledge of Him through sensible symbols. It is plain,
to this point, that we have fallen from the heaven of heaven into
this lower world of sinful darkness.

Now the text of *Genesis* obliges Augustine to explain the
prophecy of God's redemptive work figured by the creation of
the firmament. The firmament he interprets as the "firmament
of authority" God has given us in Holy Scripture. It is "stretched
over us like a skin," mantling the entire lower world into which
our fall into mortal bodies has plunged us.[94] Thus, it separates
our terrestrial world from the spiritual celestial realm, or, in
another, familiar image, it acts as a layer of cloud drawn between
our gaze and the radiance of those higher realms. Augustine
pleads with God to clear away that cloud from our eyes; his
keenest desire is directly to "behold God's face" as do those "su-

percelestial peoples" who "have no need to gaze up to this firmament" which permits only the feeble, indirect vision of God's
"word" that comes by "reading."[95] Remarkably enough, Augustine's primary reflex makes him think of Scripture as obscuring
our direct vision of the divine splendor.

That obscuring function is, however, providential: the
"natural man, like a babe in Christ" does not have eyes "strong"
enough to "gaze at the sun";[96] the firmament of Scripture has
been established to bring aid to this weakness of the lower race
we have become in consequence of our fall. By means of it, the
radiance of God's truth "reaches down to the clouds"[97]—*to*
them, but not, at this juncture, precisely *through* them. His
word appears to us, not "as it is," but in the dark image those
"clouds" of Scripture provide; we glimpse it only darkly, in-
directly, in the mirror of the heavens.[98] But we must keep our
hopes alive, for the clouds will eventually pass away, leaving
only the spiritual heavens to endure forever.[99]

It is significant that Augustine turns, in this context, to speak
of the Incarnation. The eternal Word which the "supercelestial
peoples" gaze upon directly has (like the bridegroom of the
Canticle) "looked through the lattice of our flesh," caressed us,
inflamed us to run after the odor of his ointments; but He did
not appear in such a way as to grant us a vision of Himself as
He is. For that vision, we must await the transformation that will
make us "like Him"; only then shall we "see Him as He is,"[100]
in His Light "see Light."[101] Allusive though the terms may be,
it is difficult to escape the impression that Augustine has broad-
ened his thesis on symbolic intermediaries so that it covers the
case of God's self-revelation in Jesus.

But he will broaden it still further. When he comes to discuss
the prophetic import of the "creeping creatures" and flying
"fowls" brought forth from the "waters" of our lower world, he
interprets them as divinely wrought "mysteries" (*mysteria*).
Under that term, he classifies any and all the multifarious "corporeal operations" whereby a "single thing" known by the mind
can be "set out and expressed in many ways by bodily motions."[102] Enumerated among these *mysteria* are the visible wonders wrought by God's holy ones, as well as the various "voices,"
"speeches," and "languages" God's messengers employ to bring
the Gospel to the different nations of the earth.[103]

Augustine is obviously referring to all human modes of symbolic communication. But now, in the clearest of terms, he
proceeds to identify the symbolic apparatus as arising from our

fallen condition. By these "corporeal operations," he assures us, God "compensated us for the irksomeness of our mortal senses"; they were intended to meet the "needs of people estranged from [God's] eternal Truth" by that "diseased bitterness" figured in the saltiness of the earth's seawaters.[104] For he sees *Genesis'* creation of the salt sea water as figuring prophetically the emergence of the human race, "so profoundly curious, stormily swelling and restlessly tossing."[105] Now we begin to understand the hidden implications in that much earlier remark, that the youthful Augustine, having learned the arts of speech, found himself launched out upon the "stormy society of human life."[106] For had Adam not fallen, these embittered waters would never have flowed forth from his loins, there would have been no need for God to endow mankind with the arts of symbolic communication which "gather" those waters into the sea of human society. For there would have been no need for "expressions and signs," signs that burst forth, "proceed from the mouth":[107] no need for God's ministers to "work corporeally and sensibly," to preach and speak through the symbols of "miracles, mysteries, and mystic words." For such preaching and speaking is required for "the sons of Adam, forgetful of God"—and needing reminders— for so long as they "hide themselves from [God's] face";[108] the cause of all "vocal utterance" is twofold but intimately connected: the "abyss of this world" and the "blindness of our flesh." In their conjoint operation, they account for the fact that our inner "thoughts cannot be seen," thus introducing the "need to speak aloud into our ears."[109]

Now all of this makes excellent sense on the supposition that Augustine is envisaging our present human situation in contrast to its "unfallen" counterpart, against an ideal condition in which our flesh would not blind us to each other's interior, such that our inmost thoughts could be mutually seen. And there is more reason than ever to believe that this is exactly the way he imagines the condition of those "supercelestial peoples," beyond and above the dark and cloud-covered "abyss of this world." Spiritual, lightsome,[110] unencumbered by the "mortal body" that cloaks us round with the opacity of coats of skin, the denizens of the Heaven of Heaven he imagines as perfectly transparent to one another, with no need for what Augustine considers as the painfully unsatisfying indirections of symbolic communication. From the radiant ease of that mutual transparency, he thinks, we have fallen, have become this strange amalgam of soul and mortal body, man as we know him. He would agree with Cassirer's proposal that man is a "symbolic animal," but shake his head and murmur sadly, "Yes, alas!"

The inmost spring of Augustine's evaluation of man's symbolic functioning is, I am suggesting, still located in his view of the human condition as fallen from the luminous realms of the heaven of heaven into the darkness and opacity of the bodily world. Confirmation of that suggestion can be found in how well his perplexing and difficult interpretation of *Genesis'* prophetic prescriptions for the soul's return make sense in the light of that theory.

For the *Hexaemeron,* rightly understood, is also a prophecy of the "new" creation, the economy of the Christian soul's return. It assures us that, as men are now, they must first begin in need of "corporeal rites"; they need to be initiated into that way of return through sacramental signs. Once initiated, they can make progress only if the "soul begin to live spiritually on another plane"; after the sensible, corporeal "words of initiation" they must look beyond to their "consummation."[111] That consummation brings them beyond the realm of words and symbols: for "tongues" are as a "sign, not to them who believe, but to them who do not believe";[112] among those who have made such spiritual progress, God's ministers need no longer work by "preaching and speaking" through outward signs. Once reformed in the newness of their mind, believers become able to perceive God's truth, which they have understood; they come under God's own direction and do not need men to point the way for them. They are "renewed in the knowledge of God," are "made spiritual" again, and able to judge,[113] in the light of the intelligible "forms."[114] Their power of judgment holds sway over a number of things, including all the "signs and expressions of words" men use in the interpretation of Scripture, in praying or blessing.[115]

The logic of his position would argue for Augustine's placing even the symbolic admonitions of Scripture under the sway of the spiritual man's judgment, but he refuses to do so: when it comes to God's own book, we must "submit our understanding" and "hold it for certain."[116] And yet, if our interpretation is made in the light of truth understood, under the direction of God working through divine illumination, the commanding character of the scriptural message is attenuated to some degree. Interpreting prophetically the divine blessing in *Genesis* to "increase and multiply," Augustine is emboldened to return to, and lay firmer foundation for, the position he put forward in Book XII, that the words of Scripture have multiple senses. "Observe this again," he warns his readers, and brings up the very example used in the previous book, the opening phrase of the *Hexaemeron,* on which his differences with his critics turned. There are many ways in which to understand, "various kinds of true senses" one can give of God's having "created heaven and earth."[117] More generally, there are always many ways in which any single item of intelligible understanding can be given bodily expression; love of God and neighbor, for example, is "corporeally expressed" by a multiplicity of rites, in a variety of languages, and in each language by a variety of "turns of speech." But this multiplicity works in the converse direction also: there are many ways in which the mind can understand a thing which has been given only one bodily expression—instance the various true interpretations possible of *Genesis'* "heaven and earth."[118] He mounts an ingenious argument to show that this figurative sense of the blessing to "increase and multiply" must have been Moses' intended sense: no other, more literal, sense will serve in the context.[119] And once again he traces this regime of symbolism to our sinful condition: once we fell and became the "waters of the sea," the "society of embittered peoples," our "fleshly depth" demanded, and the residual fecundity of reason made it possible, that we understand one sign in several ways.[120] The slack connection between symbol and symbolized is now far more than the provisional position outlined in Book XII; it has, in Augustine's view, received scriptural foundation, firm warrant for its being incorporated into his understanding of the faith. But the supposition underlying this understanding of symbolic operations is the same as prevailed in his earlier theory of art: every corporeal embodiment of an intelligible meaning is doomed to inadequacy, is only more or less "like the truth" it strives to image for us; the process of moving from artistic conception to symbolic expression involves, necessarily, the descent of the higher to an essentially inferior realm. Art, by its very nature, still involves a step of deterioration.

In the framework of this metaphysic, Augustine's theory of man prescribes that the soul's spiritual progress effects a reversal of this deterioration: a passage upward beyond the need of all sensible, corporeal "admonitions." The labor to which Adam and his children are condemned is paralleled by the "working" with words and symbols required of God's ministers. Both labor and work, however, recall the "general love of action" to which, in the *De Musica,* Augustine traced the soul's fall into the realm of fashioning multiple artistic imitations of the eternal Beauty that was formerly the object of its easeful contemplation. Though now more subtly insinuated, this connection between labor, work, action, and artistic creation has not entirely disappeared. It comes as no surprise that his exposé of spiritual progress earlier insisted that the soul must ascend from the stage of engaging in action—albeit merciful and charitable action—to the life of contemplation.[121]

Typically, in portraying this aspect of the soul's return, Augustine reverts to the familiar register of light and darkness. The lights God set in the firmament prophetically figure the charitable works that are the "lower fruit of action." In our ascent to the delights of contemplation we come to appear as "lights in the world," able to distinguish the day of intelligible from the night of sensible realities, as well as the light of spiritual from the darkness of carnal souls.[122] The greater light of the sun figures the Spirit's gift of "wisdom," endowed on those who delight in the "light of manifest Truth"; the lesser light of the moon betokens the gift of "knowledge"; the stars stand for the other gifts, all inferior in radiance to the "brightness of wisdom." Knowledge, as well as these lesser gifts, like faith, healing, prophecy, and speaking with tongues, are conferred to "rule the night" of "carnal souls," still immersed as they are in the realm of temporal action.[123] The gifts conferred upon them all have to do, as Augustine sees it, with the guidance of their life of Christian action. That life of action, however, is a night; though its denizens are not entirely deprived of light, their "darkness" is granted only the kind of light appropriate to the relative infancy of their spiritual development, a light "according to the measure" of their night. But night was obviously meant to give way to dawn and day, the denizen of night is summoned to emerge into the kind of light which is "not put under a measure"—to discover as his only measure that highest of all measures, the sun of eternal Wisdom that illumines the accomplished contemplative.[124]

As if to make sure we have caught his meaning, Augustine here turns to a difficult piece of exegesis: a phrase from St. Paul, only remotely connected with *Genesis,* suggests a distinction between "giving gifts" and "bearing fruit." That distinction now spells out for us as parallel with that between the gifts of Christian works of mercy, and the fruit of a right and holy will that directs this entire realm of charitable action toward the higher stage of contemplative union with God.[125] He means to drive the point home: Christian progress does indeed involve a passage from the

night of action to the day of contemplation; that same passage
involves moving from the "carnal," sense-bound stage to a stage
in which the soul moves beyond all need of sensible admonitions.
By the same token, he now informs us, the soul must strive to
pass beyond the active "restlessness" that in part prompted, in
part was intensified by its fall, to the Sabbath "rest" in God pre-
dicted by *Genesis*. "Our hearts are restless till they rest in Thee,"
rang the opening theme of the *Confessions'* stirring prelude.
Only with the diapason of his triumphant coda is the theme of
those opening bars accorded final resolution. In the peace of that
ultimate rest, the long poem of human history will at last be
silent; the *carmen universitatis,* this "whole very beautiful order
of things very good," its temporal "measures" accomplished, will
"pass away."[126] The book will be closed, the scroll, not only of
Scripture, but of human symbolisms, will be folded up; in God's
own Light, raised beyond need of any intermediary, we shall
see Light, see in His very seeing.[127] Then will our labor be at
an end, the time of works be fulfilled, action yield to the easeful
bliss of unabating contemplation. The weary nocturnal journey
of this "mortal life, living death" at last behind us, enfolded in
God's own rest, which is Himself, we shall find the rest for which
our souls were made.[128]

That ultra-spiritual view of the soul's fall and return, its
wandering converted into pilgrimage, provides, I submit, the
anthropological backdrop against which virtually all of Augustine's observations on the function and value of art become
readily understandable. Running through them all is the conviction, adumbrated in the *De Moribus Ecclesiae,* and firmly
formulated in the *De Doctrina Christiana,* that God alone is the
supreme Good to be enjoyed in restful contemplation; all other
goods are to be used along human life's journey to the soul's
celestial home.[129] But what holds for goods, Augustine here assumes holds for beauties also. Hence, when reflecting on the
experience of his boyhood education, he holds the learning of
reading and writing in higher esteem than exposure to the
poetic "fictions" of Vergil or Homer[130]—to say nothing of the
seductive immoralities of much of pagan literature and drama.[131]
The arts of human communication are useful for this life, at
least;[132] they can be put to the service of God and employed to
admonish our neighbors' souls.[133] The delights of poetry, generally, but more especially their enticing depictions of vice, like
that of Zeus and his amours, he tends to rank as dangerous al-
lurements,[134] objects of false enjoyment, deflecting the soul from

its upward path to the one true object of contemplative enjoyment, God. To grieve over Dido and her fictional sufferings or death serves only to distract the soul from the reality of its own mortal and pitiable situation; to follow the route of Aeneas' mythical journeys tends to keep the soul forgetful of its own real situation as a wanderer;[135] indeed, such "sweet but empty spectacles"[136] reinforce the very "love of this world" that, in its extreme form, amounts to no less than fornication against God.[137] Such spectacles often seduce the sons and daughters of Eve into that "mighty and hideous ocean," the torrent of "human custom,"[138] the "hellish flood"[139] that is the "sea of human society" at its depraved worst: they paint the delights of adultery as the sport of gods, to be imitated by men.[140] Hence they stimulate those "darksome affections" that keep the soul a prodigal, far from God.[141]

There is, in all this, the tone and stress of the moralist: one would expect an African bishop to warn his flock away from theatrical glorifications of adulterous love, or (in terms of another of his indictments) from the cloak of civilized refinement that can overlay the heart's cold will to do harm.[142] But there is more: Augustine is evoking the soul's condition as fundamentally out of place in this factitious human world of artistic delights; he is placing his own abilities to read and write—and, ironically, his consummate artistic powers—into the service of his fellows, admonishing them, awakening them to their sorry state, striving to convert them to return to the Father's house they have deserted, to the Heaven of Heaven from which they have fallen. Only there can they enjoy—again—the contemplative rapture from which the delights of poetry and theater, with their false claims to be legitimate objects of enjoyment, can only distract them.

As in his earlier works, Augustine juxtaposes a relatively world-affirming aesthetic of "totality" and an ascensional aesthetic of escape from the sensible realm. To reconcile ourselves to the evils we experience, we must focus, not on this or that part, but on the whole;[143] what holds for beauty, holds for good as well;[144] the ordered beauty of the world in its totality witnesses to the God Who disposes all in accord with measure, number, and weight[145]—even sinners.[146]

But the dominating movement is ascensional; the soul must be awakened to the reach of its profoundest yearning: for the "Beauty, ever ancient, ever new,"[147] "holy delight,"[148] form beyond all the grace of created forms,[149] most beautiful of beings,[150] and Beauty of all beauties.[151] Once glimpsed, the charm of God's Beauty [*decus*] can sweep the heart upward,[152] to Himself, the swelling fountain of unfailing sweetness[153] that alone can satiate the soul's deep thirst for beauty.[154]

All creation lies about us to behold, beautiful reflection of God's own beauty;[155] even the unjust cannot avoid contributing to its ordered beauty.[156] Yet, in comparison with God, its beauty is as nothing;[157] ranked in the scale of lower and higher, earthly beauties are insignificant, ephemeral and passing,[158] objects, even, of contempt;[159] our souls can only prolong, exacerbate their misery by restlessly riveting, glueing themselves to fleeting beauties "outside" themselves and God,[160] whether it be through the concupiscential lust for sense-delights,[161] or curiosity's itch for sense experience.[162] *Non teneant haec animam meam*:[163] the soul must break free of their clutch, snap the spell of their perilous, enticing sweetness.[164]

Retorque amorem. Rape ad Eum.[165] Augustine's burning zeal would enflame us to redirect our loves, detach us from the entire panoply of created beauties, fire us with that single-hearted love of God that was his own. Again, the moralist is speaking: but speaking from the platform of a definite religious anthropology and metaphysic. The beauties of nature and of art, whatever the power initially accorded them to mediate God's Beauty to our fallen state, have been steadily relativized, turned into entrapments, then virtually annihilated. All their seductive allure fades before the portrait of God's transcendent loveliness,[166] all the cadenced charm of human melody has been employed to attune our inner ear to eternal Art's ineffable silence.[167]

This is the model, interiorly perceived, which the human artist consults in fashioning his outward imitations of the supernal Beauty;[168] the rest of us, in judging some beauties higher than others, betray the fact we have not lost all memory of that divine splendor.[169] We must, Augustine would persuade us, retrace our steps along that way of memory; he is intent on freeing our entangled hearts from the "fornication" of taking this world as an object of terminal love. The God Who is Beauty is also our highest Good: He alone is large enough for our hearts' desire; He alone is to be enjoyed. How commonly the artist forgets that his creations must be used,[170] must be made to serve the soul's interior pilgrimage of return from this image-world to the radiant homeland of divine Light. Augustine is sharply aware of beauty's special power: whether in nature or in art, he views it as laying a spell upon the soul, seducing it to cease from its restless journeying, and luxuriate in the embrace of languorous delights. The artist, correspondingly, "spills forth his strength" into *deliciosas lassitudines* (luxurious weariness): art works he sees as so many siren songs, lotus islands, charming the soul to beg that the enchanting moment never end, that the weary labor of its Odyssey be postponed, indeed, forgotten.[171] Hence, while claiming to use in God's service the arts of reading and writing, Augustine remains profoundly suspicious of the distracting power of poetry, myth, theater, even of the sweet-sounding melodies of the Ambrosian psalms.[172] Such delights, he is astute enough to detect, make terminal claims upon the soul's attention and esteem. They would lull the soul into forgetting that its journey must go further, always further still. In the *Contra Academicos,* he admits to his impatience for an understanding of the faith that will lead him, he hopes, to a vision of God even during this life.[173] That hope has been dashed; the plenary vision waits at the end of our pilgrimage in the mortal body and through time, waits in another world. But the impatience for that vision is with him still, and he is striving to communicate it to us. In beauty's claims he is inclined to see a peculiarly perilous distraction, a fatal snare for the restless soul. His humanity tells him that even the sensible beauty of this world is laden with positive value; that human instinct finds theoretical expression in the liminal, world-affirming move of his aesthetic. As Plotinus himself felt, especially when responding to the Gnostic deprecation of the sense-world, Augustine knows it would be simple impiety to deprecate a world that is image of, and witness to, the splendor of divinity. And yet, with that very move toward theological justification, the relativization of sensible beauty is already underway. The second moment of theory clamps into gear: only the supreme Beauty of all beauties is worth all our heart's devotion. For this vision, Plotinus had exclaimed in words that burned themselves into Augustine's memory, the sternest combat is made the soul's chief business: nothing is of any account but this: to fail of this vision is to "fail utterly." In hopes of becoming "blessed in this blissful sight," the soul should be ready to move beyond all the joy to be found in in the sensible realm, to renounce every power and honor and kingdom, "if only, . . . straining to This, he may see."[174] The words recall Harnack's ringing summary of Augustine's spirit: "He knew his heart to be his worst possession, and the living God to be his highest good."[175] He was a divided man; nowhere do the tensions of his embattled soul show up more clearly than in his aesthetic. The very beauties that so powerfully function to lure the soul at the beginnings of its ascent, and point its faltering steps toward God, turn in the end, their value changed, into entrapments, *deliciosae lassitudines,* enticing the pilgrim soul from the unremitting labor of its homeward Odyssey.

Such was the theory of art that Augustine consciously intended to purvey to the readers of his *Confessions:* a theory which remains substantially faithful to that of the *De Musica* and *De Vera Religione.* There is, in that fidelity, a certain understandable tribute paid to intellectual inertia. Had the *Confessions* been a purely theoretical work, the matter might be allowed to stand at that.

But the *Confessions* is an undeniably great work of art. As such, it invites another mode of treatment. For as a work of art it may reveal—or better, betray—a deeper message about his experience of art, about his practice of art, than Augustine's theoretical understanding might comfortably have countenanced. The theory of art *in* the *Confessions may* be one thing; it is time to ask whether the artistry *of* the *Confessions* may not point toward an entirely different set of possibilities about art, and its relationship to Augustine's deepest understanding of human existence.

6

THE ARTISTRY

OF THE *CONFESSIONS*

THERE ARE MANY ways of approaching the art of the *Confessions;* as many as there are writers on the *Confessions,* or viewpoints those writers occupy. On could, for example, underline the mastery of *eloquentia pedisequa* Melchior Verheijen's study focuses upon;[1] or stress the resources of Augustine's "rhetoric of religion" that Kenneth Burke so brilliantly analyzes.[2] Augustine's skill both in picturesque imagery and electric expression occupies the center of Sr. Joseph Arthur's attention,[3] while Eugène Tréhorel and Guilhem Bouissou, translators of the *Confessions* for the *Bibliothèque Augustinienne,*[4] delight in drawing their readers' attention to those elevated moments when confession takes lyric flight, and Augustine's Latin begs for the contemporary typographical display that proclaims poetry.

Consider, for example, Augustine's depiction of the childlike return to God's maternal care:

Let them be turned back,
and behold Thou art there in their heart,
in the heart of those who confess to Thee,
and cast themselves upon Thee,
and weep on Thy breast after all their rugged ways.

Then dost Thou gently wipe away their tears,
and they weep the more, the more rejoice in weeping,
because Thou, Lord,
not any man of flesh and blood, but Thou, Lord, their Maker
remakest and consolest them.[5]

Or the rhythmic evocation of silence at Ostia:

If to anyone the tumult of the flesh were hushed,
hushed the images of earth, and waters, and air,
hushed as well the very heavens;
did the soul, indeed, fall silent to itself,
and mount, by not thinking on itself, beyond itself . . .
and He alone spoke, not through these things
but through His very Being
that we might hear His word . . . [6]

Or finally, that lyric that needs no introduction:

Late have I loved Thee, Beauty,
ever ancient, ever new,
late have I loved Thee!

· · · · ·

Thou didst call, cry out to me, and shatter my deafness;
Didst flash forth and shine to me, and scattered my blindness;
Didst send forth Thy fragrance, and I drew in breath and now
    pant for Thee.
I have tasted, and now hunger and thirst for Thee;
Thou hast touched me, and I burn for Thy Peace.[7]

Here, as with so many passages in the *Confessions,* even the most critical reader, however, jaundiced by the all-too-frequent prostitution of "sense-line" display, has to admit that something very like poetry in the most authentic meaning of the term, has come to flower.

The Image

For reasons that will become more evident as we go on, the approach I mean to take to the art of the *Confessions* is slightly different from those given above. Let me begin by suggesting that one of the most telling features to strike the attentive reader of Augustine's *Confessions* is the sheer power of their imagery. Here, it must be said again, Augustine's writings exhibit a gigantic paradox, much like the paradox to be met with on

virtually every page of Plotinus' *Enneads*: both men unweary-
ingly warn their readers of the dangers of image-thinking; both
proclaim the mind's ability to recover its pristine interior contact
with a purely intelligible world beyond the reach of sensible
imagery, a world beyond human language's capacity to utter.
Yet both of them achieve their most unforgettable effects precisely by being masters of the word; both lead us up to and
depict their overworld in images so evocative as to rank them
among the greatest philosophic artists Western thought has
known.[8]

To settle on a concrete example: crucial for Augustine,
though by no means absent from Plotinus, is the ever-recurrent
image of woman. Let Freudians delight if they will, Augustine's
unembarrassed reply would surely be that all the delights of
sexual encounter are themselves but images, tokens of that ecstatic union with Beauty promised us in the vision of God's
splendor. So he returns, again and again, to lead our minds upward with the aid of imagery quite unabashedly sexual: the
image of *Philosophia's* radiant loveliness[9] is transformed, in the
Confessions, into that Lady Continence,[10] again, like *Philosophia,* both mistress "chastely alluring" and inviting mother,
teeming with the fairest of promised comforts. When inspired to
confess what he loves when he loves the God of his heart, that
"Beauty, ever ancient, ever new" Augustine shifts into the same
register.[11] His first instinct is to stress the discontinuity between
our human experience of sensible enjoyment and the wholly
spiritual delight of that longed-for union with God: it is not any
corporeal beauty he loves, no time-bound splendor, perceptible
radiance, sounding melody, or sensible fragrance; no manna or
honey however sweet to taste; nor graceful limbs calling to bodily
embrace.

"And yet," that affirmation of discontinuity once on record,
he admits it *is* a "certain light" he loves, a kind of voice and odor,
food and embrace—a higher radiance that floods the soul, a
timeless music, a spiritual aroma, food for the hungry heart
that never brings on the weariness of satiety. This sets Augustine
off on another of his "ascents," upward from the beauties of the
sensible world about us, upward and within, to re-excite the
memory of that beauty whose vision once was unwaning delight
to our contemplative souls.

But, one must ask, particularly in a study of Augustine's
aesthetic, how are such ascents *really* accomplished? There is
strong evidence for thinking that the device most central to the

operation is, however camouflaged behind Augustine's theoretical denials, that powerful Plotinian instrument of the "dynamic image": one in which the mind ascends by a ladder of successive images, each correcting the one that went before it, each introducing a progressively greater sense of strain, until the vital moment when the final image shatters before our gaze, and we seem to see what the "wholly positive" must be, when stripped through this mounting process of all the negating limits endemic to the world of bodies open to our sense perception.[12] But if this be the process truly at work, it cannot be categorized as one of transcending image precisely by "turning away" from image, as though to attain a purely intelligible glimpse, radically independent of all sensual contribution to our insight. The feat would better be accounted for, not as one achieved by some kind of pure intelligence, essentially estranged in its present incarnate condition, but rather as a feat of "metaphysical imagination," a feat accomplished by incarnate spirit operating at its topmost reach—a feat of authentically aesthetic idealization.

But the principal reason for focusing initially on Augustine's imagery is that it leads straight to the center, not only of his own intention as a literary artist, but of the artistic process in its perennial essence. It was surely Augustine's intention to acquaint us, mind and heart, not only with the God of his own mind and heart, but with his own individual life as laying bare the most obstinate secrets of our shared human life. His imagery must embody not only the transcendent, but the humanly universal as well. To succeed in that communication, the imagery employed had to be familiar to us, be drawn from the store of common human experience.

Creative Imagination

But common and commonplace are far from being the same thing: the commonplace must be transformed into the significant; it must be fired in the crucible of imagination, imagination not merely reproductive, selective, illustrative, as Augustine's theory would have it, but genuinely creative. For only a creative imagination could succeed in portraying his own life as the emblem of our shared humanity, make the voice and tone of a fourth-century man address us as his intimate fellows. "To Carthage then I came": that Eliot's evocation of the twentieth-century wasteland should take so many cues from Augustine's portrait of himself as a young student strikes us as neither strained nor odd, but right and almost inevitable.[13] Drunk with his new-found freedom, "in love with love" but enthusiastic slave of lust, endlessly rationalized and inventively self-deceiving, he whispers to each of us: *hypocrite lecteur! mon semblable— mon frère!*[14] What fearful acquaintance with the heart's dreary stratagems begot that prayer he insinuates is ours as well as his: "Give me chastity and continence, but not yet."[15] We too, he guesses, have thrilled to the challenge of some personal Hortensius,[16] caught sight of some shining ideal, and then subsided into the long, haggling compromise with our inner Sancho Panza who would, we only half hoped, eventually knuckle under. Eventually, but surely not right away; like Augustine's tardy sleeper, we have blinked the sun away, murmuring *modo, modo,* "in a little while, a little while": *sed modo et modo non habebat modum.*[17]

And then, if we are fortunate, life succeeds with us. It strips us of our defenses, bares all our versatile techniques at self-deception, twists our protesting head about; we can no longer fight off beholding the self we have till now uneasily, guiltily, managed to shove behind our backs. How well Augustine sensed we would recognize ourselves in that image. How smoothly, strongly his sensitivity to language, his refinement of observation, his ebullient passion and controlled intelligence, move together in measured concert when:

So went the tale Pontitianus was telling.
But Thou, O Lord, while he was speaking,
didst twist me right about towards my self,
taking me from behind my back where I had placed myself
all that time when I refused to behold myself;
Thou didst set me face to face with myself that I might see how foul
    I was,
how twisted and dirtied, bespotted and ulcerous.
And I beheld, and recoiled in horror,
but there was nowhere I could find to flee from that self.
And if I sought to turn my gaze away from myself,
on and on that man intoned the tale he was telling,
so that once again Thou didst set me face to face with myself,
didst thrust that vision into my very eyes
that I might discover my iniquity and loathe it.
Recognized it I had,
but pretended that I did not, forced my eyes away, made it sink from
    memory.[18]

Language

It is more than doubtful that Augustine's theory of imagination could account for the magnificent achievements of his artistic imagination. But doubts arise from another quarter as well: can the function he attributes to language truly account for the stunning ways his sensitivity to language operates, lending not only expression, but texture, dynamism, color and—again that term—"musical" coherence to his thought? Consider, once again, the powerful orchestration of the woman-image; when tracked through all its sinuous turnings, it reveals not only Augustine's imaginative affirmation of the feminine quality in God, it strongly suggests that many, if not all his imaginative characterizations of God have crystallized, constellated about the varied meanings and images suggested by a single, multivalent Latin word: *fovere*.[19] Dotting his earlier works with near-bewildering frequency, the word expresses first the action of *Philosophia,* mistress-mother of Augustine's soul; next it applies to that other mistress-mother figure, the Church; Augustine's powerful imagination then begins to envisage the supernal Truth-Beauty itself in mistress-mother terms, and the word *fovere* comes to express God's gentle providential care for wandering souls. Used not one single time in the earlier books of the *Confessions,* its range of meanings and images nonetheless crop up, proliferate, call to each other, and subtly overlap on virtually every page. The nurses of his infancy nourish him at the breast, care for him, foster his growth: a moment later we are assured that God Himself was doing all this in and through them. Nurses yield to Monica, Monica to Mother-Church, but always the secret agency is God's providence maternally omnipresent, omnipresence maternally providential, warming, healing, caressing, suckling, nourishing, fostering the growth of nestlings into fledglings, infants into adults, carrying them until they become able at last to walk, to run, to fly. Then, for the first time in his story, at the crucial moment of conversion, the term itself appears: to express the dizzying complexities of God's patient dealings with him, dealings all designed to make him a child again,[20] lure him back to the maternal comfort of the divine breast. Augustine's imagination could have hit upon no better symbol than this: *Fovisti caput nescientis,* he confesses; his headstrong pride had turned him away from God, turned him into a sick, mad, querulous fugitive; it had, until then, kept him from knowing what motherly care so fondly, faithfully pursued him at every stage of his runaway attempts at evasion, from Thagaste to Madaura, Madaura to Carthage, from Africa to Rome, and finally to the fateful encounter God was preparing for him at Milan. *Fovisti*: the ice of his sinfulness has been melted, the tumor of his pride reduced; now the petulant, angry tears are gently brushed from his eyes; his still feverish head is stroked, caressed, tenderly turned back, converted, to God's consoling breast; he drowses off in sleep to all the world of vanities that formerly bewitched him with their deceptive promise; and he awakes in God, sees at last the radiance of that beauty he had all the while, unknowingly, been seeking.

There may be other ways of proving that Augustine was more than a consummately talented rhetorician; I know of few pieces of evidence more compelling than this explosive display of evocative power, coming exactly where only an incomparable poetic imagination, working at depths profounder than all conscious planning, beyond all calculation of effect, could have managed it.

Again, Augustine's art provokes an altercation with his theory of art. The working of imagination, he would have us believe, is a relatively pedestrian thing, essentially selective merely, and reproductive; words, he would claim, are little more than vessels of meaning previously conceived and conceived without any intrinsic dependence on the weird alchemy those words exert upon the very genesis of thoughts, images, and all their luxuriant combinations, interconnections, surprising transformations. But were this the case, would the writing of the *Confessions* ever have been possible? Kenneth Burke's ingenious study of Augustine's religious rhetoric[21] highlights the abundant materials for thinking quite the opposite: from the teeming ambiguity of the prefix *in-*,[22] through all the transmutations possible with terms like *vertere*,[23] *facere*,[24] *sinus*,[25] *haerere*,[26] to humbler punning possibilities like *Karthago-sartago*,[27] *peritus-periturus*,[28] *accendimur-ascendimus*,[29] all these and other instances beyond numbering suggest that the resources of the Latin language were *there*, that Augustine was particularly sensitive to them, and that they functioned as that "terministic screen" Burke talks about,[30] a filter of vision coloring, texturizing his every perception, image, and conception.[31] Precisely at those critical points where his artistic theory asserts discontinuities—between image and meaning, word and conception, sensibility and understanding—his artistic imagination builds bridges of continuity and subtly gives the lie to theory. His mesmerizing art could scarcely have existed were his theory of art, and of symbolism generally, an apt account of its uncanny alchemy.

The Discipline of the Arts

Nor, I submit, can his theory account for what we may safely guess was Augustine's lifelong experience of art and beauty. He tells us much about his education, about the dawnings of his youthful sensitivity to beauty: these pages of his *Confessions* he has penned in retrospect, exploring the landscape of his past through the straitening lens of theory. We must read them with that theory in mind, and consequently, with tongue in cheek.

His youthful education had exposed him, he informs us, to the "fictions" of both poetry and theater: how much less useful, these, when compared with the "more certain" studies that taught him to read and write![32] Again, one stricture he lays upon them any moralist would readily understand: not only the frequently lascivious "shows" of the ancient world but instances of their drama as well, could exert an immoral influence on the immature spectator.[33]

A contemporary mind would protest: there must have been more to the poetry, theater, and literary training, even of Augustine's time! Yet even if this were so, his indictment continues, these shows and spectacles pander to our "curiosity";[34] real as shows and spectacles, they are essentially false as imaginative imitations of life: "sweet fictions",[35] they amount to no more than a webwork of tales, inane and untrue,[36] that vainly pretend to slake our hunger for the solid food of verity,[37] presenting (when compared with Scripture) "trifling subjects", like Juno's passion, to exercise the student-*rhetor's* nascent powers of reproductive imitation.[38]

The feelings of grief they conjure for our paradoxical delight in grief are therefore equally false, a simulacrum of that compassion we are urged to show toward the true misery of real persons;[39] not only false, they are shallow also, since the grief we so yearn to feel over the miserable fortunes of fictional personalities is one we would never choose to experience in our own lives.[40]

Augustine's larger theory of man allows him to dispense, then, with virtually every justification that could be offered for such imaginative creations; allows him, indeed, to rule out of court the entire realm of poetic fiction or semblance. And yet, he insists, his adolescence was powerfully drawn to the delight in grief and pity experienced in theater.[41] There are mingled echoes

here of Plato's sometimes ruthless strictures on mimesis; along
with them come hints, however, of Aristotle's theory of tragedy's
catharsis through pity and fear:[42] hints and echoes, both firmly
recast in the mold of Augustine's own personal theory. Obviously, he is having none of Aristotle's more benign analysis of
drama's effect upon the spectator; that very rejection compels
the reader to speculate on whether an Aristotle would not render
a juster account of how his youthful poetic and theatrical experiences truly affected Augustine.

Instead of agreeing with Augustine's claim that "the more a
man is moved" by the emotions aroused in drama, "the less he
is free from such passions,"[43] the Aristotelean would point to the
elevating discipline and refinement of the crude emotions of
everyday that dramatic catharsis effects; he would insist on this
as the deepest instinct giving rise to imagination's truly creative
activity of artistic mimesis.[44] Precisely by transporting us into the
realm of "fiction," such a view would hold, the artist, whether
poetic or dramatic, affords us a larger, graver view of reality,
not everyday reality, studded with banalities and blurred with
distracting irrelevancies, but that reality purified to its essential
lines, brought to the grander scale that enables a Dido suddenly
to stand for all of weeping womankind, an Aeneas or Ulysses to
symbolize the pain, the pathos, the noble bravery that man can
bring to the trials of the human pilgrimage—or an Augustine
to embody the murky struggles and shining flights of that *grande
profundum, homo,* that mighty abyss that is "man." This is not
falsity, but life become, if anything, more real than actuality; become "poetically true," the object of man's solemn attentiveness,
aesthetic delight, ushering him into the hushed world of tragic
wonder. The contemplative pity and fear such fictions arouse in
us do not immediately move outward into sympathetic action,
certainly; but this hardly makes them count as less deep than
the everyday counterparts of such affections, as Augustine would
have it; quite the reverse. The usefulness of such experiences
must not be judged from the standpoint of their immediately
pragmatic, action-oriented goodness—again, the way of beauty
affirms its right to be kept distinct from the way of good. The
impatient moralist's demand that art be didactically useful in
this immediate sense would accomplish the death of art, drama,
and poetry. It would banish from our world this profoundly, but
peculiarly useful—or better, priceless—medium of humanization—and the Augustines with it.

For the report of the centuries is as peremptory as it is accurate: nothing impresses us more than Augustine's thorough and profound humanity. But it is important to seize upon the peculiar stamp of the humanity that makes for his perennial contemporaneity and roots his unfailing power. Certainly there is justice in speaking of that mercurial quality called "African temperament";[45] yet, we must not be deluded into thinking that the mere inherited capacity for passion, for emotion stormy and raw, is what commends Augustine to human beings of every age and place. Each time this surfaces, as occasionally it does throughout his career, he frightens us rather, vaguely alienates us; we feel for a fleeting instant he is no longer our familiar. We knew those qualities were in him, slumbering but never quite asleep, always fueling with life and fire the most measured cadence of his prose, the most disciplined flight of thought or imagination. Artists, it has been said, are born: without that underlying turbulence, Augustine could never have become the potent artist he was. But just as art is more than unfettered expression of emotion, crude and unrefined, so no great artist is ever merely born; he must endure the long patiences of apprenticeship, wondering sometimes whether they are effecting anything, and partially because their effects go deep into the dark of that subterranean self, subtly, imperceptibly forming it with cadence, discipline, or, as Augustine himself would have it, order, number, measure.

This, I submit, was an essential part of that humanization process that produced the Augustine we recognize as the ageless brother of our race, a part that could only have been played by his adolescent and youthful experience with poetry, theater, and art more generally. Without this development of the artist's special mode of observation, without this attunement of his sensibility, his *Confessions* would have been little more than a tiresome litany of everyday banalities, or a pouring forth of raw, unformed emotions.

Yet even the most untutored reading finds them more than that. Closer study reveals how much not only Augustine's expression, but his powers of observation, sensibility, and artistic conception, owe to the way the images, music, and poetry of the *Psalms,* the mighty images of the Bible, had penetrated into the deepest recesses of his being. But the same thing holds, in sometimes subtler form, for the cultivating influence of pagan literature at its best. Could Cicero's *Hortensius* have stirred so deeply any and every nineteen-year-old, simple and fresh from the fields of Thagaste? How often one finds that the passages of Plotinus' *Enneads* that leave their strongest traces on Augustine's sensibility and imagination are precisely those in which the master is displaying his own consummate gift for imaginative conception and poetic expression.[46] Indeed, one of the central triumphs of the *Confessions* is the way in which Augustine's own creative imagination has wedded the paradoxical properties of the Greek and Biblical notions of divinity, presenting us with that portrait, awesomely majestic and irresistibly endearing by turns, of an Omnipresence that is providential, a Providence that is omnipresence, all the while a God transcendent and immutable, yet a God intensely personal, whom the heart can address as *tu,* "thou," confide in as a God who genuinely cares. Again, conceptualization would tend to keep these features of God distinct, even inimical to one another; but Augustine's soaring artistry boldly establishes continuities where theory would press divorce proceedings.

So much, then, for the Bible and Plotinus. Could an Augustine less thoroughly sensitized by the solemn pathos of Vergil's *Aeneid* have produced that moving portrait of Monica, daughter of Eve and Christian Dido, weeping on the Carthaginian shore as her new Aeneas, having tricked and deserted her, sails off in quest of the city of his heart's high dream?[47] Could a man untutored to the poet's occult power of universalizing the particular, have told of his friend Alypius with such seeming factuality, and yet brushstroke by subtle brushstroke, made him in the end emerge as a timeless portrait of the man of "curiosity"?[48] Did his devotion to the theater contribute nothing to his evocation of the garrulous Pontitianus' rolling tones, droning on and on: *immoratus est in eo sermone . . . pertendebat ille et loquebatur adhuc . . . narrabat haec Pontitianus . . . narrabat ille quod narrabat;* well intentioned, surely, yet just that trifle self-complacent, piously obtuse, so taken up in the telling of his edifying tale as to ignore entirely the storm it was stirring in the depths of his tormented listener?[49] Only a man sensitized, not merely schooled, to the ways of drama, could have portrayed that final crisis of conversion in the garden at Milan. Augustine is describing the pull of his former habits, the growing counterpull of the continent life, and the resulting rending of his interior being. That struggle could so easily have turned into an interplay of pale abstractions; instead, the scene is dramatically alive with things and people: chains, scourges, women of memory whispering seductively, and that shimmering Lady Continence, addressing her alluring invitation not only to brain, but to heart, sense, and fantasy, all at once.[50] Only an accomplished dramatist could ever so strongly have engaged us in those desperate struggles of soul that came upon him after the death of his youthful friend—his name a lesser artist would have told—but if he had, we would not then so sharply scent a world entire reeking with the stench of death, shudder in the grip of those moments when sorrowing alone was sweet to us, peer into the faces of every advancing crowd, search hopelessly at every crossing for our own dead friend, until we reel in the grip of a sudden vertigo that makes us, too, a "great riddle" to ourselves.[51]

And finally, sweet fiction though he may have thought it at a certain level of his consciousness, Homer's tragic vision of human life nevertheless provides Augustine with the key images for transmuting his own life, too, into much more than an individual career; all the great artists of the ancient world, in fact, with their strange power of seeing the concrete individual as archetypal, have conspired to help him see his life in its essential features as one with our own: an Odyssey, whose uncanny strangeness, echoes of remembered promise, aching loneliness for far, far places, can burst upon our souls in just those moments when we were being lulled into feeling most at home in it; the restless Odyssey of the Christian soul, of Everyman.[52]

Only a long and sensitizing apprenticeship with art, an extended discipline in surprising the essential lines of human action, perceiving the apparently random "tears of things" as secretly moving to the solemn cadences of God's own providential poetry, could have produced a power of vision so controlled, majestic, and in the end, contagious. Of that apprenticeship and of its subtle workings, the Augustine of the *Confessions* tells us little or nothing; the rigors of his theory scarcely permit him to see, much less articulate them. But his battle with the resistant points of theory continues; the later Augustine succeeds in providing hint after hint toward how he himself might better have understood, and how we may understand the twin spell of art and beauty; understand it, and situate it in the scale of values keyed by those crucial parameters of the Christian existence: creation, Incarnation, and resurrection.

7

AUGUSTINE'S

LATER AESTHETIC

Augustin, one scholar has observed, *a ses tiroirs:*[1] when faced anew with a familiar question, or stimulated to treat some issue he has onced worked out to his satisfaction, he tends to trust the beaten pathways of his earlier thinking, to reach into memory for the familiar response, even where shifts in his thinking would question his continuing right to do so. The psychology of intellectual inertia is not hard to understand, particularly as it would affect a very busy bishop, the press of whose duties would scarcely stimulate him radically to rethink the aesthetic system he had once elaborated.

So it is that throughout his later works, aesthetic observations continue to flow frequently from Augustine's tongue and pen, but mostly as adornments, illustrations, or applications of the strictly religious and pastoral themes that more and more engage the center of his attention. The result is that substantial continuity in his aesthetic thinking, which Svoboda, despite some tendentious interpretations, has objectively presented for the most part.[2]

But there is another result: Augustine's pastoral zeal induces him repeatedly to underline certain selective features of his aesthetic, already present in far from latent form in his earlier writings. In consequence, the spiritualizing side of his theory of art receives more insistent emphasis, thereby creating the overall impression—for impression it largely is—that his entire aesthetic has become more spiritual as his life proceeds.

But the ground-bass from start to finish plays the identical fundamental theme: the ardent yearning for vision, the impatience with what he considers second-rate beatitudes, these are Augustine's hallmarks from the Cassiciacum writings onward, through the *Sermons, Enarrationes,* and *De Trinitate,* up to and beyond that paean of exultant hope with which he ends his *De Civitate Dei*: "There we shall rest, and shall behold; beholding we shall love; and loving, praise. See what shall be our end without ending!"[3] His heart will settle for nothing less than that; as pastor, despite the rigors of his predestinationism, he strives fiercely to prevent that "stray sheep" from cheating him- or herself, as for years he had consented to do.

This pastoral zeal, then, accounts to a great extent for the selective emphasis on Augustine's part which persuaded Svoboda to trace his curve of progressive spiritualization. A few concrete illustrations may help make this clearer.

As in his earlier works, Augustine repeatedly calls attention to the aesthetic of totality; particularly when dealing with the Manichees' outright rejection of the material world, he counters with the need for considering not just the good of this or that part, but the beauty and goodness of the whole.[4] Even bodily beauty is beauty; wherever found, and rightly contemplated, it displays that numerical symmetry and harmony of parts that stands as signature of the God Who forms the entire panoply of creation in order, measure, and number and weaves the beauties of time into a single grand poem.[5]

But bodily beauty is lowest on the scale of beauties; not only does Augustine admit this to his adversaries, he hammers the judgment home to his spiritual children.[6] There is no absolute unbeauty,[7] yet when compared with higher, spiritual beauty, the beauty of the material and fleeting temporal world is relatively unbeautiful,[8] worthy, even, of the soul's contempt.[9] Augustine's impatience for the vision is never too far in the background, his momentary world-reconciling moods already throb with, soon give way to the ascensional demands that the quest for vision imposes upon the soul. Even when seriously revising aspects of his earlier anthropology in the *De Trinitate,* he starts with the thesis that our souls are hungry for that vision[10] and not unnaturally concludes that the central identity of man—man when

considered precisely as created to God's "image"—is soul: not
active soul, or soul endowed with powers of sense and imagination, but contemplative soul, candidate for the bliss to be found
only in that ultimate vision of God.[11] "For that vision of God is
a vision of such great beauty, worthy of such great love," he tells
us in the *De Civitate*—and goes on with disarming candor to
cite one of his enduring inspirations for thinking so—"that Plotinus does not hesitate to call that man most miserable who fails
of it, endowed [though he be] with a wealth of whatever other
goods."[12]

Hence the enthusiasm which enlivens his tongue, drives his
pen, when discoursing on the beauty of God and beauties of that
other, higher world; once glimpsed, he assures us, they will turn
our love for human beauties to something verging on contempt.[13]
Hence, too, the frequent contrasts between interior and exterior,
the beauties of body and those of the soul:[14] what pastor has not
had occasion to warn his children (of every age) against the skin-
deep charms of a shapely bust or a well-turned thigh; but Augustine's warning is couched in terms entirely coherent with the
dichotomies of his earlier aesthetic. Even the incarnate Christ,
he seems occasionally willing to admit, was outwardly ugly to
the sight of men, while gleaming all the while with the inner,
invisible beauties of justice, love, and with the hidden splendors
of divinity.[15]

The human artist, he repeats, must work from glimpses of that
higher world of beauty, imitating what he sees there, imposing as
best he can the traces of supernal form upon the refractory materials on which he works.[16] The crucial moment of creative intuition remains, then, intellectual: imagination in all its workings is tethered to the realm of reproducing, rearranging and
combining images from sense.[17] So, too, the converse process of
appreciating beauties requires a judgment, now only rarely accorded to sense, but—far more consistent with his earlier theory
—a judgment of intelligence in its capacity to intuit the world
of Forms beyond all sense-embodiments.[18]

The various *artes,* as he understands that term, are accorded a
place quite in keeping with Augustine's scheme of values:[19] the
art of rhetoric comes in for frequent mention—not a few of his
critics have leveled suspicious comment on the famed eloquence
attached to Augustine's name—and the former *rhetor* freely admits to the ambiguous power of charming expression; justification for it can be found only in its alliance with truth; it must
be used rather than simply be enjoyed; the hungry soul is, as

always, bidden to seek, not the delights of sounding words or figured speech, but the solid nourishment of their inner, higher meaning.[20] The same dichotomies of inner and outer, bodily and spiritual, continue to command his remarks on *musica*.[21] Augustine's overall evaluation of art in our modern sense, man's symbolic adornment of this fallen world, remains substantially what it was in the *De Quantitate Animae*;[22] but his remarks on painting and sculpture are, despite Svoboda's heroics on both counts, so sparse and elusive as to tell us almost nothing of his opinion of them as art forms.[23] The repeated focus of his condemnation remains the theater: the seductive power of the divine immoralities is lashed again and again; the origin of pagan theater is traced to the demons, its spectacular charms aimed at appealing to the fallen soul's inveterate "curiosity."[24]

Spiritual enough all this is, admittedly, but with the spiritual note appropriate to a fervent bishop laboring a field sown richly with the stubborn persistences of paganism, a paganism that leaps to a sudden surge of desperate, dying life on the occasion of the fall of Rome.[25] The armature of Augustine's thought, however, remains essentially what it always was; the moral, pastoral, and religious applications, not the cast of thought itself, are what convey whatever impression there may be of a greater spiritualization than was there before.

All the while, in fact, on the deeper, anthropological level, Augustine's thought is running strongly in a counter-direction: toward what, for want of a better term, we might call a despiritualization. The spiritual tone of his early aesthetic, we have seen, was both corollary and reinforcement of a view of man as soul, fallen into the bodily realm of darkness, mutual opacity, and all the attendant need for symbolic operation. That way of accounting for symbolism leaves Augustine with a peculiar anomaly to explain: why is it that the incorporeal truth we seek affects us not less, but more powerfully, when alloyed with image, allegory, symbol? The phenomenon was one Augustine himself had keenly experienced, but the breach his anthropology has set between the bodily and spiritual, the thoroughly pedestrian role it assigns to imagination, force him into a variety of ways to explain the power of this perennial human mode of poetic, artistic communication. The myths and fictions of the poets he may choose to spurn;[26] the symbolisms of poetic theology he analyzes and reduces to a hopeless shambles;[27] the mythopoeic strain of Manichee theology he criticizes and discards as so much sensist, earth-bound folly;[28] again and again he urges his flock to seek the God whose beauty and greatness lie beyond all the power of human imagery to grasp or to convey.[29] All this his earlier theory would lead us to expect from him; and yet, he cannot dispense with the problem easily: one may wonder whether an irksome uneasiness compels him to return to it often and forces him to try such a diversity of explanations. Why does the truth, when wrapped in images, figures, or cloaked in allegories, exert an even stronger appeal to our humanity than when exposed in simple, expository terms?

All his attempts to unravel this enigma continue to suppose the breach between the order of sensible, exterior symbols and the higher, intelligible meanings to which the inner, spiritual eye attains:[30] but despite the consistency of their common root, the variety of his solutions arouses the suspicion that Augustine's disincarnate view of man cannot come satisfactorily to grips with the phenomenon. He suggests that the allegorical figure, in all its sensuous corporality, is a kind of condescension to the depths to which our souls have fallen: our earthy hearts, like torches in need of shaking, require the excitation that comes from earthy images;[31] just as the sounding songs of voice provide a stepping-stone toward the higher spiritual music our souls long to hear.[32] Or, in another family of explanations, simple exposition of the truth can tend to bore us, leave us lazy; it does not exercise our questing intelligence enough; we need the difficulty involved in searching for the truth hidden in such enigmatic figures, need to be rewarded by that thrilling pleasure of discovery.[33]

It would never occur to Augustine to say—the suggestion would have disconcerted him—that the marriage of truth and image was simply the index of the human soul's substantial kinship with the sensible, corporeal order. Aristotle's theory of the soul as entelechy, as form of the body's matter, he has met with early in his career, quite misunderstood, confusing it with the Stoic thesis of the soul's essential materiality.[34] Again, his *tiroirs* function consistently: the soul's essential spirituality, its hierarchic superiority to everything material, remains to the very end, despite all the anomalies it raises for him, the central strand in his view of this puzzling amalgam of soul and body, the human being.[35]

The *De Trinitate* illustrates this point admirably. Augustine is faced with another form of the very difficulty we have been treating. He is querying the process whereby we come to love someone like the Apostle Paul.[36] We do not love him for his body, he begins predictably: we love him inasmuch as he is a "just soul." Our knowledge of soul is simply enough explained, he thinks: we each have souls, which know themselves as souls. Whence do we derive our knowledge of what justice is? Not from any outward sense- or memory-image, he argues in his usual fashion; such knowledge must come by the interior way of insight into the form of justice itself. Justice as the unchangeable norm for how a good man should conduct his life we "see within ourselves, or rather, above ourselves in the Truth itself"—our love for Paul reposes on the belief that he lived his life in accord with the form which, intellectually, we see.[37]

Thus far Augustine's habitual thoughtways carry him; but now comes the perplexing question: how is it we are inspired to even greater love of this form of justice through the belief we have that men like Paul actually lived that way? It is easy to explain why the love of the form would bring us to love the just man's manner of life; how is it, though, that our belief that this was any individual just man's manner of life, can excite us to an even more fervent love for the form of justice itself? Augustine is faced with a human phenomenon that analysis cannot reduce; it leads him to conclude, happily enough, that faith is a powerful help toward our loving God, as well; but the workings of his disincarnate noetic leave him disarmed before the difficulty he has raised in such sharpened terms. The logic of his position should persuade him to conclude that the mind's direct, unmediated grasp of the form's intrinsic beauty should suffice unto itself; the sensible embodiment of justice in a man whose interior can be grasped only through belief should in theory contribute nothing to our more ardent love of that higher, spiritual reality; we should, rather, to be consistent with his frequent urgings, turn within and upward, rise above, assert the intuitive mind's sovereign independence of the world of sensible embodiments and their liminal, admonitory function. And yet, his human experience has taught him this is not the case; and with that disarming candor only great and honest thinkers can afford to manifest, he raises a telling difficulty to the logic of his own position; "I do not know how" the thing is to be explained, he confesses, and lets the matter stand.[38] The aesthetician, though, is not entitled to let the matter stand at that: he finds himself here confronted with a richly suggestive item of human experience, one that dimly clamors for profound alterations in the noetic, and anthropology which nourish Augustine's aesthetic, and which it nourishes in its turn.

Along with these continuities in his aesthetic observations, along with his continuous wrestling with a nagging anomaly his aesthetic confronts him with, there are still other important revisions going forward on deeper levels of Augustine's thought. Most crucially, his view of man as fallen soul, so closely bound up with his theory of symbol, is thrown up for serious question, and in the end, meets with his rejection. The story of this rejection is a complex one,[39] its exact timing, for one thing, being somewhat cloudy. But it seems to have been somewhere in the neighborhood of 415 that Augustine, stimulated by the Pelagian controversy, comes to interpret a text from Paul's Epistle to the Romans as implying that souls cannot be thought of as having either merited or sinned before their birth in this embodied existence. The mainspring of his theory of pre-existence is thereby snapped; from this point on, he abandons his preference for this way of accounting for the ignorance and difficulty the soul experiences in fighting its way toward the naked vision of Truth.[40] The *De Trinitate*, it has been suggested,[41] represents his effort to adjust the heavily Plotinian cast of his earlier theory of man: that suggestion may, I submit, have considerable merit. It should not, however, becloud the fact that while revising, Augustine is at the same time determinedly attempting to salvage many of the essentials in his earlier, spiritual view of man's condition and end; the upshot of the revision is that man remains essentially soul, and soul contemplative.[42] The Beauty for whose vision the soul was made is still an archetypal Beauty' to be grasped without the intermediary of sense;[43] our fall may not have been from some disincarnate spiritual pre-existence, yet the need for sensual symbolism is still connected with our present, fallen condition.[44]

That firm connection of symbolism and fall assures that art retain essentially the inferior value attributed to it in his earlier theory. But there are other serious tremors unsettling the Augustinian landscape. Having abandoned his disincarnate view of man's beginnings, Augustine is compelled to portray man's end in more and more incarnate terms: the Christian doctrine of the final resurrection of the body makes progressively greater inroads on his thinking.[45] Firmly he rejects the "Porphyrian" depiction of our return: our business is not to take flight from every type of body, from all dependence on the deliverances of sense; it is the "mortal" body, the deceptions of the "carnal" senses proper to our penal condition, that we must leave behind, in hopes of being vested in the immortal bodies of that final resurrection.[46] Those immortal bodies, it is clear, will be of a different, higher quality than the bodies familiar to us from our earthly experience;[47] Augustine's tendency to attribute a kind of celestial body to the angels, also, may have encouraged him to label the transformation of resurrection as angelic.[48] More frequently, now, we watch his mind inquiring about, praising, presenting for our admiring contemplation, not only the thoroughly spiritual world of his earlier yearnings, but the world of risen bodies as well—the new heaven *and* the new earth![49] And in one late text at least, he boldly asks a question that would stun the reader of his early works: could the bodily senses, in the world of resurrection, themselves be empowered to glimpse the radiance of divinity?[50] That his answer to the question is uncertain, even reserved,[51] should hardly occasion surprise: what surprises is the very seriousness with which the question is posed, the sympathetic care with which it is discussed.

The circularity of his earlier portrayals of our fall and return is now firmly discarded: our renewal, renovation, is not simply the recovery of a state that Adam and Eve enjoyed in Eden, it is a renewal *in melius,* an arrival at a condition superior to the pristine, prelapsary human condition.[52] But that condition is definitely, now, incarnate; however superior in quality to the bodies of our present, mortal sojourn, however heavenly in certain respects, those bodies will be in some genuine sense material.[53] And the way is paved, at least in principle, for a far more sympathetic appreciation of the incarnate features, and values, of the human scene.[54]

The anthropological underpinning of his aesthetic is tested at yet another vital point; we have seen how Augustine's impatience with the provisional beatitudes to which created beauties tempt us found intellectual articulation in the *De Doctrina Christiana's* distinction between use and enjoyment (*uti* and *frui*): God alone is the terminal object in whose vision the soul must find restful enjoyment; all other beings are to be used in pursuit of that beatific vision. The very cleanliness of this distinction is inviting, but even when generously interpreted, it presents serious difficulties. And Augustine is not entirely unaware of them.

Even in the *De Doctrina Christiana,* a trace of embarrassment shows: are we to love our neighbor with essentially the same category of love that extends to bread, clothing, shelter? Must we class the delights of human friendship with such patent objects of sheer use? The logic of his distinction would seem to impose such a conclusion, but his great humanity, so often touched, thrilled, and enlarged by the intimacy of friendship, momentarily protests: we may enjoy our fellow humans, but enjoy them in God—in such a way that our enjoyment does not slow or deflect our journey to Him, enjoy them with an enjoyment which can only in a forced sense (*abusive*) be termed *frui* in the meaning implied by his original distinction.[55]

Theory has been challenged, but for the moment at least, has reasserted its claims. The *De Trinitate,* however, still betrays a lingering discomfort: inferior creatures are to be used, but creatures equal to ourselves may, even must, be loved with a love of *frui,* enjoyed, but in God;[56] we are still on a road toward ultimate happiness, but just as the foot can be said to rest at each step of its continuing progress, so too the will may find restful delight in another creature even while pursuing its onward course toward God: resting, that is, not like a pilgrim finally arrived at his native land, but like a traveler taking refreshment, even temporary lodging, in view of his further journeying.[57]

One must appreciate the sensitivity that dictated this compromise solution: a compromise which, taken with other difficulties Augustine is brought to confront,[58] raises doubt about the very framework in which the question has been posed. Augustine has been led to acknowledge the quasi-terminal claims of interpersonal love, and yet he is nervous about letting our delight in fellow souls become absolutely terminal: our enjoyment of them must never entice us, in terms of the linear image he is working with, to halt or deflect our tireless Odyssey. Were we to allow the charms, the *amoenitates* of the human landscape to do that, they would amount to a variant of those luxurious languors (*deliciosae lassitudines*) to which, he is persuaded, created beauties also solicit us.[59] If life be a journey, then rest, enjoyment in the genuine sense, is subject to a postponement after death.

But even accepting the *uti-frui* framework, it is tempting to ask, would not a similar compromise solution suggest itself in respect to created, even created bodily beauties? There is every reason to think so; Augustine's firm conviction is that Good, Truth, and Beauty are at bottom identified in God; that conviction encourages him, in works both early and late, to affirm that the hierarchical order of truth and beauties is the same as the order of goods; this in turn leads him to assume that the ordered pursuit of Truth and Beauty is subject to much the same rules as the pursuit of the Good; hence he inclines to assign the same relative evaluation of intermediate truths and beauties, as he does to intermediate goods.[60] There is much in that final assumption that needs further probing, and probe we must, in time. But for the moment, this much is clear: Augustine's sensitivity to the phenomenon of human friendship, a sensitivity undoubtedly enhanced by his concern with the Christian law of love, has led him to make a momentary adjustment of his categories touching the order of goods—an adjustment that tends precisely to accord the created human scene a greater value than a rigorous application of that order of goods would logically warrant. Pursued to the end, and applied to the realm of beauty, this sort of thinking would seriously have attenuated the uncompromising spiritualization that marked his earlier aesthetic, and in holdover fashion continues to characterize the aesthetic of his later works. The result would have been, undoubtedly, a franker acknowledgement of the quasi-terminal claims of those human phenomena, so strangely akin, friendship and created beauty—leading, one may think, to a renewed attempt to situate those quasi-terminal claims in a system now accommodated to make place for them. Perhaps Augustine was more than vaguely aware of this: his later depictions of our heavenly felicity lay stress not only on our ultimate enjoyment of God, but our enjoyment of one another in God;[61] the promise of human (and Christian) friendship attains the fulness of its reality in the blissful community of the resurrection; from another point of view, heaven has become a truly human place, and Augustine's thought a thought in the truly human mold.

But is the joy of friendship, then, merely promise after all?— merely *pignus,* or, in St. Paul's expression, that denser, weightier thing, *arrhae,* actual foretaste? Augustine asks the question directly of the charity that links us even now with God; he could, though, have asked it of the entire panoply of those experiences that lend to Christian existence its peculiar quality: experiences of joy, hope, peace, and fleeting bliss. These, too, he could have said, "grow from a latent state, growing become perfected, and perfected become eternal" (*latendo crescit, crescendo perficietur, perfecta permanetur*).[62] As foretastes, not merely promises, they are inchoations, gifts of the very reality whose fulfillment is promised in the giving of them. Enjoyment of the ultimately terminal Good need not, accordingly, be thought of as the ever-during-this-mortal-life-postponed. The swift dichotomies that leap so readily to his tongue and pen may call for re-examination.

It may not adequately reflect the complexities of the Christian pilgrimage to repeat (as so regularly he does) that this life is the place for unremitting labor, action, yearning fundamentally unassuaged, while only "there" shall we have rest, contemplation, and the joy of possession.[63] Not merely *sacramenta,* they may be *res* as well, realities to be regarded as such, *res et sacramenta*; acknowledging their sacramental function, as pointing to spiritual realms beyond, must not exact a depreciation, to near-evaporation, of their own created reality.

Here Augustine's progress as a Christian exegete compels him to another awkward hyphenation of categories that his earlier thought tended rather to oppose one to another. The letter of Scripture's sacred text must be respected for itself, not treated all too prematurely as a trampolin, occasion for an impatient leap into the disincarnate realms of spiritual interpretation.[64] But if the letter deserves that respect, then the things the letter designates must in their turn be acknowledged as real, historical things: the earth and sun, the trees and birds, the man and woman of *Genesis'* creation account cannot be sublimated into symbols quite so briskly as the earlier Augustine tended to sublimate them.[65] The mind both may and sometimes must pause over them, investigate them for themselves, and in doing so, implicitly pay tribute to their genuine reality. To dwell upon the sensible world of admonitions, he is being led to see, is not necessarily to make them objects of mere curiosity. The later Augustine must actually develop a new category to designate the mind's legitimate inquiry into this world of temporal realities: now they become objects of *scientia,* and worthy, as such, of the Christian's careful attention.[66] An attention, surely, that never loses sight of the other world to which they point; but one which dimly recognizes that their ontological status and density exact a more patient, respectful attitude than his single-minded quest for vision would formerly have accorded them.

The development of Augustine's later aesthetic is, therefore, a far less unilateral affair than Svoboda's curve of spiritualization would suggest. The formally aesthetic observations that leap from his tongue and pen are, for the most part, holdovers from the frankly spiritual accent of his earlier theory; his pastoral concern explains the selective emphasis he lays on aspects of that theory appropriate to moral and religious exhortation. He grapples with a central difficulty in that theory, the power of sensuous image and symbol; he may have dimly guessed that the bout was inconclusive, for his anthropology at crucial points was steadily shifting toward a more incarnate view of man: embodied in his beginnings, man will remain embodied in the fulfillment of resurrection. Will our bodily senses, then, be elevated to the vision he has regularly reserved for pure intelligence? And is there a way of articulating the order of love so that our human delight in sensuous beauty ranks, along with the delights of friendship-love, as a kind of legitimate *frui,* genuine foretaste, *arrhae,* realities, not merely sacraments, of that world of risen splendor?

It would be rash to press Augustine's almost parenthetical asides on these matters, to the point of elaborating them into a full-blown later aesthetic. For the Christian thinker, though desirous of learning at Augustine's school, it would be philosophical sclerosis to ignore their suggestive power. Perhaps the justest summary of the case might be the modest conclusion: glimmering on the horizon of Augustine's later thinking, tremulously, hesitantly, but glimmering nonetheless, is the pale dawn of another aesthetic entirely. At crucial junctures markedly in contrast with the spiritualist aesthetic of his earlier works, it teases the mind to think of sensuous beauty as there, not for disincarnate souls to glance at merely, and hurriedly turn away from, but for human beings to dwell upon, contemplate, not simply look at, but genuinely to *behold.* And beholding, enjoy a foretaste, even now, of our "end without ending."[67]

Augustine is not an utter stranger to the quite peculiar attitude of soul that permits us to behold the world of sensuous beauty: an attitude in which acquisitiveness, desire, the eagerness to possess are lulled into a solemn stillness, suspended in a silence of detachment, of receptivity pure from all anxious self-concern; when man's whole being seems to become enraptured eye, attentive, hearkening ear. This is the attitude to which he summons us so often, when urging us to prescind from the evil of this or that annoying, harmful, or poisonous part of the sensible universe we find about us, to suspend our considerations of the *aptum,* and dwell upon the *pulchrum,* the musical harmonies disclosed even in the finely articulated members of the flea. His insight on the matter is, I have suggested, an unsteady one: despite his frequent explicit reflections on it, he never fully draws out its implications. Constantly interfering is his other, profound conviction that the good and the beautiful (read, for our purposes, the fitting and the beautiful, the *aptum* and the *pulchrum*) are fundamentally identical, *in re.* Hence the frequency, not to say regularity, with which his hierarchical portrayals of the order of beauties slide over into becoming descriptions of the order of goods; hence, too, the wavering in his awareness that the subjective response beauty elicits is distinct from the desire for union, embrace, possession he associates with our soul's hunger for enjoyment of the good. Beauty, as such, becomes the object of the eudaemonistic quest, and—here he received ample encouragement from Plotinus and others in the ancient world—the way of the soul's progress up the ladder of beauty becomes identical in its working with the way up the ladder of goods.

Yet, in his finest moments, Augustine knew better. And in their operations, deeper reaches of his soul occultly obeyed that knowledge: I suggest that the aesthetic that was struggling for expression in his later works is much more adapted than his earlier theory, to the task of discovering the workings of his own artistry, particularly in the *Confessions*. That later theory, too, responds far more exactly to what we can confidently guess was his youthful, indeed, his lifelong experience of art and beauty.

But the younger Augustine was determined to elaborate an aesthetic fitted to the task he felt that Christian spirituality had every right to assign it. Hence the occasional simplicities, unyielding rigors, the uncompromising thrust toward vision incorporated in his earlier view. Yet had this later theory, fully unfurled, been at his disposal sooner, it would, I submit, have performed the task he exacted of it not less, but far more cogently than his earlier theory did, or could.

8

TOWARD A CONTEMPORARY

AUGUSTINIAN AESTHETIC

THE TITLE OF this chapter must tease the reader's mind with questions. Is it really possible to discern the indispensable lines of an Augustinian aesthetic? The preceding chapters have implied so much criticism of various features of Augustine's own theory and evaluation of art and beauty: is it an illusion to think one might now pronounce a confident *nevertheless,* show that the features criticized are dispensable after all, and argue that a conscientious Augustinian thinker could, on reflection, gladly, or at least resignedly dispense with them? Thus chipping away, one could congratulate oneself on removing only the excrescences that mar the statue's beauty, eventually laying bare the contours, firm, clear, and impressive, of the essential or perennially valuable features of the Augustinian aesthetic.[1]

The project is, at very least, a tempting one: no great thinker is entirely wrong, there are always points at which he is splendidly, powerfully right. The instinct that prompts us to strain out the gold of genius from the dross of human failing is surely one of the most powerful driving forces for progress in philosophical thinking. When it is a question of Augustine's aesthetic, however, a project of that kind involves peculiar difficulties. From the outset, it would appear that many of the most appealing and characteristic strengths of Augustine's view of art and beauty are inextricably interlocked with what must be considered vital weaknesses.

Augustine's Other-Worldliness

To begin with what I take to be the central point of all: no thought could claim Augustinian fatherhood unless it remained in some genuine sense faithful to his other-worldly stress. For it is, in Marrou's words

certainly true that in the thought and above all in the spirituality of St. Augustine there is an impatience, as it were, an urgency to mount, and to leave behind the lower rungs of the hierarchy of beings, to neglect secondary causes and subordinate ends, and to press forward as directly as possible towards Him who is both First Cause and Highest Good—Cause of all that is, and Final End which fills to overflowing all need, all aspiration, all expectation.[2]

The whole of Augustine's thought clusters about the deep desire of man's soul for a vision that will beatify him; the "restless heart" is what contributes the hallmark character to his view of man, hence of beauty, and of art. However suspect that heart might be to him, he knew at least the extent of its reach: its highest good was nothing less than the living God,[3] a good to be possessed in a vision that is equivalent to embrace, of clinging to, cohesion with its divine subject-object. But equally central to his mature thought would seem to lie the conviction that the vision is attainable here only in briefest snatches, momentary, anticipatory glimpses: *frui*, enduring enjoyment of God's enchanting beauty, is reserved for there—for that other world toward which all human life is voyage, journey, pilgrimage.[4] All this accounts for the feeling-tone that pervades the Augustinian world-view: an aching sense of alienation here, in this world, and a hankering impatience to arrive there. Extract that nerve of other-worldliness, and the personal pulse beat is no longer recognizable as genuinely Augustine's. And yet, retain it, and immediately two quite ambiguous features of his aesthetic would appear to follow.

The first of them is Augustine's attitude toward aesthetics: theories of art and of beauty must be subordinated to, placed at the service of, a philosophy of the happy life; aesthetics is called upon to contribute, as *de facto* it does in Augustine's work, to this all-preoccupying way toward the beatific vision. It receives its marching orders at the outset, from the nonaesthetic concern of the Augustinian system; willy-nilly, and cost what it may, its order of business is laid out for it to construct a ladder of beauties leading to that highest beauty, to lure the soul to leave lower beauties behind as it mounts upward toward the ultimate goal of its quest.

This brings in the second ambiguity, not to say weakness, that Augustine's otherworldly stress entails: created beauties, whether natural or artistic, must consent to be placed in service, reduced to objects of use rather than of genuine enjoyment. But then misgivings come in swarms. Has beauty been properly respected precisely as beauty? And has aesthetics, thus pressed into service, been short-circuited, flogged into hurrying its essentially contemplative interrogation for beauty's proper name, harried into missing out on beauty's peculiar properties? Has sensual beauty, particularly, lost its special character through this insistence that it be squeezed into the category of an image-truth, an intermediary good?

Tracing the development of a much more incarnational view of man and of Christian eschatology, I have suggested that a new, and in ways superior aesthetic view, showed signs of dawning on the older Augustine; but then the question only returns in altered form: would the completion of that development have so changed his thinking as to sap, or at least seriously dilute the "restless heart" emphasis that is so characteristically his, thus transforming his Augustinianism into something quite alien to itself?

Surely there are some contingent features of his view with which he, and Augustinians generally, would be willing, almost cheerful, to part. His later disaffection toward the view of man as fallen soul, if fully unfurled and resolutely pursued to its logical conclusions, would dispense with the corollary that man's appeal to symbolic knowledge, communication, and action, must be traced to the fall of the contemplative soul into the alien world of body, time, and action. No longer then, would the very existence of art need to be accounted for by the pride that plunged the soul into a temporal career of perversely imitating the divine world and artfully dominating fellow souls in the fallen world. Pursued further, Augustine's disaffection with the fallen-soul theory might have snapped the link between curiosity and the soul's itch for restless action: a more benign judgment on man's tendency toward gratuitous, solemnly playful contemplation—and enjoyment—of the sensible universe, and the connected justification of an equally joyful re-creation and artistic celebration of that sensible world, such corollaries, one may think, would not have trailed far behind. Indeed, even in Augustine's thought as it stands, artistic enjoyment and creation are already pressing their demands as legitimate human activities.

Symbol and Symbolized

Once completely disentangled from the fallen-soul theory, those activities might conceivably have beckoned Augustine's mind to re-examine not only their titles to legitimacy, but their inner working as well. At that juncture, his entire theory of symbolism would have to come under review. Here, the first item of agenda could well have involved querying the slack relation his theory sets up between symbol and symbolized, between the images of the sense-world and the other, true world of intelligible archetypes. The claim that each sensible symbol can have any number of intelligible referents, and vice versa, warrants Augustine's frequent appeal to allegorical interpretation. The allegorical imagination, however, readily assigns meanings to sensual symbols in a fashion that, on examination, turns out to be both arbitrary and mechanical. The claim, for instance, that the whales of *Genesis* must symbolize the miracles worked by God's messengers, or that the sea-waters must figure human society, rightly strikes us as arbitrary, even capricious. The logic involved has none of the inevitability that marks the workings of the genuine poetic imagination. If a logic is present, it is one deriving from the exigencies of a theory—Augustine's view of the soul's fall and return—that commands and imposes the meanings it requires: what initially appears an arbitrary interpretation turns out, in fact, to be a mechanical one.

The genuinely poetic imagination, on the other hand—and Augustine frequently shows himself eminently capable of this—would give itself over to the patient, welcoming, appreciative contemplation of the sense-realities in presence, until, unforced by intellectual theory seeking confirmatory instances, the "inscape"[5] of the sensible reality discloses itself, its inmost imaginative identity yields itself up as symbolic of a spiritual realm to which the mind rises, not by fleeing, cutting loose from the sensible concrete, but by remaining silently with it, interrogating it without preconception, returning to it again and again until its depths are plumbed, its secret revealed. But now, quite contrary to Augustine's theory, yet quite consonant with his most effective practice, the spiritual reality suggested, symbolized, is grasped not merely beyond, but through and in the sensible concrete.

Augustine would have it that the birds of *Genesis* figure the voices of God's Gospel messengers, and our imaginations experience a wrench, a feeling of dislocation. When, on the other hand, Wordsworth attends to the skylark's song and finds it full of a "madness and "joy divine," lifting his earthbound traveler's heart with a "hope for higher raptures, when life's day is done";[6] when he returns to it again—"ethereal minstrel, pilgrim of the sky"—and follows it soaring into its "privacy of glorious light" and finds it now "Type of the wise who soar, but never roam";[7] when Shelley in his turn explores both song and flight of this "blithe spirit" and discovers there the "clear keen joyance" of a love that "ne'er knew love's sad satiety,"[8] the reader is struck by the naturalness of the move our minds have been invited to make: symbol and symbolized are in easy, unforced consonance; we hear the ring of imaginative inevitability. Here are birds imaginatively understood.

But, ironically, the reader is struck by something else as well: both metaphors are distinctly Augustinian in flavor and import. We find ourselves transported to another world, as Augustine would have insisted we must be. But that world is far from the purely spiritual world to which Augustine in his earlier aesthetic, the thoroughly disembodied world into which even the Christian poet Hopkins seems to be inviting us, when in his turn he finds the caged skylark imaging man's soul shut up in his "bone-house, mean house." It is far more a world "true to the kindred points of Heaven and Home," in which the echo of the skylark's song rings on, the lift and plunge of its flight leave delicate, unfading after-images traced upon the "new heaven, new earth." Such is the world of Augustine's later resurrection theology, to which this earth and heaven point as both sacrament and epiphany; a world where, as Hopkins concludes, man's spirit will be found, in its pinnacle state, both "flesh-bound" and "unencumbered".[9]

Augustine tells us in the *Confesisons* of a temptation.[10] Passing through a field, his eye is caught by a hare escaping a pursuing hound. The sensitivity we know was his is immediately awakened. Unless God soon warns him to "rise quickly" from this indulgence of his "curiosity," he avows, he stands there "vacant-minded," his eye following the movements of the chase. Those movements come, he must admit, from the "wondrous creator and orderer of all things"; even from such humble incidents he can "advance to praising" God. But theory enters to short-circuit sensitivity: the point, he is convinced, is to "rise quickly"; either to "rise up from the sight to [God] by some reflection, or to spurn the whole incident and pass it by." One can scarcely suppress a wish that he had not been in such a hurry. The entire incident betrays his sensitivity to the charm of things, his poet's eye; it recalls his power of imaginative evocation as well. But for his haste, he might have left us a gem-like vignette of one small, frightened creature, leaping, turning, darting toward some dreamt-of haven of life; in its lightsome swift grace describing timeless figures of resurrection.

It would, of course, be purest speculation to suggest that Augustine s own development would ever have led him this way, and this far along this way. My real point is that the Augustinian thinker of today should be willing and ready to discard such features of his thought as I have been dealing with here and do so with a clear conscience of remaining faithfully Augustinian.

Number

Could one, though, so easily discard the centrality of number in Augustine's aesthetic? The answer here is far less clear. The least that can be said, I submit, is this: the contemporary thinker has the right and obligation to be wary of the dead, impersonal quality that a numerical, geometrical aesthetic is constantly in danger of assuming. The passage from the relatively congealed world of number and geometry to a personal Logos as the ever-living font of that world is, I have suggested, a difficult one for the mind to navigate, if navigated it can be at all. Here however, Augustine's own emphasis on the numbers of time and motion— how often he applies his insight to the rhythms of verse, to the "tuneful-turnings" of time and history—furnishes a remarkable counterbalance to his views on architecture, where number and symmetry go static and dead. Applied to the pulses of history, to the plunging beat of a poetic line, numbers come alive, are transformed in the handling of them to capture the shifting patterns, the rhythms of life itself. In this understanding of them, numbers suggest the living form that is at the heart of all artistic creation.[11] To pass from this world of living forms to an ideal divine world characterized primarily by the quality of immutability as it so regularly is for Augustine, is the very inverse of the problem considered a moment ago: but putting the question in terms of living form might have challenged the ease with which he reaches for immutability the moment it becomes a question of designating the primary perfection of the divine world. It can be argued that Augustine's unquestioned axiom, that the immutable is superior to the mutable, is itself an unacknowledged corollary of an aesthetic in which the static, dead quality of number has prevailed and exacted its revenge. Again, the argument would run, more careful attention to the peculiarities of the aesthetic field would perhaps have prompted Augustine to a more dialectial, nuanced approach to his other, divine world, and this world's relationship to it. In any event, if number is to be retained as an element in the essential Augustinian aesthetic, a certain retranslation of it must be made—one sanctioned by Augustine's own most frequent application of the notion—so that it becomes an index of living form.

But retranslations of a similar sort are in order for other features of his theory as well. I have been brought to criticize, in the wake of others, the rationalist tone that pervades Augustine's aesthetic, especially in his earlier works. He would have the artist work from a knowledge of pure (we would say abstract) number; the artistic judgment of appreciation, correlatively, must focus on that same realm of disembodied number: *non numerosa faciendo, sed numeros cognoscendo*, knowledge of numbers, is the key to both operations. Here again, the Augustinian finds himself in a field calling for generous interpretation: to conclude, as Augustine does, that the flutist cannot be a genuine artist unless he has this quasi-scientific knowledge of numbers presiding over his artistic activity goes down a bit hard indeed.

The contention can hardly be saved in its entirety; but the truth Augustine is trying to get at should not be missed for all that. However maladroit the expression, it betrays his keen perception, following the Neo-Pythagoreans, that artistic expression is not a matter of sheer instinctive spontaneity; that the artistic emotion is formed, disciplined emotion; that artistic appreciation in its turn must be able to discern this quality of form. But to discern it in perfect abstraction from its embodiment in a particular song, a concrete movement of dance or verse, is this entirely required? The early Augustine's rationalistic tendency, along with his dichotomized view of sensual symbol and intelligible archetype, combine to present it that way. And yet his acknowledgment of a "judgment of sense," his concessions in the *De*

Musica to the near-inerrancy of the "practiced ear," suggest a more incarnate approach to the matter, one that would involve the total human subject in the acts of creation and appreciation. Such a view, drawn to its logical extensions, would represent the working of man's mind as in constant vital contact with the concrete singular existents that nourish its operations, would question, and even reject the pretension that we ever grasp pure form in clean divorce from some concrete embodiment.

Sense and Mind

Arguable across the entire epistemological front, that stress on the intimate marriage of sense and mind is peculiarly applicable to, and finds its most crucial confirmation from, the art-experience. Vermeer does not permit us to lose contact with the rich concreteness of this particular Flemish woman, sensually depicted to be sensually beheld, in this individual room; yet, precisely because of that, he succeeds in presenting us with the lights, textures, the aura of human moods that qualify the world, the timeless, unbounded universe into which his painting invites us. Without ceasing to be individual, this woman and this room have become universal, typical: without ceasing to be perfectly concrete, the scene has been structured, with a structure that does not freeze, but musically accents the flow, movement, beat of everyday life. Let the rationalistic structuring, on which Augustine so frequently insists, be understood in these more incarnate terms, and his concern that we must apprehend such formal structures is both legitimized and transposed: translated, if you will, into a language expressing the precise kind of living form that transmutes the banal concrete into the stuff of art.

Again, Augustine has applied a questionable epistemological principle to the aesthetic field, where its application breaks down in most dramatic fashion; a more patient sensitivity to the peculiarities of the aesthetic experience would perhaps have led him to question his entire disincarnate epistemology. That questioning might conceivably have led to the more incarnate aesthetic sketched out, albeit only allusively, above. But again, my real point is that the contours of the aesthetic experience invite the contemporary Augustinian to something like this retranslation of the master's rationalistic utterances.

But if the art experience provokes a revision of Augustine's rationalistic statements, it poses *eo ipso* a serious question to that other pillar of his epistemology: the contention, inherited from

Plotinus, that we come to our grasp of the intelligible world by turning away from the presentations of sense. Questionable in almost every area of our cognitive activity, that contention founders completely when applied to aesthetics. The most rudimentary phenomenology of this form of experience must conclude to its peculiar faculty of charging the conjoint operation of sense and intellect with the power to attain to one of its highest, if not its highest cognitive achievement: the envisagement of intelligible ideals as embodied in and suggested by, the imaginatively transformed sensuous concrete. The case has been made that the Platonic forms themselves are in fact a residue of aesthetic experience;[12] Augustine, I have argued, especially in his depictions of that highest of ideal realities, God, follows a similar approach: he employs something very like the "dynamic image" found in Plotinus' writings. Instead of turning away from the sensual, as he so often professes to do, he imaginatively transforms, projects, idealizes the sensual concrete, driving it to the point of "shatter" where it yields its ultimate disclosure—as all great artists do, and as even metaphysicians must.

That would include the contemporary Augustinian metaphysician, quite particularly. I have more than once been brought to criticize what I conceive to be Augustine's oscillation from a stress on God's omnipresence (hence immanence to created reality) to a counter-insistence on God's transcendence (couched, more often than not, in language much like that of Plotinus' emanation imagery).[13] Never, to my knowledge, does he consciously attempt and clearly succeed in expressing the dialectic of immanence-transcendence "in one act of thought." The result, I have tried to show, is that despite all his best intentions and all his stress on omnipresence, the emanation register is forever threatening to take over: created reality runs the constant risk of being "folded up like a scroll," of collapsing back into the transcendent reality of God.[14] Here too, an exploration of the kinship between the aesthetic relation between symbol and symbolized, and the mediaeval metaphysician's insight into the analogy between created beings and the Creator-Being, would be worth pursuing further than would be appropriate here. But briefly put, the suggestion would run that the metaphysician espies the symbolized (Creator-Being) never as merely *in* (more precisely, immanent *to*) the symbols (created beings *qua* created). As in the art intuition, the beyond is caught precisely in *and through* (and therefore beyond) but never as "pure beyond," always as trancendence undivorceable (in the given world of our experience) from omnipresent immanence. Again, Augustine's failure to take the peculiarities of aesthetic symbolism as explicit focus for reflection leaves him with a "radically defective theory of sensibility,"[15] which exacts its revenge at the very heart of his metaphysic.

Action and Contemplation

Augustine would seem to be on questionable ground in putting forward still another of his cherished dichotomies: when he contrasts the activity, the imitative *actio* of the artist, with the serene leisure (*otium*) of philosophic and religious contemplation. Here, too, one can appreciate the truth disclosed in that contrast from the extreme cases he obviously has in mind: we have all had experience of that mindless, unreflective itch that occasionally plunges us into a disorganized, and further disorganizing round of activities; we unthinkingly yearn to escape from the inner vacuum of our often intolerable selves by doing something, doing anything—just to be *on the go*. The result is that *effusio ad exteriora,* that frittering away of our inner spiritual resource that Plotinus compares to a seed uncoiling its interior riches into the wasteful prodigality of what only seems a larger life—an image (as I suggested earlier) that Augustine may well have had in the corner of his eye when he speaks of artists who scatter or sow their inner forces into *deliciosas lassitudines.*

How, though, counterbalance that wasteful loss of self? Augustine's taste for antithesis goes to work again, urging us to collect, unify ourselves in contemplation. This would be all to the good, if it did not suppose a good deal about how the *activity* of human contemplation operates. For if what has been argued above makes any sense, contemplation is precisely that, a process and an activity, in which the mind does not merely receive passively the self-disclosure of an object it gazes upon but engages, rather, in a dialectical operation of welcoming reception and creative idealization that permits and promotes the self-disclosure. Now if the evidence of the aesthetic realm is to carry any weight, the peculiarities of artistic activity may furnish a showplace for seeing in clearest terms how action and contemplation may coincide, mutually enable and fructify each other, in one and the same activity.[16]

Explaining this contention, though, involves challenging another of Augustine's cherished notions which is closely connected with his view of artistic activity. Augustine, it will be remembered, proposes that the artist works from some direct, disincarnate insight into the pure forms of the intelligible world, and that the ensuing activity of embodying those forms implies an inevitable step of deterioration, degeneration. Augustine's own practice as an artist suggests an opposite view: that the artist's activity—and the art appreciator's in an analogous way —is an intense marriage of contemplation and action; that the "art-idea" does not stand forth full-blown at the beginning of the effort at artistic embodiment. On the contrary, it comes to full articulation in the artist's consciousness only at the final term of the artistic process. Inchoate, half-formed, dimly soliciting rather than clearly commanding the artist's activity, the art-idea must be pursued, hunted down, in a process wherein (to use the example of painting) the artist's every brush-stroke conspires with mind and eye, directed and corrected by turns, as mind and eye interrogate each stage of the product for the contenting expression being sought, enriched at each succeeding stage in their capacity to see more fully the next step in the process. The painter's mind is at the "end of his brush," as it were. The active process of creation, therefore, and the medium chosen, are both intrinsic and essential to the artist's way of coming to see his idea: a poetic idea is precisely that, an idea *for* poetry's linguistic expression; a musical idea is inseparable from the music for which, and in which, it stands forth, finally, as finished idea. The sense of inadequacy the artist so frequently experiences does not entail a consciousness that a gap exists between the pure idea he envisages in contemplation and the necessarily flawed embodiment that emerges from his art activity; that phenomenon can just as easily and far more realistically be explained in a theory that views the other world of artistic aspiration as a thoroughly incarnate world, after all, one to which the artist gains access only through the labor of the idealizing imagination: a labor that remains incarnate from beginning to end; a process of artistic creation that is not now contemplative, now active, but contemplative-active throughout.

Peculiarly intense, and hence most easily identified in the art experience, it could be argued that this wedding of action and contemplation, this human capacity to become contemplative *in* action, is analogously realizable in the other realms of accomplished human activity. Especially close to Augustine's preoccupations is the moral realm, and though it may at first sound odd, his conception of the soul in its resurrected state, its contemplation overflowing undistractedly into graceful bodily action, becomes, in this connection, richly suggestive. The aesthete would be inclined to translate that conception of human fulfillment into a prescription that men should aim at acting much as artists do, with that self-possession, self-collectedness, that lucid calm absorption with the ideal-to-be-embodied in activity, such that their acts become morally beautiful acts. But then, a similar dialectic of action and contemplation comes into play. Augustine's own stress in the *De Ordine* on a "discipline of *mores*"-is a way of pointing toward the deep truth that only the developed moral *agent* can even hope to see valid and compelling moral ideals, in a seeing that—like aesthetic vision—implies kinship, resonance, "connaturality" with those ideals.[17] Penetrated through by their attractiveness and commanding beauty, with sensibility, affectivity, and intelligence brought into harmony, the "divided man" progressively becomes unified in a questing response to his highest dream; thereby, in Augustine's phrase, morally beautified through attunement to moral beauty, he would at length arrive at the *facillima vita* of easeful contemplative activity.

The Discipline of the Arts

The retranslations suggested above—an incarnate aesthetic and its natural corollary, the artistic marriage of contemplation and action—might also provide a language for re-expressing Augustine's cherished ladder of the *artes*. As they stand, particularly in his earlier works, the *artes* function to exercise the mind rather than the complete man, raising it stepwise toward grasping the numerical laws that govern beauty's workings: the function of rationalization Marrou so rightly criticizes. And yet, another more incarnate function is entirely thinkable: the contemporary Augustinian might legitimately transpose these ladders into ascending grades of aesthetic, moral, and theological idealizations—forms never become abstract, sensuous concretes progressively informed. They would lead the incarnate subject from the relatively humbler know-how of the practical arts, upward to the beauteous ideals toward which human action, ensouled by contemplation and undivorced from it, continually aspires. The ladder of the *artes*, then, no longer conceived of as a school of quasi-mathematical abstraction, would become what Augustine's deepest intention wanted it to be, an *exercitatio* in progressively refined sensibility, leading toward the greater and greater harmonization of the total self. The abstract cast of mathematical ideals would then be recognized as differing markedly from the ideal-concrete character that attaches to both moral and aesthetic ideals. It was right that Socrates, when striving to communicate the nobility of his own courageous fidelity in the face of death, should conjure up the figure of Achilles— a concrete man, poetically transformed by Homer's creative imagination into the very embodiment of courage for the sensitive Athenian.[18] For in morals as in art, the rightful task of *exercitatio* can never be the total abandonment of the definite,[19] but rather the contemplative-active plumbing of its depths, until the "inscape" has been brought to disclose itself.

The Definite and Its Beyond

But, in that moment of disclosure, what occurs is something not entirely unlike what Augustine strives to express when telling us that the musical ascent brings us ultimately out onto the soaring heights of silence: something there is in the process that initially tempts one to think that intellectual activity has in the end yielded to total passivity, that ascending grades of the definite have at last been left behind. And yet, a closer analysis reveals that the silence is not purely negative, it is full—like the silence of that breath-taking rest in Beethoven's *Hymn to Joy*— its fulness assured by the persistence—Augustine would say, in memory—of the melody that has led to it, and still contributes its pulse beat to the silence. Again, the effect is closely parallel to that of Plotinus' technique of stretching our metaphysical imaginations through the successive stages of his dynamic image until the image shatters.[20] At the very point of shatter, the mind, moving with the momentum of the process that has led it up *to and through* that point, reaches insight into what lies beyond the world of image, beyond the realm of the concrete definite. But the moment of insight remains an active moment, its apparent passivity only the relative passivity, the unstrained ease of activity brought to a consummatory peak: the self-disclosure of the silent transdefinite chimes through an atmosphere still vibrating with the rhythms of the process that conditioned its final bursting forth upon the welcoming "eye of the soul."[21]

The Language of Art

Augustine's somewhat balder insistence that we hear this infinite word only in a silence beyond all created words is partially

linked with his inclination to dichotomize the sensual and intelligible, the temporal and eternal. But there is a companion
root to this way of viewing the matter; he assumes that meaning
relates to the art work in much the same way as meanings attach
to the words of our everyday language. If what I am suggesting
has any merit, that assumption is highly questionable. If everyday language sufficed to say all that men feel compelled to say
about the world of our highest experience, then metaphor,
poetry, music, and art as we know them might never have been
dreamt of. One special property of these languages is the keen
awareness that accompanies their most authentic employment,
the awareness of strain, the consciousness of the "barely sayable"
that envelops, like an aura of luminous darkness, a "cloud of
unknowing," all their attempts at utterance. "That has done it,
more or less," our greatest works of art implicitly murmur, "but
let me have another try." The hearer or beholder is put on notice
that all artistic expressions "strain, crack, and sometimes break"
under the weight the artist lays upon them; they invite us to
prolong their statement into an answering silence, and at the
same time send the artist back to his "intolerable wrestle" with
the symbolic materials of his trade.[22]

Nowhere more self-consciously than in art does human language recognize, and recognizing, point beyond, the limits of
language; nowhere is the moment of negativity so ingredient to,
so seamlessly interwoven with the intention of positive expression. The language of art becomes, accordingly, far more than
the "outward vessels" of "inner meanings"; rather, to revert to
that other Augustinian metaphor, once briefly entertained but
then so soon discarded, the symbols of artistic creation function,
not like so many opaque clouds that hide the sun from view.
Much more, and much more than in any other form of human
discourse, the symbols themselves become the "luminous clouds"
of transfiguration.

Art and Reverence

Transposed in such a way, the Augustinian *exercitatio* of the
artes could serve as a school of genuine humanization, rather
than a technique of rationalization. Its efficacy would resemble
that of the "island's music," working on the Caliban in each of
us, awakening the slumbering inner man to the beauty that sur-
rounds us everywhere, until we "cry to dream again"; and dream,

indeed, as Augustine would have us do, of those otherworldly harmonies that come to us here and now, in and through, the concretized, embodied modulations of everyday.

But along with that leap of aspiration, that nostalgic yearning, the attunement to beauty must be seen as inspiring a deep sense of reverence—the "awe and reverence" of the lover in the *Phaedrus*[23]—so akin to the religious shudder Augustine speaks of when he tells us that the momentary glimpse granted him at Milan left him trembling *amore et horrore*: "with love and dread."[24] Beheld in that attitude of reverence, the world about us takes on its real importance; created, it leads our hearts and hopes beyond itself to the Creator; but also, precisely as creation, not despite but because of that, it is perceived as the Creator's ever-renewed gift to us, participation of the very being, holiness, and beauty that is omnipresent to, mysteriously ingredient in its every humblest item. As such, creation itself commands our reverence, brings us to a "point of rest in ourselves," asserts the "sacred independence" which, acknowledged, permits a "tree [to] become a mystery, a cloud a revelation."[25] Out of that reverent posture, created reality is beheld as not just *there,* but as coming to us each moment—"the sun grew round that very day" —as the everyday miracle Augustine loved to discourse about.[26] Reverence before creation's beauty, the heart's leap of welcoming wonder at the surprise that any of this should be at all, are attitudes, both of them, closely akin to the spirit of thankfulness Augustine includes as one meaning of *confessio;* a spirit he proposed as indispensable condition for man's coming to a recognition of the God Who unaccountably made everything to exist simply because He loved and is love.[27] These neighbor attitudes conspire in that dialogue of free divine gift and free human response that liberates, arouses the self-concerned soul from its jaded sense of deception, inciting it to "become a child again."

Viewed out of this cluster of attitudes, however, creation is more than the landscape of our journey, of an impatient pilgrimage we are meant to make across, and ultimately away from it. It becomes genuinely our home, created gift eliciting our own creative giving, worthy of our reverent attention, cultivation, adornment. In that way the furnishings it boasts, and those our art equips it with, can speak to us, reveal through the workings of our human providence, that divine providential care of which our world, in one of Augustine's dearest and most enduring insights, is the unfailing arena.

Tragic Wonder

But, and again Augustine's profoundest intention is superbly right, if we are to find our world the disclosure of God's providence, we must become perceivers properly attuned—attuned to accepting the dark in the cosmic painting as well as its lights and flashing colors. Taken on a superficial level, this aesthetic justification for the evils we experience can seem a cheap evasion. Speak to a mother who has just lost her child in terms of painting and poetry, and the size, the poignancy of her personal tragedy may at first seem trivialized. Doubtless, in the history of theodicy, even in one or other appeal to it by Augustine or Plotinus, there are instances of this aesthetic justification of evil which smack of that bloodless trivialization. Yet there is a depth at which the comparison may be entertained where it is the furthest thing from an evasion, a cheapening of the pang of human misery.

One knows, at least, that Augustine himself was sensitive to that pang: his appeals to this aesthetic illustration were meant not to take our eyes off the darkness in the cosmic canvas, but to focus them upon it, embracing it in a wider, deeper, not less but more sensitive view. But the sensitivity being summoned into play is, once again, not the raw capacity to react to pain or pleasure. We are being asked to respond, not merely to react, and to respond with an emotion formed, disciplined, modulated, penetrated with intellectuality. We are being asked to see the arena of human events with the artist's eye: the eye of a Vergil who could sing of life's incurable pang, the *lacrimae rerum,* and still assure us that our keenest sorrows can be transfigured in remembrance *(forsan et haec olim meminisse juvabit)*; the eye of a Sophocles who could conduct us through the pain and horror of Oedipus' self-destructive quest for himself, yet lead us at the end to that upland plain from which we view both heroism and horror synoptically, experience that strange exaltation at the one, the solemn, serene acceptance of, reconciliation to, the other. From that spectacle we return to our everyday round more capable of seeing the tragic wonder of the world we live and struggle, rejoice and die in.

One has to think that such a process of attunement to the solemn grandeur of human life is a more appropriate propaedeutic for the faith Augustine preached and lived than any voyage through the empyreans of abstraction, number, and geometry: it was, one guesses, part of what equipped him with the seasoned sensibility that enabled him, in time, to snap the spell of Manichaeism's harping on the fact of evil in the world and to accept that world as the battleground of God's redemptive love in Christ.

Conversion

But such acceptance involved, for Augustine, conversion or, more accurately, a series of conversions.[28] The perception of the world as shot through with providential care is a faith perception, one that the perceiver freely decides, consents, to make his own—a gift to which he is summoned to surrender.[29] Here again, the aesthetic analogue casts a privileged light on the inner mechanics of the long labor of conversion. For the seasoning, the slow refinement of sensibility, up to the point when the developed subject has been formed, this is a process demanding consent every step of the way. We must yield to an invitation in order to enter the world of artistic vision in the first place, in some obscure manner decide to filter out both the angry stridencies and sheer frivolities of immediate experience—to drift into a "slumber of soul" (*consopitum est anima mea*)[30]—in order to be recollected in this peculiar tranquility. But then we must willingly pass from easy comicbook thrills to the more muted, weightier excitements of Shakespeare or Dostoevski; we have to suspend our attachment to the more facile appeals of a Norman Rockwell, to Tschaikovsky's melodic charms, in order receptively to entertain the Olympian measures of Beethoven, the searching, troubling question of Rembrandt's self-portraits. Any passage from more facile artistic renderings of the human thing to renderings that must at first appear to us as more austere, demanding, less immediately rewarding, requires of us a docility, a welcoming openness—a free consent.

And the progress of sensibility recorded in Augustine's *Confessions* was, it would seem, something on this order. He grew from the child he was, petulantly squalling whenever his wants went unattended, through that puerile stage of Manichaeism so noisy with complaints about the world's evils, to a humbled, mature acceptance of our world as the arena of Providence. But in order to do so, he had to record a progress similar to Wordsworth's: the quicksilver reactions of his youth outgrown, his maturer ear can catch the sound of that

> still sad music of humanity
> nor harsh nor grating, though of ample power
> to chasten and subdue.[31]

This, I submit, is a world not unlike the world of Vergil, Homer, and Sophocles; the world of our experience, but beheld through the lens of tragic wonder. The graduated consent required for entry into it is not unlike the sort a Socrates demanded, or a Buddha, or (in a way one is perhaps permitted to consider quite unique), a Christ. Acceding to its demand exacts, in Plato's term, a conversion of the whole soul;[32] hesitant at first, and fearful, but growing in confidence and boldness as we follow the invitation of that savior figure who would draw us from the familiar shadows of our cave existence, strip us of those cozy, easy estimates of reality to which we were so attached, compel us to admit that our complaints against his liberating violence arose, at first, from an unavowed complicity with the dark surrounding us, a secret infidelity to our truest, highest selves. From the cave to the sun, every upward step is pain, incipient revolt, tempered and checked by growing consent. Only at the price of "leaving our older selves behind"—again, *cessavi de me paululum*—of accepting, more and more fully consenting to the childlike self that is being born in us, to the fresh appreciations, values, and importances, in short, only at the price of saying yes to the spiritual eyes that come with that new self, can we eventually come to see.

The aesthetic of Cassiciacum assures us that the harmony of our universe and of its historical unfolding is the work of divine Reason, that the discovery of our true selves implies our coming to see our soul's kinship with that overarching Reason.[33] What a less rationalizing aesthetic could have justified more naturally, I submit, is the half-uttered implicit in Augustine's invitation to Romanianus, and to us, that we join him in the recollected tranquillity of *Philosophia's* haven:[34] that our kinship with providential Reason is not merely a kinship of mind or disembodied soul, but one embracing our whole reality as sensuous, affective, perceiving and understanding human beings. That kinship, too, is in the last resort something on which we must decide, something to which, in faith, we must consent. And once we have consented, we can then accept the sense-world freshly beheld as bathed in this new light; in accepting it we have, in deepest truth, passed beyond its buffetings and pains, but without any movement of contempt, without for a moment being brought to despise either it, or the senses that conspired in the achievement of this vision. Reconciled to the sense-world, we are reconciled to our incarnate selves, and to God, "creator of the visible and invisible."

The Aesthetics of Belief

Had Augustine's aesthetic been more incarnate, I am suggesting, or had he more fully exploited some of the incarnate features underlined above, he might have come to a more persuasive rendering of his own progress in believing. By the same token, his theory of belief in its relation to understanding would, I submit, have gained in cogency. Faith, in his early thought, is of "things unseen"—its work is first to assure us that the unseen exists, then to purify, to strengthen the eye of understanding for a glimpse of that splendorous spiritual world, the world of eternal patterns that preside over the unfolding of the visible and temporal.[35] The *De Musica* shows another tendency emerging: the contingent facts of our visible, temporal world become the object of opinion: they pertain to *haec opinabilis vita*. Hence the historical happenings of the Gospel must be taken on authority, must be believed.[36] The *De Utilitate Credendi* represents, among other things, a valiant attempt to persuade an Honoratus who, it is supposed, is among the few already capable of understanding insight into the invisible world, that he must nonetheless join the many, the crowd of believers.[37] Valiant the attempt is, but Augustine is successful only at the price of invoking a quite extra-systematic concern for the human community, the *societas humana;* his dichotomies have so disjoined the realms of seen and unseen, historical and eternal, authority and reason, that the move from one to the other simply is not a natural one.

Transpose his spiritual world into the register of an incarnate aesthetic, however, and these problems lend themselves to natural unforced solutions. The forms or intelligible patterns we glimpse as presiding over the course of human history are no longer realities glimpsed by leaving sense behind: they become aesthetic distillations, grasped by the metaphysical imagination; they represent the idealized paths of human action, the artistically envisaged norms for the "way things ought to be," at once transcending, and yet caught glimmering through the rhythms of the sensible, historical. These are the terms on which the Christian assents, his eyes opened by the risen Christ on the road to Emmaus, that the historical facts related in the Bible, all the song and pathos, the triumphs and defeats of God's people in the checkered course of history—even the dark reality of Calvary —disclose, when properly beheld, a mysterious sense: it was *right* (*oportet, dei*) that a loving God decree that it all happen that way.[38] And then, those same eyes turned upon the events of our present, everyday world, they understand it in the same terms, assent to finding in its tortuous turnings the same rhythms, the same mysterious, providential logic. This, significantly, is the logic Augustine eventually discerned as originating from beyond, but discoverable *within* the very stuff and texture of his life experience. This is not the logic of Greek necessitarianism, but something far closer to what Aristotle's aesthetic hints at as the "possible which is probable or necessary," the seemingly (and even possibly) merely chance happening which, viewed under a different light, intimates an air of design after all. For if it be credible that God does not toss dice with His universe, it is equally clear that his dealings with mankind are scarcely governed by a logic which is mathematical. How grasp the profoundly interpersonal cast of God's providential logic in dealing with His children? Again, I am suggesting, an incarnate aesthetic may well furnish a most appropriate key.

The Aesthetics of the Interpersonal

The same incarnate register, too, takes far more naturally into account the centrality of Christianity's concern for the *societas humana*. For the refinement of sensibility we have been describing takes on a special urgency in the interpersonal encounter, a focus that Augustine's thought instruments cope with only awkwardly. When Reason asks him, in the *Soliloquies*, whether the knowledge he seeks of God is anything like the knowledge he has of his dearest friend, Alypius, his disjunction of visible and invisible forces him to contend that he has no direct knowledge of Alypius' true identity, his soul.[39] The *De Trinitate* shows him grown uneasy with that kind of solution: how indeed is justice seen and loved, embodied in the Apostle Paul?[40] The theoretical cast of his earlier reply has partially come home to him; he suspects that there is something desperately unreal about the theory. How do we get to know our friends? Are their real selves somewhat like so many ghosts in the machine of their outward bodily covering—a covering whose opacity precludes our piercing to their interior?[41] We have seen

Augustine repeatedly revert to a model very like this: his interpretation of the knowledge that arises in the interpersonal encounter runs on the same theoretical paths as his aesthetic, as his more comprehensive way of relating outward sign to inward reality. His conclusion: that the consonance between outward expression and inward reality is matter for faith—a faith grounded in a charity that urges us to believe that the outward truly expresses the interior.[42]

But then, can I ever know that another person loves me? Surely, for a Christian, the question is a crucial one: what more privileged revelation of God's love and care for us than the love and care extended by the brethren? But the kind of knowledge to be sought here cannot be of a mathematical, geometric, rationalist variety:[43] the type on which Augustine's aesthetic is modeled. Again, transpose his aesthetic into another key, and fresh resources come immediately to hand. We *discern* that the words and gestures, all the outward expressions of unfeigned love, truly reveal an interior attitude that neither remains utterly unseen behind its opaque covering, nor ever becomes totally transparent to us; the truth of the matter is that the other's interiority becomes *translucently* manifest in, and through, its symbolic expressions. In the first surprise moment when another insinuates he loves me, there has to come a catching of breath, a tremor of disbelief: this would, indeed, be good news, but almost too good to be true! Like the Apostles after the Resurrection, we cannot but be tempted to "disbelieve out of sheer joy."[44] In the very next instant, however, we dimly realize that this offer of love implies reciprocity; it calls for both respect and response; it is both offer and solicitation; as with each step into the aesthetic unknown, it asks us to decide, consent, to trust that each new offer is genuine, and to respond with an answering offer.

Then, however, as the original encounter is succeeded by another, others, a series of encounters that gradually bind our lives together, a self-confirming pattern is formed; I can find that my initial belief has gradually been validated; my friend has become, in the deepest sense of the world, my familiar; I begin to find such a consistency, such a reliability expressed in his symbolic behavior—I can sense, almost clairvoyantly, when a word or gesture betrays that he is "not himself"—that my interpretation, in Augustine's term, my "understanding," of his interior becomes a kind of knowledge: not unlike the kind of knowledge I have that Sophocles, or Rembrandt, or Mozart—or

St. John the Evangelist—when grappling with the meaning of life, read the riddling sense enmeshed in its mystery, caught something of it, and each in his own way "got it right." Always the same factors are at play: a series of consents, freely made, "willing suspensions of unbelief"[45] if you will, to accept a meaning not at first obvious, but discovered at last, not in some disembodied world beyond the reach of sense, but in and through the symbols accessible to us as total, incarnate, affective perceivers.

The Sacramental Universe

Few concerns are closer to Augustine's heart than his preoccupation with showing us that the entire universe, open to the eyes of the believing—and understanding—Christian, is a truly sacramental universe: a forest of signs figuratively disclosing the creative and redemptive work of the Trinitarian Godhead.[46] Yet constantly standing athwart his efforts in this direction is the tendency to portray the sign as a kind of veil, interposing its opacity between the sensuous beholder and the spiritual, invisible reality behind it. All the suggestions put forward above call for a decisive modification of this fundamental schema: they point to how one may envisage the sign in terms more consonant with the Johannic *semeion*[47]—as itself translucent, at once both revealing and concealing the Truth-Beauty fashioning the living forms, the musical rhythms of our experienced world, into cosmic poetry; a Truth-Beauty that now more easily, naturally, assumes a personal character.

The World of Resurrection

Connected with Augustine's view of the sign as a veil is his persistence in viewing our human exterior as hiding our interior, and his connected insistence on envisaging the ideal corrective to this situation in terms of a perfect spiritual transparency of our several interiorities to each other. That ideal situation, we have seen, he promises will be realized in the world of the resurrection: a world that, in consequence, he is compelled to portray in terms that come dangerously close to suggesting a purely spiritual world, shorn of the embodiment that his thinking associates with opacity. His dogged altercation with the Porphyrian "flight from the body" leads him, in time, to suspect this tendency in his own earlier thinking, and yet, despite all manner of rethinking the matter, never (to my knowledge) does he determinedly confront, deliberately undercut, the dichotomy of exterior-interior that originally led him down this pathway of thought. Yet undercut it must be, if the spiritual body is to become the perfect expression of the risen soul; if the question is even seriously to be posed whether our senses in the eschatological world can conceivably be empowered to glimpse the divine splendor; if the glorious body of the risen Christ, the full flowering of His incarnation even "there," is to confer an *ewige Bedeutung,* an everlasting meaningfulness, on His, and our, incarnate careers in time and human history.[48] But once again, undercutting this dichotomy, in order to arrive at a mode of thinking of the body's risen condition, implies a sensitive readjustment of all those other key dichotomies that we have seen come so readily to Augustine's pen and so regularly command his thinking: bodily and spiritual, visible and invisible, action and contemplation, temporal and eternal.

Augustine and the Perennial Value of Platonism

If I might hazard a summary of this chapter, of this entire book, and indeed, of all that I have previously written about Augustine's thought, it might come to this: few facets of his work cry out more eloquently for readjustments than his aesthetic theory; and yet, once readjusted, no single facet provides such a rich series of suggestions as to how analogous readjustments could rejuvenate the entire organism of his thought; rejuvenate, and liberate all that is most authentic and perennially valuable in his towering contribution to the Christian task of understanding the faith.

For Augustine's perennial hold on the human spirit, in the aesthetic area and in other areas as well, derives at least as much from what he does as from what he claims to be doing. Jean Guitton was making a similar point when he sat himself to disengage Augustine's Christian "spirit" from the husk of ancient-world "mentality" and "language" that often threatens to betray, rather than translate it.[49] The metaphor itself is characteristically Augustinian; what has been written here on the relation of words to meanings would raise some doubts about its entire appositeness; and yet the metaphor communicates, even when a precise understanding of it eludes us. That, I have suggested elsewhere, is something very like what Augustine succeeds in doing: genuine poetry, it has been claimed, "can communicate

before it is understood";[50] the greatness of Augustine, and of
the major figures in the Platonic tradition more generally, is
that they manage to speak to man at a depth where more is communicated than is explicitly understood. Great literary artists
all of them, Plato, Plotinus, and Augustine accomplish more
than they could ever have intended on the conscious level, more
than they could ever have reflected upon, and laid out in so many
theoretical claims, clearly expressed. It was almost inevitable,
then, that Augustine never found a language adequate to express
what he was actually doing: had he not *done* it with such power,
finish, contagiousness, he would never have underlined so forcefully the relative poverty of the theory he evolves to explain what
he *thought* he was doing.

Augustine and the Task of Philosophy

The very richness of the Platonic psyche, then, accounts for
the richness of contact it makes with the psyche of everyman
in every age: it speaks not only to our brains but to our hearts,
our senses, our affectivity. It challenges and masterfully over-
rides the fancy that philosophizing is a purely cerebral business.
But the triumph is not merely psychological: it reflects the dim
awareness that being itself is richer in resources than mere brain-
work could ever elicit from it. In the folds of its mysterious unity
lurk other treasures: it confronts us with that disarming variety
of faces to which Augustine and the mediaevals after him assigned the names of truth, goodness, and beauty.

The pursuit of truth has always brought with it the concern
for solid evidence, rigorous method: man wants to be sure, be
confident that he has seen it aright. That preoccupation has led
again and again to the ever-renewed choice between empiricism
with its careful survey of the atomic evidence, for what "is the
case," and rationalism with its conviction that man's mind can
gain some insight into what "must be the case." Neither method
in its pure state has ever gotten very far: Kant's first critique
may be thought to have shown their limited tether.

But this only brought Kant to push his inquiry farther: practical reason involves itself with being's visage as the "good"—a
face of being no true philosopher is at liberty to ignore. Is it an
illusion to think that being holds out to man not only the
promise of intelligibility, but the promise of ultimate satisfaction
as well? Does the heart have reasons which reason cannot legitimately be expected to understand? Is the pragmatist's insistence

that the world make "moral sense"[51] only a more sophisticated version of Hamlet's bantering remark, advising us that there is more to life than is dreamt of in philosophies dominantly preoccupied with the evidently true?

But is the insistence that the world make moral sense exclusively a belief in being as good? Or has another face of being subtly asserted its claims, one that Kant came to contemplate in his Third Critique, being's face as beauty, beauty, that elicits the judgment that the picture is "right," in the profoundest sense, "decorous" just as it *decet*, "ought to be"? Here there enters, as Augustine unsteadily saw, a property of the whole that requires our suspending for the moment all our aspirations toward satisfaction, that forbids us to lay claims on a being that now reveals majestically its peremptory claims on us, laying upon us the sacred obligation of beholding the panorama before us in the silent reverence that accepts it as it is, consents that it be so.

Philosophy, it has been said, begins in wonder. But all too often that wonder is interpreted as something verging on inquisitiveness: the spur of puzzlement that leads us to want to banish the darkness of ignorance or confusion, to inquire, to get to know and thus—apparently—eliminate the very wonder that gave inquiry birth. In other connections, our ignorance or confusion may be seen as touching on our thirst for satisfaction: we yearn to understand why we are unhappy, how we may attain to our restless heart's desire.

We have witnessed both these types of wonder—about being as true, about being as good—active in Augustine's thought: the Truth-Beauty he aspires to see answers not only to the mind's yen for inquiry, but to the restless heart's aspiration after bliss. As such, it better deserves the name of truth-good: being as promising beatitude to the contemplative mind. The Augustine whose first concern would appear to be to exorcise the residual hold of academic doubt upon him, whose *si fallor, sum* ("if I err, I must exist") has so often been compared to Descartes's *cogito*,[52] assures us at times that his method of banishing doubt is that of Christian Platonism, but straitened in the heavily rationalistic mold of Pythagorean mathematicism. But there is more than propositional truth and certainty involved; *De vita nostra, de moribus, de animo res agitur*, Augustine exclaims,[53] life, morals and the destiny of the soul are all at stake. Hence the seeming rigor of method gives way at a crucial point to the leap of aspiration: it is Truth, subsistent and transcendent he aspires to glimpse, in a vision promised him by the radiant

feminine figure of *Philosophia,* one toward which the Lady
Continence, so "chastely alluring," invites him to advance in a
movement that is surrender; to the vision of a God who sums up
in Himself all the enrapturing charms of feminity. Even as we
read his rationalistic assurances, our minds glide easily over
them; we catch the beat of deeper vibrations; we know better;
there is more than rationalism here, there is imaginative appre-
hension, aesthetic envisagement running far beyond what rigorous method would honor as evidence. The heart, we are convinced, is right in so responding to being's opulent promise; the
eye of faith has truly penetrated to something more than meets
the questing eye.

Augustine's intermittent, but recurring confusion between
the beautiful and the good persuades him that his rationalistic
method will furnish him tools for erecting an aesthetic theory,
too, construct a ladder of beauties that will promote the soul's
ascent to the realm of its deepest desire, to the other world of
beauty naked and unveiled. These assurances, too, we glide over:
here too we sense there is at work something more, the unspoken
but clairvoyant sensitivity to beauty as distinct from good, to
beauty as bringing the soul to a pause of stillness, free from self-
concern, as exciting not so much *amor* as *horror,* the recoil of
reverence; as laying its sovereign claims upon a third variety of
wonder, one that descries that beauty glimpsed brings with it
that imperative so operative in Platonisms of every stamp: that
this is how we must strive to make ourselves, and our world, to
be. Even as we read Augustine's assurances the beauty can be
approached by the same routes as truth and goodness, we know
him too well, we supply what we have glimpsed in other places
of his work, and half-consciously correct the exaggerated claims
of his confident rationalism.

And we are right to discount a number of his explicit claims:
fifteen hundred years of thought should make us at least be
methodologically more sophisticated, more aware of these possible confusions than he, understandably, could have been. But
returning to a Plato, a Plotinus, or Augustine is like returning
to Homer and the world of ancient myth, to the sense of exu-
berant vitality our forbears possessed. We are suddenly reminded
that method, sophistication bring other dangers with them: the
constricting preoccupation with epistemological refinements,
with rigorous analysis, fine distinctions, can induce philosophic
anemia. We can, in Plato's phrase, be robbed of the capacity,
when the situation calls for it, to "lose our heads," to take the

daring manic step that being as good and beauty would in their deep consonance invite us, command us, to take.[54]

The philosophic task in any age is not a happy one: rigor of method, care for evidence must always keep us honest, prevent our aspirations from leading us into mere sentimental wish fulfillment. It must discipline the idealizations, chasten the constructions of our metaphysical imaginations so that they do not drift off into insubstantial fantasy. But the epistemological preoccupation, become imperialistic, can also hobble our advance, clip the wings of philosophic flight, prevent us from coming to know the very good our hearts most deeply yearn to know; it can, in the tones of a perverse kind of piety, interdict our recognizing the commanding beauty that, as moral beings, we must be ready to assent to. Philosophical thinking, then, to retain its vitality, to maintain itself in readiness to respond to the riches of being, must consent to become a constant series of decisions, interlocking and mutually correcting—epistemological, ethical, and aesthetic.

Among those claims being makes (Augustine would remind us) is the religious claim. Answering to, correcting, and eventually overriding his rationalistic assurances to provide our minds with unquestionable certainties, there is the deeper admonition to which he insistently returns: *nisi credideritis, non intelligetis,* unless ye believe, ye shall not understand. The cry of a Christian apologist, merely? No: the ensign of an extraordinary human being, who came to discover—with eyes and ears, with imagination, mind, and heart—that the harmonies of being and the melodies of temporal variety could be caught only by one who had, in the depths and heights of the self, become attuned to the solemn cadences of the *carmen universitatis,* the riddling poem of human history, in all its fulness.

If I may chance a final series of retranslations: it is only when the conscious rational mind renews its vital contact with the deeper regions that he calls memory; only when it yields to the invitation toward ideals that reside in that part of the soul subject to divine illumination; only when it comes to know, with more than rational conscious knowledge, the secret kinship that links the philosopher's moments of reasoning, poeticizing, even taking mystical flight—only then can the human and the Christian come to coincide, and the God of the philosophers be glimpsed as the living God of Abraham and Isaac and Jacob. A large claim, surely; one Augustine more eloquently issues by what he does than by what he tells us he is doing; but one to be tested by the application of more resources than mere analysis can offer.

For we judge philosophers and what they bring to us in far more subtle fashion than is generally acknowledged. We listen as much for the intimations of their unsaid and unsayable as to their explicit affirmations, methodological or otherwise. We listen for the attunement of a genuine humanity, hearken to the ring of being—truth and goodness, goodness and beauty all enclosed in its mysterious folds—pealing forth steady and round from one total human subject to another. We judge philosophies, in short, much the way we judge great poetry, drama, or symphony. When the harmonies are rich and disciplined enough, we know the master "got it right." Judged on these canons, despite all the criticisms the centuries have leveled at him, Augustine's perennial vitality is assured.

And appreciated in this light, even the otherworldliness that seems at first to militate against his aesthetic finds itself at home. Expressed as he often does express it, it could lead to a depreciation, a near-evaporation of this world of sensible beauty; to an instrumentalization of both beauty and art; to the hasty, impatient call that we leave all this behind us in our single-minded journey toward the "alone," the *unum necessarium,* the not-to-be-rivaled God of our ultimate enjoyment. Yet this is Augustine's language when in the grips of being as good, when goaded by the restless heart in pursuit of its lasting bliss. That wavering, unsteady insight we have seen him possess into beauty precisely as beauty would immediately introduce a corrective: for being as beauty demands attention, calls for that patient beholding we know Augustine the artist practiced. It may seem strange at this juncture to compare him with that determined anti-supernaturalist, John Dewey. Yet the comparison speaks persuasively of Augustine's undeniable modernity, precisely because the parallels between them are too striking to ignore. For Dewey, too insists on a kind of attunement to the universe we behold, a "natural piety" as affective precondition for our seeing the world as it truly is. Like Augustine, he exploits the idealizing power of "imagination" as projecting from experience, sensitively gathered, the ideals that solicit human striving and, more strongly, lay claim on man's allegiance. It may be significant that the logic of aesthetic experience led him, eventually, to a striking formulation that seems, for one flashing moment, to loosen his grip on militant naturalism; it seduces him, in fact, to an utterance that is strangely Augustinian in flavor.

Beheld aesthetically, Dewey tells us, any object of experience can introduce us into a totality that is "commemorative, expectant, insinuating, premonitory"—into a universal background that "qualifies everything in the focus." This property of aesthetic experience, he goes on to say,

explains the religious feeling that accompanies intense aesthetic perception. We are, as it were, introduced into a world beyond this world which is nevertheless the deeper reality of the world in which we live in our ordinary experiences. We are carried out beyond ourselves to find ourselves.[55]

We glimpse another world, indeed, but on condition that we adopt an attitude that expressly forbids our short-circuiting this world; a world that does not cheapen, but enhances, lends an added aura of grace, preciousness, and value, cloaks the immediately sensible with a penumbra of gift, surprise, reverence-inspiring wonder.

This very body that we bear, Augustine's resurrection theology insists, will be transformed to become our risen body—the body that will be itself, but come to the consummation toward which its every graceful action now dimly aspires. But the same must be said of the world the Christian beholds, "groaning in its great act of giving birth,"[56] shot through with "eager longing" for its fulfillment in the new earth and new heaven.

So much for the world as Augustine invites the Christian to behold it. But is that vision the exclusive prerogative of the Christian?

No, Augustine would answer, and the contemporary Augustinian would echo him. For nothing is more at the heart of perennial Augustinianism than the claim that Christian faith and human understanding are in fundamental concord; that between them they conspire to generate the one *vera philosophia*.

More than a century ago, Matthew Arnold disconsolately gazed from his window over Dover Beach and contested that claim, eloquently. Thousands have followed him since. The strident cry of human suffering, the apparently senseless clangor of cosmic perversity must, for those of us born in the past few centuries, must and cannot but be a cacophony infinitely more disorienting than the sound that "Sophocles heard upon the Aegean." The world that we behold, "so various, so beautiful, so new" seems obdurately to defy our Sisyphean efforts to make sense of it. "A darkling plain, where ignorant armies clash by night"; into its absurdity, give them this credit, the Manichaeans stared, and struggled to a mythic understanding of it. That understanding, the mature Augustine was eventually forced to reject. And much more we. Yet the clangor and its stridency still assail our ears, our hearts, our understanding. It is conceivable, indeed, truly possible, that this world we experience is the absurdity Augustine was once very close to believing it was.

But how is one to decide? That same world Arnold beheld, and after him Camus and Sartre and a hundred others: is it, when properly beheld, as "commemorative, expectant, insinuating, premonitory" as Dewey's "natural piety" pronounced it to be?

As one man's personal answer to that question, I may be forgiven a final translation of Augustine's thinking. It hearkens back to that image, so exceptional in his works, with which in many ways this book began. And yet, I have tried to show, it is the image towards which Augustine's aesthetic explorations tend, as to some culmination providentially ordained.

If we are commemorative enough, and free enough from self-concern, pious enough to behold, pay genuine attention, we may come to find our world "insinuating, premonitory" after all. We may find it hinting at quite another consummation than the blank, unanswering darkness, the *una nox perpetua dormienda*. Out of that recognition, we may be called upon to act, as well: so to reverence our world, so to respond to the call of beauty in the homely fabric of everyday, that our hearts are ready to translate our filtered artistic vision into caring for, adorning, bringing to completer formfulness the world of inchoate forms that lies about us. Maybe only then can we hope to be disposed by the conversion that Platonism has always held to be the cradle of the philosophic quest; disposed to distinguish, at first "through a glass darkly," but then, perhaps, to glimpse more confidently, through the "luminous clouds" of our rare transfiguration moments, the shifting shapes, glimmering outlines, of that other world aborning.

Appendixes

Notes

Index

Appendix A

CONTRA ACADEMICOS I, 3:

PER LUCIDAS NUBES

ONE OF THE most striking features of this text is that image of clouds as "light-filled," so that Augustine can say that *through* them the personified *Philosophia* was granting him a glimpse of God (*Deum . . . ostentare dignatur*). In his later, and more habitual employment of the cloud image, Augustine tends to depict the light of the higher world reaching downward *to* them; they function as cloud cover, so to speak, intercepting that light, providing us with shadow (*umbra*) so that our weakened eyes will not be blinded by the brightness of that light. They symbolize, therefore, the entire regime of authority, which provides us with *indirect* messages from the "light," the eye of our reason being too weak or dimmed to gain access to a direct vision of it.[1] How account for this unusual variant on Augustine's customary symbolism?

First, the relevant sections of the text: Augustine is addressing his former patron, Romanianus:

Illud ergo, illud tuum . . . quod in te divinum nescio quo vitae hujus somno veternoque sopitum est . . . secreta Providentia excitare decrevit. Evigila, evigila, oro te.

Ipsa [Philosophia] me nutrit et fovet . . . [Et] Deum . . . jam jamque quasi per lucidas nubes ostentare dignatur.

That, that [part] of you . . . [that] divine [part] that has been lulled
by some kind of sleep or lethargy of this life . . . a secret Providence
has decreed to rouse up. Awake, awake I beg you.

[*Philosophia*] herself nourishes me and makes me strong . . . [and]
deigns very soon to reveal God to me, through light-filled clouds,
as it were.

Nutrit ac fovet: an array of elements points to the *fovere* image
which flowers at the central point of the *Confessions*.[2] There he
describes God's *fovere* action as "lulling him to sleep" (*consopitum est insania mea*) to this world of "vanities," until he awakes
in Him (*evigilavi in Te*) to a new spiritual vision of Him. Soon
afterwards, he depicts that same vision as a vision "from afar,"
as though from the height of some hill (*cacumen*) whence the
traveler can only catch a glimpse of the happy fatherland
(*patria*).[3]

Sleeping, waking, a *fovere* action, and a consequent vision;
but, on the one hand, a vision from a height, *cacumen*; on the
other, a vision through light-filled clouds. Could there be some
other source that provides a connecting link between these two
portrayals?

That link, I suggest, is the transfiguration scene as described
by Matthew (17:1–8) and Luke (9:28–36)[4] and commented on
by Ambrose in his *In Lucam* (VII, 8–20). The vision enjoyed by
the chosen Apostles took place on a mountain (*mons*), and Ambrose comments (VII, 12) that unless we ascend to the height of
a higher prudence (*cacumen*; cf. *Conf* VII, 27) "Wisdom" will
not show itself to us. Wisdom, for both Ambrose and Augustine,
stands for the eternal Son, whose "face" in the transfiguration
shone like the sun (*sol: Matt.* 17:2). And we are reminded that
the Ambrosian hymn Monica quotes—*fove precantes, Trinitas*
—at the climax of the *De Beata Vita* (35), describes the Son as
splendor paternae gloriae, the "splendor of the Father's glory";
and Monica herself is described as *evigilans in fide,* "awakening
in faith," in order to see the Trinitarian point Augustine was
driving at.

But the Apostles, too, slept and woke. Luke tells us they were
"heavy with sleep" (*gravati sunt a somno,* 9:32), and Ambrose
interprets their drowsiness in terms that Augustine evidently
took to heart: "the incomprehensible splendor of divinity presses
down (*premit*) upon our bodily senses; for bodily sight cannot
bear up against the brightness of the sun" (*solis radium . . .
corporea nequit acies sustinere,* VII, 17); how could our corrupt

mortality, imprisoned in the body, bear the brightness of the divine light (VII, 17 and 18)? For so long as we are in the body, a certain "slothfulness of mind" (*desidia quadam mentis*) keeps us from this vision (VII, 18).

But awaking (*evigilantes*), Luke tells us, the Apostles "saw his majesty" (*viderunt maiestatem eius*, 9:32); a moment later, a "cloud" overshadows them (*obumbravit*). But what Luke tersely describes as *nubs,* Matthew specifies as *nubs lucida,* the "light-filled cloud" of the *Contra Academicos.* And again, Ambrose may well have pointed to that connection, for this cloud, he explains, was a *lucida nubs,* like the *Shekinah*-cloud of God's power that enshrouded Mary at the incarnation, its function being to impregnate with faith the minds of men (VII, 20). From out of the cloud comes the voice of the Father commending obedience to His Son.

Here, I submit, we have the elements of sleeping, waking, and vision of the divinity common to both the *Confessions* and *Contra Academicos* texts. But we have, in addition, the mountain or "height" (*cacumen*) of *Conf* VII, 27 in linkage with a cloud, both "shadowing" and, as in Augustine's words to Romanianus, "light-filled." Much more could be said about Augustine's debt to Ambrose's commentary and hymnology, to confirm the view I am proposing; but let it suffice for now to suggest that, behind both these descriptions of Augustine's access to vision, there lies the image of transfiguration.

Appendix B

THE DATING
AND INTERPRETATION
OF THE *De MUSICA*

SVOBODA's interpretation of the *De Musica*, as I have observed, follows in the main the interpretation that Edelstein accorded it before him. But for both of them, it is necessary to suppose a considerable time gap between the first five and the sixth book in order to sustain their interpretation. Both would have us believe that the first five books had been composed at Milan, when Augustine was in the full fervor of his enthusiasm for the *disciplinae*; but then, as Augustine's conversion proceeded, as the *Wandlungen* of his early strides in understanding the faith brought him more and more to being a "convinced Christian," his ardor for the pagan disciplines cooled. Evidence of this coolness is to be found in the opening (and while we are at it, the closing) paragraphs of the sixth book. It is no longer the convert of Milan, bestriding uncertainly the fence between Christianity and Neo-Platonism, now it is the deep-dyed Christian (read "the ecclesiastic") who is leveling a sterner judgment on the value of the liberal *artes*, and on *musica* in particular. This development must have taken time, however; to lend the thesis credibility, therefore, reason must be found to insert a time gap between the first five books, with their enduring admiration of *musica,* and the sixth, where the results of the postulated development have had time to show. Thus far Edelstein and Svoboda.

Neither of them tends to attach great importance to Augustine's own indications of chronological sequence and dating, as he reports them in the *Retractations*. To that question of extrinsic evidence we shall return shortly. The evidence Edelstein relies upon is largely "intrinsic": once granted his theory of Augustine's gradual conversion—drawn largely from the works of Alfaric and Thimme—he finds a number of doctrinal emphases, in Book Six especially, that, to his mind, set the tone of that book sharply against the preceding five. Those features include:

1. The fact that Augustine values religious authority above the *disciplinae*; authority, when it is the authority of the Christian Scriptures, carries greater weight in the believer's pursuit of truth than such works of "reason" as the liberal arts represent. Edelstein (p. 120) is able to cite the opening paragraph of Book Six to support this contention, but no other citation to that effect is forthcoming.

2. Coherent with the above Edelstein thinks (pp. 120–121) is the fact that Augustine's citation from pagan authors throughout Books One to Five suddenly yields, in Book Six, to his musical meditation on Ambrose's hymn *Deus Creator Omnium*. This goes along with a much freer and more frequent appeal to scriptural texts, as well.

The Extrinsic Evidence

The first step in evaluating Edelstein's theory must be a consideration of the extrinsic evidence for dating the sixth book as he finds it necessary to date it. And one such item of extrinsic evidence Edelstein thinks he has: *Letter* 101, dating from the year 408/9, represents Augustine's reply to Memorius the Bishop, who had asked for a copy of the *De Musica*. He cannot put his hand on the first five books, Augustine informs his correspondent, but he is sending along a copy of the sixth book, *emendatum*. Edelstein is forced to an interpretation of that phrase that will treat his theory most kindly: the emendation can be understood as having left the book substantially "unchanged" (Edelstein, p. 118); hence the ecclesiastical spirit of Augustine the Bishop could remain content with this version of Book Six, while leveling stern criticism against the tenor of the first five books.

What, though, of the chronology and dating indicated in the

Retractations? Here Edelstein remains more discreet. But what does Augustine say? He speaks of the *De Musica* not once, but twice.

The first mention (*Retr.* I, vi) occurs when he is telling of the project *De Disciplinis* he had conceived of while still at Milan, in 387. One of the classic seven disciplines he meant to bring into play, in order to lead the mind "through corporeal things [upward] to the incorporeal," was *musica.* The work he conceived of in this connection would treat only of one part of *musica,* to wit, *rythmus,* or "meter." The finished work consists of six books. The project was conceived of at Milan, Augustine tells us,

Sed eosdem sex libros iam baptizatus iamque ex Italia regressus in Africam scripsi; inchoaveram quippe tantummodo istam apud Mediolanum disciplinam.

But those same six books I wrote when already baptized and already returned from Italy to Africa; I had only started on that discipline at Milan.

In his later mention of the work, he places it after the *De Genesi contra Manichaeos* and just before the series *De Magistro, De Vera Religione,* and *De Utilitate Credendi,* all of them identified as from the early African period. Speaking of the *De Musica,* he says:

Deinde [i.e., after writing the *De Genesi contra Manichaeos*] ut supra commemoravi [in the text alluded to above, *Retr.* I, vi], sex libros de musica scripsi, quorum ipse sextus maxime innotuit. (*Retr.* I, xi, 1).

Then, as I recalled above, I wrote six books on *musica,* the sixth of them being the most noteworthy.

Twice Augustine informs us that he wrote all six books after he returned from Italy to Africa. He had only made a start (*inchoaveram quippe tantummodo*) on his work on that discipline while at Milan. Ambiguous enough term, if it stood alone: it could mean anything from a few programmatic jottings to the composition of one or even several books. But it does not stand alone; in both texts Augustine removes the ambiguity to this extent at least: whatever kind of start he made, it was not the kind that would prevent him from saying that he wrote all six books in Africa, and indeed, after having completed the *De Genesi contra Manichaeos*: a formidable objection to any attempt to hold that five books date from Milan, while the sixth dates from a period of "ecclesiastical" fervor in Africa.

What, though, of Edelstein's appeal to Letter 101, to Memorius? That question can be answered, and in a way that respects the data of the *Retractations,* by accepting Marrou's later interpretation of the nettling term, *emendatum.*

In Appendix D of his *Culture Antique* (pp. 580–583) Marrou takes up the question of this *emendatio.* In doing so, he focuses our attention on the fact that the change in Augustine's attitude toward the *artes* is reflected in two, and only two paragraphs of the sixth book of the *De Musica*: the first (VI, 1) and the last (VI, 59). There is no evidence in any other portion of Book Six as it survives to indicate a cooling of Augustine's attitude toward the *artes.* Nor has Edelstein been able to produce any evidence from other portions of the sixth book, bearing precisely on this issue.

Marrou's proposed solution to the *emendatio* question suggests, accordingly, that the extent of Augustine's *emendatio* was precisely to write a new opening and a new closing paragraph, both reflecting the more "ecclesiastical" viewpoint that was his, not in the year 390, but in the year of his writing to Memorius, 408/9. That proposed solution permits our honoring the chronological data of the *Retractationes*; in doing so, it permits our viewing the two items of extrinsic evidence on the chronology of *De Musica* VI as perfectly consistent with each other. And, finally, it warrants our introducing a time gap, but one that touches only these two paragraphs, and one that stretches, not from 387 to 390/1, but from 390/1 to 408/9.

The Intrinsic Evidence

One thing we know about Augustine's intellectual development is that the theory of conversion to which Edelstein and his forebears Thimme and Alfaric gave credit has not stood up under investigation. The Dialogues of Cassiciacum, and notably, the aesthetic of the *De Ordine,* is far more "Christian" in intent and content than these men were able to see. His theory of conversion prompts Edelstein to view the *De Ordine* aesthetic as *autonom-philosophisch,* the aesthetic of *De Musica* VI as *christlich* (Edelstein, p. 121). It is this perspective, I suggest, that leads him to illuminate, and by that illumination faintly to distort, the evidence he then proposes for his interpretation of the work.

From the opening paragraph of Book Six—quite probably, if we accept Marrou's proposal, "emended" in 408/9—Edelstein argues for the superiority of scriptural authority (*auctoritas*) over the way of "reason" represented by the ascent through the liberal *artes*. This interpretation he then extends to the whole of Book Six: his interpretation can only be answered by another. I have tried in my own interpretation to show that *De Musica* VI—its opening and closing paragraphs apart for the moment— remains faithful to the view Augustine propounds in Books One to Five and indeed throughout the works of this period. The reader must judge whether that interpretation makes sense of Book Six as it has come down to us. But we must return to this question shortly in another context, when examining whether Edelstein is warranted in drawing his theory even from the *emendatio* paragraphs.

Augustine's hard-won regard for Scripture and for Christian sources more generally, Edelstein then argues, accounts for his shifting from "pagan" verse citations through Books One to Five, to a meditation on Ambrose's *Deus Creator Omnium,* and to the proliferation of scriptural texts that generously punctuate *De Musica* VI. But here again, we are dealing far less with "evidence," far more with an interpretive perspective that accords to certain factual items a significance that is highly questionable: illuminate those items from another interpretive perspective, and they take on another significance entirely. Again, I must refer the reader to the text of my own interpretation: the "pagan" citations are really moralizing verses which Augustine, even when he has borrowed them, has reformed to fit his own purpose; they "lead the mind" progressively upward throughout Books One through Five to the "fruit" of that gradual ascent, a fruit to be culled only in Book Six. The thrust of the *exercitatio animae* remains what it always was, from the *Contra Academicos* onwards. And what was the climax of the "ascent" of the *De Beata Vita?* From academic, through Stoic, through Neo-Platonic notions of the happy life, Augustine leads his reader to Monica's rapt appeal to Ambrose's *Deus Creator Omnium!* Augustine's shift into that Christian register is far less novel than Edelstein's conversion perspective would allow him to see; the Cassiciacum works are as *christlich* as the *De Musica,* and the *De Musica* as *philosophisch* as the works of Cassiciacum.

The Teaching of the Emendatio *to Book Six*

Thus far, however, I have been conceding for the sake of argument—*dato sed non concesso*—Edelstein's interpretation of *De Musica* VI, 1, and VI, 59: conceding, that is, what he conceives to be the "later" attitude which Augustine the "convinced Christian" betrays toward the liberal arts, and toward the ways of authority and reason. "Later" that attitude most probably is: but even as late as 408/9 is it the attitude Edelstein thinks it is? The death blow to his theory, I submit, is dealt by a closer scrutiny of those very paragraphs.

Is Edelstein really entitled to think that Augustine's regard for the way of the disciplines has, even by the time he wrote the *emendatio,* been entirely eclipsed? He interprets, for instance, the hard language of Augustine's introduction to mean that the work is addressed *solely* to those who are outside the faith and who are deceived by heretical promises of reaching God by "reason" and "knowledge" (*ratio, scientia*). For the Christian, Edelstein claims, Augustine commends Scripture as the "highest authority"; the implication would seem to follow that the Christian should have nothing to do with the way of reason and science. But could Scripture be the highest among authorities and still, *qua* authority, rank as subordinate to the way of "reason"? And could some Christians, at least, find the way of "reason" appropriate to them?

This touches, once again, on the whole question of authority and reason, but now as Augustine proposes their relationship in the years 408/9, when he wrote his *emendatio.* To make a first step toward an answer to that question, to whom does Augustine *now* address his work? Does he mean it, as Edelstein maintains, *only* for those outside the faith? Here, we must read Augustine very carefully. He hopes his lengthy exercise in the trivialities of the first five books will be excused by "men of good will" as a labor his office imposes on him (*officiosus labor*). It was written, he adds, so that "adolescents," or men of any age whom God has endowed with a good natural capacity (*bono ingenio*), might under reason's guidance (*duce ratione*) be torn away, not quickly but gradually (*quibusdam gradibus*) from the fleshly senses and letters it is difficult for them not to stick to, and cleave (*adhaerescerent*) with the love of unchangeable Truth (*incommutabilis veritatis amore*) to the God and Lord of all . . . (VI, 1). Thus far, those "adolescents" could be either believers or non-believers. But Augustine continues.

His sojourn on this "lowly way" (*vilis via*) was, therefore, a question of "the necessity of wayfaring" (*iterandi necessitas*) toward a "possession" far from lowly (*possessio non vilis*); but then he adds, significantly, that "this way we, too, not very strong ourselves, have preferred to walk in company with lighter persons, rather than to rush with weaker wings through the freer air." It would be odd, at least, were he condemning outright a way which he admits to have taken himself: he only warns those "steeped in the sacraments of Christian purity and glowing with the highest charity for the one and true God" but at the same time "not educated (*eruditi*) to understand these matters," not to "descend" to them; they have already "passed over all these childish things" and can "by flying, pass over difficult roads and obstacles in their path." These are liable to become unduly discouraged by a journey for feet (*pedibus*) when they have already learned to fly. It would appear, then, that the *eruditio* and *ingenium* so important at Cassiciacum have, by the year 408/9, become the equipment for a voyage of an inferior kind.

But things are not quite that simple. For what of those *qui . . . nullas alas habent*: who do not possess the "wings of piety" which allow the above class to take the route to God more appropriate to them? The answer depends on whether "because of infirm or untrained steps they cannot walk here"—that is, on whether they possess the intellectual equipment for this way of the disciplines. If not, let them not "involve themselves" in the troublesome inconvenience of this way, but rather "leave behind the labor and dust of this road" and "nourish their wings with the precepts of the most salutary religion and in the nest of the Christian faith." So doing, "more intent on the fatherland itself than on these tortuous paths," they will fly rather than walk to God. Twice thus far has Augustine excluded certain souls from embarking on this "way," and in both instances his exclusions have been grounded precisely on their lack of training and erudition: without these, they cannot profit from this way at all. But this leaves the question open: those possessing that training and erudition may still profit from this way; and, if they lack the "wings" of a developed piety, it could quite conceivably be a way appropriate to them. And Augustine has not excluded believing Christians from that number.

The concluding paragraph of Book Six, again part of his *emendatio,* might seem at first to strike a different note. This book, he says, was written for those "much weaker" (*multo infirmioribus*) when compared with others who follow the "au-

thority" of the two Testaments, venerating and adoring the
Trinity by "believing, hoping, and loving." These latter are
"purified, not by flashing human reasoning, but by the effective
and burning fire of charity." In following the way of reason "we
go more slowly," he admits, "than holy men who in their flight
deign not to pay heed to the ways we have been considering."
Why, then, has he consented to dawdle on this winding way?
Because he did not think those souls should be "neglected"
whom "heretics deceive with false promises about reason and
knowledge." And he has precedents, for "many pious sons of
the Catholic Church, best of mothers, who in their youthful
studies have sufficiently developed the faculty of speaking and
arguing, have, for the confuting of heretics" done the very same
thing that he has done here. Taken alone, *De Musica* VI, 59,
seems to argue that Edelstein was right: Augustine was writing
for the non-believer.

And yet, the autobiographical note is unmistakable: the Augustine of the *Confessions* will repeatedly harp on his "weakness"; on his refusal to acknowledge the Church as "best of
mothers," to consent to strengthen his wings in the "nest of
the faith." "Deceived" he was by the "false promises of reason
and knowledge" held out to him by the "heretical" Manichees;
he was fired by his "youthful studies" to value above all the
rhetorician's arts of "speaking and arguing."

The "way" he preferred for himself was not the Catholic way
of "believing, hoping, loving"; and yet, as he allusively implies
in *De Musica* VI, 1, the "way of reason"—*vilis via,* perhaps, but
to a far from *vilis possessio*—was the one that eventually led
him back to the nest of the faith. The love of "unchangeable
truth" had never quite died in his heart, so that God was able
to profit from his very *eruditio* to bring him, at the last, home.

And that is exactly the purpose he has set himself. "These
books," he says,

are written for those who, given up to secular letters, are involved in
great errors and waste their natural talents (*ingenium*) in vanities
(*nugis*), not knowing what delights them in such things (*quid ibi
delectet*). If they did notice it, they would see how to escape those
snares, and what is the place of happiest safety (*quisnam esset beatis-
simae securitatis locus*, VI, 1).

For those much like what he had been himself, therefore, Augustine addresses his book. To non-believers only? Or to those
whose belief remains ill formed, who are tempted by what seem

more inviting roads to truth and beauty, with the love of that Truth-Beauty still a smoldering fire deep in their souls? Or even to believers, erudite and intellectually trained, but lacking the spiritual strength to "fly" as saints prefer to fly? Or, to any and all of these? Who are these *infirmiores*, these "weaker ones" to whom Augustine refers in *De Musica* VI, 59? Read without any sense of Augustine's own biography, and excluding all connection with *De Musica* VI, 1 (part of the same *emendatio*), one might be tempted to agree with Edelstein: the *De Musica* is directed "solely" to non-believers. But set in this fuller context, it becomes far more coherent to include the wavering believer as well.

For Augustine had experienced what it meant to be endowed with *ingenium,* the native talent that equipped one for the ascent of reason (*duce ratione*). He had come to "see" what delighted him in the "carnal letters" to which he had become attached, to see that his delight in them was clearly linked with the "love of unchangeable truth," which, in Augustine's present understanding of the matter, still served as a good definition of "charity." Such souls he would lead gradually (*quibusdam gradibus*) along a way he freely confesses he himself has walked: the way described in his project on the disciplines as leading upward "through corporeal realities to the incorporeal."

But if he can entertain such high hopes for the efficacy of a reasoned ascent for such as these, if that way was effective in his own case, then clearly it could also prove effective in the case of believers who possessed the necessary "erudition," particularly when bereft of the "wings" of developed piety. Even as late as 408/9, therefore, Augustine has not utterly abandoned his regard for the way of the disciplines.

Charity and Truth

The reason is not far to seek: crucially, it lies in his conception of charity. It may still be spoken of as the *amor incommutabilis veritatis*—the love of a loftier Truth, Light, Beauty; the *erôs* which exists in the depths of every soul and explains even the fascination "vanities" of flesh and body can exercise upon the mind and heart. Once the soul is brought to recognize that all beauties "here" derive their attracting power from the subsistent Beauty "there," then detachment from these lower beauties becomes thinkable; the drawing power of that higher Beauty will act as a purifying fire which helps us rise to the "place of happiest safety." "My weight is my love": *pondus meum, amor meus*. The very position from which Augustine feels obliged to devaluate this "way of the disciplines" serves, upon examination, to ground (and prevent him from denying) the continuing legitimacy of that way. On the surface, his words seem to imply the "contempt" of the disciplines which both Svoboda and Edelstein have read into them; but deeper down, that condemnation is far from unambiguous; nor is it really so significant as these authors have imagined.

Even in 408/9, therefore, there is still room in Augustine's synthesis for a way of "reason," a gradual ascent of the mind through the "disciplines." But the *De Musica* entire, exclusive of these deprecatory remarks, embodies an even firmer and higher evaluation of the "disciplines." It, too, is based upon the intellectualist notion of charity incorporated in the *emendatio* remarks. Just shortly before, in writing the final paragraphs of his *De Genesi contra Manichaeos*, Augustine found it necessary to interpret what was meant by the Cherubim with flaming sword; both of these, he assures his reader, symbolize the way back to paradise. The Cherubim signifies the "fullness of knowledge" (*plenitudo scientiae*), the sword symbolically urging us to bear up patiently under the evils of temporal existence (*tolerantia molestiarum*). All of us must certainly do the latter; but it would seem that "the fullness of knowledge comes to a few" (*paucioribus*); not all return to paradise by that route. But then, did not the Apostle speak of "charity" as the "fullness of the law" (*plenitudo legis*)? The somewhat verbal coincidence encourages him a few lines later to equate the two and speak of the soul's return "through the fullness of knowledge, that is, through charity" (*per plenitudinem scientiae, id est, per caritatem, GenMan* II, 36).

Verbal at first, the coincidence is forged more firmly later by identifying charity with the "love of immutable truth"—the intellectual *erôs* we have seen legitimating the way of the disciplines and underlying the ascensional thrust that runs from first to last through the *De Musica*.

What value, then, does the *De Musica* accord to "art" in our modern sense of the term? Edelstein is not entirely misguided in thinking the answer to that question will partially depend on the value Augustine accords to the "disciplines"; he is even closer to the truth in thinking that this second question will turn on the relation of authority to reason. His *a priori* respecting Augustine's conversion leads him to think that the sixth book of the *De Musica* shows that Augustine has abandoned the high estimate of reason he held at Cassiciacum (before becoming a "convinced Christian"); reason is now made subject to the "highest authority" which is Scripture.

But precisely the contrary is true: the *De Musica* from start to finish supposes the same relation of authority—even scriptural authority—to reason, that is elaborated in the works leading up to it, and propounded in the early African writings, which, on Augustine's own say-so, bracketed it in time: the *De Genesi contra Manichaeos, De Moribus Ecclesiae, De Magistro, De Vera Religione,* and *De Utilitate Credendi.* For the great majority of men, the way of authority must be walked before the soul is ready for the way of reason; but there is a stage in the soul's progress when faith in authority may, and indeed, perhaps ought to be left behind and the way of reason taken up: the way of authority precisely prepares the mind for the eventual vision of those eternal realities which is reason's highest performance.

For the way of authority is a condescension to the soul's weakness in its "fallen" state: all of authority's utterances are "admonitions," reminding the soul to turn "inward" and "upward" to where the eternal light of truth-beauty resides, still accessible to the soul's eye, once it has been strengthened and purified to "see."

But the doctrine of the two "ways" Augustine proposes during this period of his production, I have detailed more fully elsewhere. The reader must judge whether it illumines, or distorts, the interpretation of the *De Musica* presented here.

Notes

Introduction

1. New York, 1951.
2. *Conf* IV, 20.
3. *Conf* X, 38.
4. See Étienne Gilson, *The Christian Philosophy of Saint Augustine* (New York, 1960), pp. 33–34 and 115–116. Cf. also Ragnar Holte, *Béatitude et sagesse* (Paris, 1962), and, for this theme in Augustine's preaching, Aimé Becker, *De l'instinct du bonheur à l'extase de la béatitude* (Paris, 1967).
5. Vernon J. Bourke, *Augustine's Quest of Wisdom* (Milwaukee, 1944).
6. *Lib* II, 35–38.
7. *Saint Augustin et la fin de la culture antique* (Paris, 1938), (hereafter cited as *Culture antique*).
8. *L'art dans Saint Augustin*, 2 vols. (Montréal, 1944), I, 149–150.
9. *A History of Esthetics*, by Katharine Gilbert and Helmut Kuhn, 2d ed. (London, 1956).
10. *Ibid.*, pp. 139–140. Cf. F. Van der Meer, *Augustine the Bishop* (New York, 1961), trans. Brian Battershaw and G. R. Lamb, pp. 317–337 and 561–565; H. I. Marrou, *Culture antique*, pp. 331–356.

11. *Ibid.*, p. 140; cf. pp. 121–122.

12. Paris-Brno, 1933 (hereafter cited as *Esthétique*).

13. *Ibid.*, pp. 195–196.

14. J. LeBlond, *Les conversions de saint-Augustin* (Paris, 1950), pp. 285–294 (hereafter cited as *Conversions*); see also Maurice Pontet, *L' exégèse de Saint Augustin prédicateur* (Paris, 1944, pp. 255–304 and 565–566 (hereafter cited as *L' exégèse*).

15. *St. Augustine's Early Theory of Man, 386–391 A.D.* (Cambridge, Mass., 1968). For a test of this same hypothesis as it applies to the *Confessions,* see my *Saint Augustine's Confessions: The Odyssey of Soul* (Cambridge, Mass., 1969). (I shall hereafter cite these two books as, respectively, *Early Theory* and *Odyssey.*)

16. "Augustine and Plotinus: A Reply to Sr. Mary Clark," *International Philosophical Quarterly* 12:604–608 (1972); "*Confessions* VII, ix, 13:xxi, 27," *Revue des Etudes Augustiniennes* (hereafter cited as *REA*) 19:87–100 (1973); and "Augustine's Rejection of the Fall of the Soul," *Augustinian Studies* 4:1–32 (1973).

17. New York, 1939 (hereafter cited as *Beauty*).

18. *Ibid.*, p. 103, note 2 to Chapter 2.

19. *Commonweal* 30:166–167 (1939).

20. *Beauty*, pp. xii-xiii.

21. Heverlée-Leuven Augustijns Hist. Institut, 1967. The book has scarcely enjoyed the diffusion that would make it readily accessible to the English-reading world. It is, however, substantially identical to Tscholl's series of articles in *Augustiniana,* though chapter and article divisions do not always exactly correspond. Hence, I shall refer to the pagination of the articles, with the corresponding pages of the book appended in parentheses (abbreviating the book title as *GS*). The articles (listed under their full titles, then with the abbreviated titles I shall employ for reference) appeared in *Augustiniana* 14:72–104 (1964), "Augustins Interesse für das körperliche Schöne" ("Das körperliche Schöne"); 15:32–53 (1965); "Vom Wesen der körperlichen Schönheit zu Gott" ("Vom Wesen zu Gott"); 15: 389–413 (1965), "Augustins Aufmerksamkeit am Makrokosmos" ("Makrokosmos"); 16:11–53 (1966), "Augustins Beachtung der geistigen Schönheit" ("Die geistige Schönheit"); 16:330–370 (1966), "Dreifaltigkeit und dreifache Vollendung des Schönen nach Augustinus" ("Dreifaltigkeit"). Sober, systematically repertorial, and showing occasional flashes of critical insight, Tscholl takes little account of the *development* of Augustine's aesthetic that will occupy much of my attention in the following pages.

22. Projected as part of a five-volume study, Mayer's first volume (no. 24, vol. 1, in the *Cassiciacum* series, Würzburg, Augustinus-Verlag, 1969) was published simultaneously with my two books, referred to earlier. I knew nothing of his work, and there is nothing to argue to his having depended in any significant way upon mine. (Even the references in his second volume allude only to my claims for Augustine's dependence on specific *Enneads* of Plotinus). The treatment of

Augustine's sign theory in the pages to follow, already launched in my interpretations of Augustine's *Confessions,* was elaborated in total independence of Mayer's findings, and all of what I have written here was composed before I had any opportunity to study Mayer's important contributions.

Now that I have read Mayer's several articles and the two volumes which have appeared (cited hereafter as *Zeichen* I and *Zeichen* II; the second volume appeared in 1974 and covers Augustine's anti-Manichaean works composed before 405), I have deliberately chosen to change nothing in the text of this book. First, because Mayer and I are in substantial agreement: with a far more exhaustive display of philological detail than I have presented (and with good sensitivity to Augustine's development), Mayer demonstrates convincingly that Augustine's sign theory is essenially commanded by a Neo-Platonic metaphysic. Second, it seemed wiser to preserve the independence of our testimonies on that significant thesis. Third, since Mayer has not yet furnished everything he has to say on the subject, it seemed better to leave any adjudication of both his work and mine to others, who will have had the benefit of his completed study. I will, however, refer the reader to his treatment where appropriate.

It should be noted that while Mayer traces Augustine's sign theory to his Neo-Platonic "ontology," he refrains from pronouncing one way or another on the Neo-Platonic "anthropology" so intimately related to that ontology, i.e., the view of man as "fallen soul." But I find nothing in his study which would militate against or cast serious doubt on the anthropological thesis I have been proposing.

23. Note the title of his article, "Philosophische Voraussetzungen und Implikationen in Augustins Lehre von der Sakramenta," *Augustiniana* 22:53–79 (1972), and the final pages of conclusions. The same stress on the commanding role of the Neo-Platonic framework, out of which Augustine is working, is maintained in Mayer's subsequent articles: *"Res per signa"* (On the Prologue to the *De Doctrina Christiana*) in *REA* 20:100–112 (1974), (see his summary, pp. 111–112); and "Signifikations-Hermeneutik im Dienste der Daseinsauslegung," *Augustiniana* 24:21–74 (1974), where he demonstrates (see his summary, pp. 73–74) the continuity of the *Confessions*' sign theory, Books X–XIII, with that contained in the *De Magistro* and in early portions of the *De Doctrina Christiana.* In all of this, as I read it, Mayer and I are of much the same mind.

24. *Early Theory,* p. 288.

25. *Le temps et l' éternité chez Plotin et Saint-Augustin,* (3d ed., (Paris, 1959), pp. 31–34.

26. *Ibid.,* p. 170.

1. Cassiciacum

1. *Vita* I, 6. For some sensitive observations on this stay at Cassiciacum see André Mandouze, *Saint Augustin: L'aventure de la raison*

et de la grâce (Paris, 1968), pp. 122–123 (hereafter cited as *L'aventure*).

2. John J. O'Meara, *The Young Augustine* (London, 1954), p. 131. O'Meara does, of course, call attention to the valuable knowledge of Augustine's development that emerged from this long controversy.

3. Svoboda, *Esthétique*, p. 75: "Augustin parle déjà [in the *De Musica*] en chrétien convaincu." A very similar theory of Augustine's "gradual" conversion to Christianity presides over Heinz Edelstein's *Die Musikanschauung Augustins nach seiner Schrift "De Musica"* (Ohlau, 1929) especially pp. 118 and 121 (hereafter cited as *Musikanschauung*).

4. Already seriously undermined by Jens Nörregaard's *Augustins Bekehrung* (Tübingen, 1923) and Charles Boyer's *Christianisme et néo-Platonisme dans la formation de Saint-Augustin* (Paris, 1920; 2d ed., 1953), the anachronistic opposition between Christianity and Neo-Platonism, on which this view of Augustine's conversion rested, was finally shattered by Pierre Courcelle's *Recherches sur les Confessions de saint-Augustin* (Paris, 1950; 2d ed., 1968). Especially telling are the numerous intimations of a Trinitarian theology more recently unearthed in these early Dialogues by Olivier du Roy, *L' intelligence de la foi en la Trinité selon Saint-Augustin* (Paris, 1966), pp. 109–206 (hereafter cited as *Trinité*). See also *Early Theory*, pp. 184–257.

5. *Esthétique*, pp. 46–47.

6. *Early Theory*, pp. 193–197.

7. *Ibid.*, pp. 197–200.

8. *Acad* II, 7.

9. *Ibid.*, II, 6–7.

10. *Ibid.*, II, 5. The expression is used referring to the effect his readings of the *platonici* had on Augustine.

11. *Ibid.*, II, 3–6.

12. *Ibid.*, I, 3–4.

13. *Ibid.*, II, 5. See *Early Theory*, pp. 70–80.

14. *Ibid.*, III, 7.

15. *Ibid.*, III, 13.

16. *Ibid.*, I, 1. Augustine is quite possibly already looking forward to the writing of the *De Ordine*.

17. *Early Theory*, pp. 169–170.

18. *Ord* II, 14–17 and 24–25. See *Early Theory*, pp. 125, 191–193.

19. *Ibid.*, II, 35–44; see I, 15–21, for earlier intimations of this identity.

20. *Esthétique*, pp. 46–47.

21. Augustine is here echoing in his own fashion the traditional Platonic strictures on purely "imitative" art.

22. *Esthétique*, p. 47. Nor did the ancients make our distinction between the "useful" and the "fine" arts.

23. *Ord* II, 41. For Augustine's treatment of the seven *artes*, see *Ord* II, 35–42, and H. I. Marrou, *Culture Antique*, pp. 211–275.

24. *Ord* II, 53–54.

25. I use the term "abstraction" without necessarily implying any prejudice, at this point, to Augustine's theory of "illumination."

26. *Esthétique*, pp. 36–38. Tscholl, "Vom Wesen zu Gott," *Augustiniana* 15:33–35 (1965), rightly underlines the importance of "unity" in Augustine's numerical aesthetic.

27. *Ibid.*, pp. 18, 36–38, 43. See also, *Early Theory*, pp. 7, 9, 73, and J. J. O'Meara's translation of *Against the Academics*, *ACW* 12 (Westminister, Md., 1950), pp. 160ff (hereafter cited as *Academics*).

28. *Enn* I, 6, 1; see the Notice to this treatise in Émile Bréhier's *Plotin: Les Ennéades*, I (Paris, 1954), 93–94.

29. *Acad* III, 37–42; see *Early Theory*, pp. 193–197.

30. *Vita*, 22–32; see *Early Theory*, pp. 194–195.

31. *Acad* III, 42.

32. See H. R. Schwyzer, article "Plotinos," *RE XXI*, 1, cols. 547–548.

33. See Bréhier's Notice to this treatise in *Les Ennéades*, III (Paris, 1956), 17–23; also Henri-Charles Puech, "Plotin et les gnostiques," in *Entretiens sur l' Antiquité Classique*, Hardt Fondation 5, "Les Sources de Plotin" (Vandoeuvres-Geneva, 1960), pp. 161–190. The presentations and subsequent discussions by E. R. Dodds and Willy Theiler, in the same volume, are also highly suggestive in this regard.

34. See O'Meara, *Academics*, pp. 160ff. For a more general presentation of the evidence, see Aimé Solignac in *Les Confessions, BA* 13 (Paris, 1962), pp. 682–689.

35. *Esthétique*, pp. 22–23.

36. See my "The *Enneads* and St. Augustine's Image of Happiness,' *Vigiliae Christianae* 17:129–164 (1963); for a condensed version of the same evidence, *Early Theory*, pp. 203–226. Cf. Solignac in *BA* 13, pp. 687–688.

37. See *Early Theory*, pp. 162n18, 166n20, 194.

38. *Vita Plotini* 24–25.

39. *Ord* II, 34; see *Esthétique*, pp. 25–26.

40. This was a commonplace for the ancient world; see *Esthétique*, pp. 39–40. See also Mayer, *Zeichen* I, 170–220.

41. *Ord* I, 32.

42. See *Lib* I, 4, where Augustine underlines its importance both for the Manichee apologetic and for his own youthful religious conceptions. The *Confessions* later supports this view.

43. *Ord* I, 1. See Tscholl, "Makrokosmos," *Augustiniana* 15 (1965), esp. pp. 389–393 (*GS*, pp. 57–61).

44. See Henri-Charles Puech, *Le Manichéisme, son fondateur, sa doctrine* (Paris, 1949), for an excellent presentation of Manichee teaching; also, in briefer compass, Peter Brown, *Augustine of Hippo* (Berkeley, 1967), pp. 40–60.

45. *Ord* I, 1.

46. Indeed, Augustine is willing at this stage of his career to state the case more strongly: the very existence of evil is necessary for the existence of good; see *Ord* I, 18.

47. *Ord* I, 2–3, 18; II, 12–13. See Svoboda, *Esthétique*, pp. 20–23, and Tscholl, "Das körperliche Schöne," *Augustiniana* 14:74–75, 84–85, and 101–102 (1964), (*GS* pp. 5–6, 15–16, 27–28).

48. *Ibid.* Note that this all requires that relative "detachment" of view already called for by Augustine's youthful work, *De Pulchro et Apto*; see *Conf* IV, 20. See also Tscholl, "Das körperliche Schöne," pp. 86–91 and 96 (*GS* 17–23 and 28).

49. *Ord* I, 1; see *Early Theory*, p. 125.

50. *Ord* II, 11–13 and 18–23.

51. *Ord* II, 14–17 and 24–51. Augustine's rehandling of this entire problem in the *De Libero Arbitrio suggests* he was not fully content with his abortive treatment of it in the *De Ordine*.

52. See notes 34 and 36, above.

53. See Plotinus' references to "mud" and "filth" and his association of "ugliness" with "earthiness" (*Enn* I, 6, 5, 26–59). Compare, also, his image of the pig-sty (*ibid.*, 6, 1–7) with Augustine's references (in the "outhouse" episode, *Ord* I, 23) to the *coenum* and *sordes corporis*. See also *Acad* I, 11 (*corporis labes*), III, 42 (*sordes*), and compare the contexts and language of *Acad* II, 7 (*viscum*), and of *Sol* I, 24.

54. *Enn* IV, 8, 1.

55. *Early Theory*, pp. 152–155.

56. See the article by H. C. Puech cited in note 33 above.

57. *Ord* II, 11–13, 18–21; cf. *Vita* 1 and *Sol* I, 4. See *Early Theory*, pp. 169–173 and 189–190.

58. *Early Theory*, pp. 156–183. It has been objected by various critics that Augustine's exegesis of *Genesis* might owe much to Ambrose, Basil, Origen, Marius Victorinus, and others. True enough: but (quite apart from the lack of evidence that Augustine in this early period of production was exposed to anyone in that list except for Ambrose) the Neo-Platonic cast of these men's thinking would have been likely to encourage rather than deter Augustine from pursuing the Plotinian understanding of the faith he presents in his own first *De Genesi*. See *Early Theory*, pp. 156–157.

59. *Early Theory*, p. 123.

60. *Esthétique*, pp. 24–29.

61. *Early Theory*, pp. 116–117, 121–131, 185–186.

62. *Ibid.*, pp. 112–131.

63. See Paul Henry, *Plotin et l' occident* (Louvain, 1934), pp. 126–133. For more recent confirmation, cf. Solignac in *Les Confessions, BA* 13, pp. 682–687.

64. *Enn* V, 1. See *Immort* 24 and *Quant* 69 for clearer evidence of this; cf. also *Early Theory*, pp. 122–131.

65. *Early Theory*, pp. 130–131.

66. *Sol* I, 2–6. See O. du Roy, *Trinité,* pp. 198–206; also Mandouze, *L' aventure,* pp. 530–536.

67. *Ibid.,* I, 7–8.

68. *Ibid.,* I, 17, 22–23.

69. *Ibid.,* I, 12–14.

70. *Ibid.,* I, 22. For an analogous expression of Augustine's "impatience" for understanding and vision, see *Acad* III, 43. One already begins to sense that his will be an "aesthetic of impatience," as it were; not, perhaps, the most recommended attitude for grounding a genuine aesthetic.

71. *Sol* II, 1.

72. *Ibid.,* II, 31–32.

73. *Ibid.,* II, 34–35.

74. *Ord* I, 14, 25–26.

75. *Ibid.,* I, 25.

76. Compare, in this connection, Tscholl, "Das körperliche Schöne," *Augustiniana* 14 (1964), esp. pp. 76–80 and 94–96 (*GS* pp. 7–11, 25–27), and "Vom Wesen zu Gott" entire, *ibid.* 15: 32–53 (1965), (*GS* pp. 35–56), with the analyses presented by Mayer, *Zeichen* I, 284–330 and 349–359, and the article cited in Introduction, note 24, above. I may be excused for thinking that Mayer's keener sensitivity to the philosophic instruments at play enables him to detect and set forth more clearly the import of Augustine's *admonitio* doctrine and the associated ontological weakness (*Schwäche*) of the sensible signs that function to admonish the soul. I do not mean to suggest, however, that Mayer would necessarily agree, or imply, that Augustine's is a sign theory elaborated for fallen souls, as I understand that feature of Augustine's anthropology.

2. Art, the Arts, and Eternal Art

1. *Sol* II, 34–36.

2. *Ibid.,* II, 34.

3. *Ibid.,* II, 35.

4. The expression also puts us on notice that—theme for later investigation—this Truth-Beauty is not merely some*thing,* but some*one.*

5. Augustine does have some insight, albeit a wavering one, into this distinction; see *Esthétique,* p. 46.

6. *Ibid.,* p. 47.

7. A usage in the singular would, of course, present no difficulty, as for instance *ars grammatica, ars dialectica.* For Augustine's list of the *artes,* see *Ord* II, 35–42, and the comments of Marrou referred to above, Chapter 1, note 23.

8. *Ord* II, 43. See Chapman, *Beauty,* pp. 13–26, and Tscholl, "Vom Wesen zu Gott," *Augustiniana* 15:32–41 and 45–48 (1965), (*GS,* pp. 35–44 and 48–51).

9. I refer to Pierre de Labriolle's translation of the *De Immortalitate Animae*, 6, in *BA* 5 (1948), p. 180. His translation is partially justified by Augustine's reference, in the preceding paragraph, to *ars* as being in the soul of the *artifex*. But the somewhat surprising term here, *eruditus*, advises us of how Augustine conceives of the genuine musical "artist's" way of going about his business.

10. It might be claimed, with some justice, that my explanation of the Forms in relation to artistic activity is more Plotinian than "classically" Platonic, but the point is secondary for our purposes here. Plato's complaint, in the Tenth Book of the *Republic*, that the artist produces only a "copy of a copy," is sometimes quite conventionally understood by Plotinus, but it gradually yields to the view presented here; see Eugénie de Keyser, *La signification de l' art dans les "Ennéades" de Plotin* (Louvain, 1955), pp. 29–52 (hereafter cited as *Signification*). On Augustine's application of the theory, see Chapman, *Beauty,* pp. 56–66, and Tscholl, "Vom Wesen zu Gott," *Augustiniana* 15:40–53 (1965), (*GS* pp. 43–56). (How Plato himself intended his theory of forms is, of course, another question.)

11. *Mus* I, 1–9. Here, especially in 6 and 9, Augustine shows a trace of Plato's theory of the mimetic artist.

12. *Ord* II, 49.

13. For Plotinus' stress on this, see especially *Enn* V, 8, 5, 19–25. See also Chapman and Tscholl, cited in note 10 above.

14. *Ord* II, 48–50.

15. *Sol* I, 27–29.

16. *Ord* II, 51.

17. *Symposium,* 210 E, and Plato's *Letter* 7, 341C. See the valuable discussion in Paul Friedländer, *Plato: An Introduction* (New York, 1964), pp. 59–84 (also published as vol. I of his three-volume *Plato* (New York, 1958–69), trans. Hans Meyerdorff (hereafter cited as *Plato*).

18. *Conf* VI, 6.

19. *Acad* III, 21.

20. *Ibid.,* III, 23–24. For the importance of such "enduringness" to Augustine's aesthetic, an enduringness in which the mind in quest of truth and certainty could find "rest," see Tscholl, "Das körperliche Schöne," *Augustiniana* 14: pp. 76–80 (1964), (*GS* pp. 7–11).

21. *Esthétique,* p. 43. Tscholl, "Vom Wesen zu Gott," *Augustiniana* 15:33–40 (1965), (*GS* pp. 36–43), points up the dynamic reference to the divine Unity as the secure and unchanging "home" of Beauty. Note, however, how the epistemological theme of the mind's quest for certainty resonates throughout and colors to a large extent the theme of the heart's longing for an unchanging abode of rest and peace.

22. *Sol* I, 9–11, II, 33–35,

23. *Quant* 10–21; *Immort* 1, 6. Cf. also the discussion in *Lib* II, 20–24 and 30–32. Marrou's remarks on all this are excellent, *Culture*

antique, pp. 262–266 and 302–308. None of this is meant to deny Augustine's even higher evaluation of the *ars dialectica;* but even this latter has a strong mathematical cast.

24. *Ord* II, 53–54.

25. *Sol* II, 34–35; cf. I, 9–12. Note that, from the very first, the "memory" theme, far from being opposed to, is linked with the theme of "illumination." Cf. my "Pre-existence in Augustine's Seventh Letter," in *REA* 15:67–73 (1969), and *Early Theory,* pp. 154–155 and 191–193.

26. *Lib* II, 25–29.

27. See above, notes 20 and 21.

28. Marrou, *Culture antique,* pp. 23–26.

29. *Ord* II, 34.

30. See above, Chapter 1, note 41.

31. *Ord* II, 40.

32. *Quant* 71; cf. 73; *Lib* I, 18–19; II, 12, 35–38, 41–44. Alert to the earlier distinction and its import, Tscholl is less so on this slippage. But see "Das körperliche Schöne," *Augustiniana* 14:72–75 (1964), (*GS,* pp. 3–6).

33. See above, note 32; also *Quant* 4, 24, 54, 73, 76; *Lib* I, 31–32; *Mor* I, 20–21, 37.

34. See Marrou, *Culture antique,* pp. 47–83, for details on the education of the rhetorician and on its persistent influences on Augustine.

35. *Sol* I, 11.

36. *Ibid.,* also I, 15.

37. *Lib* II, 41–42.

38. *Ibid.,* II, 29–32.

39. *Sol* I, 8.

40. For the "subjective factors" required for aesthetic appreciation, see Tscholl, "Das körperliche Schöne," *Augustiniana* 14:84–85 (1964), (*GS* pp. 15–16).

41. See Charles Couturier's study of *"Sacramentum* et *Mysterium* dans l' oeuvre de saint-Augustin," in Henri Rondet *et al., Etudes Augustiniennes* (Paris, 1951), esp, pp. 189–194. See also Maurice Pontet, *L' exégèse de Saint Augustin prédicateur,* pp. 127–128, 132–134, 255–304. Despite his reserves on certain features of Couturier's study, André Mandouze's "À propos de *'sacramentum'* chez S. Augustin," in *Mélanges Christine Mohrmann* (Utrecht, 1963), pp. 222–232, does not weaken the point being made here: see, for example, the language he applies on pp. 229–232. See also Mayer's articles cited above in note 24 to the Introduction and *Zeichen* I, 185–220.

42. *Sol* I, 22; *GenMan* I, 33. Compare the analogous images of the "clouds" that obscure our view of the sun (*Mor* I, 1, 3, 11–12; *GenMan* I, 37; II, 4–6) and of the "mortal" body as concealing the movements of the soul (*GenMan* II, 32). See, in this connection, Jean Pépin, "Saint Augustin et le symbolisme néoplatonicien de la vêture,"

in *AM* I, 293–306, and "Le problème de la communication des consciences chez Plotin et Saint Augustin," in *Revue de la Métaphysique et de la Morale* 55:128–148 (1950) and 56:316–326 (1951). See also Mayer, *Zeichen* I, 185–210.

43. See Friedländer, *Plato,* pp. 3–31.

44. See John A. Stewart, *Plato's Doctrine of Ideas* (Oxford, 1909), pp. 128–197, and Friedländer, cited in note 43 above; also my "The Unknown Socrates' Unknown God," in *God Knowable and Unknowable,* ed. Robert J. Roth (New York, 1973), pp. 1–22.

45. *Enn* VI, 6, 18. Compare Plato's remarks on the "due measure" in *Statesman* 283B–284D.

46. *Sophist* 249A

47. See Paul Henry's Introduction to *Plotinus: The Enneads,* trans. Stephen MacKenna, 3d ed., rev. B. S. Page (London, 1956), esp. pp. lxiv–lxvii; also, R. Ferwerda, *La signification des images et des métaphores dans la pensée de Plotin* (Groningen, 1965).

48. See de Keyser, *Signification,* pp. 53–65.

49. *Enn* V, 8, 4–6, 11. See de Keyser, *Signification,* pp. 53–65.

50. Émile Bréhier, "Images plotiniennes, images bergsoniennes," in *Études de Philosophie Ancienne* (Paris, 1955), pp. 292–307.

51. *Enn* V, 8, 9.

52. *Ord* II, 51.

53. *Early Theory,* pp. 58–59. A. H. Armstrong has called my attention to *Enn* VI, 7, 1–15, where Plotinus develops the ontological side of this: everything "here" is present, in more authentic form, in *noûs.* Hence at our arrival in the intelligible, we find that nothing— including sense-perception—has truly been "left behind." It would be fascinating, but I fear also very difficult, to "prove" that Augustine studied this very rich treatise.

54. *Ibid.,* pp. 59–61.

55. *Ibid.,* pp. 227–232.

56. *Ord* I, 22–23.

57. *Conf* IX, 17–37. See *Odyssey,* pp. 106–118.

58. P. M. Löhrer, *Der Glaubensbegriff des hl. Augustinus* (Einsiedeln, 1955), p. 111. See also *Early Theory,* pp. 250–257.

59. *Sol* I, 12–13.

60. *Ibid.,* I, 22.

61. *Lib* II, 38. See *Early Theory,* pp. 250–278, for a fuller discussion of this view of faith, as it relates to Christ incarnate and eternal, respectively.

62. *Conf* VII, 26.

63. *Ibid.,* VII, 25.

64. *Vita* 2 and 5; see *Early Theory,* p. 219. Augustine's failure to develop this theme may partially stem from the iconoclastic temper widespread in the Church at his time.

65. *Enn* V, 8, 11, 17–19; cf. *ibid.,* 4, 4–6 and 42–44.

66. *Laws* 930E–931A, 899B, 966E–968A. See also my discussion of this in the article cited in note 44, above.

67. *Phaedrus* 250D.

68. *Colossians* 2, 8.

69. *Acad* I, 3.

70. See Appendix A for fuller details.

71. Tscholl's generally careful study does not seem so attentive to chronology and to the possibilities of Augustine's development, as most recent studies demonstrate is both warranted and necessary.

72. For fuller developments on this suggestion, see below Chapter 8.

3. Groundwork for the De Musica

1. *Retr* I, 5, 1.

2. *Early Theory*, pp. 138–139. Compare, for this entire time period, Mayer, *Zeichen* I, 220–359, especially his summary, pp. 349–359.

3. See Pierre de Labriolle's Introduction to *BA* 5 (1948), pp. 18–20; also, *Early Theory*, pp. 135–136.

4. *Early Theory*, pp. 138–139.

5. *Ibid.*, pp. 154 and 166–168.

6. Compare the list of questions posed in *Quant* 1 (and the allusions of *Quant* 7, 22, 34 and 81) with the "traditional" list of *de anima* questions outlined in A. M. Festugière's *La révélation d' Hermès Trismégiste*, 4 vols. (Paris, 1944–54), III, x and 1–26

7. *Retr* I, 8, 1.

8. *Quant* 4–25.

9. *Ibid.*, 69.

10. *Ibid.*, 70–78.

11. *Ibid.*, 72. For the implications of this usage, see below, note 85.

12. *Ibid.*, 76. Note the characteristically Plotinian touch in the suggestion that this "arrival" resembles nothing more than a "cessation" of activity (*Quant* 55) and that the soul may well exercise all these grades of activity at once (*ibid.*, 79). See *Early Theory*, pp. 166–168.

13. See my *"De Libero Arbitrio* I: Stoicism Revisited," in *Augustinian Studies* 1:49–68 (1970).

14. *Lib* I, 28–29.

15. *Ibid.*, I, 10.

16. *Ibid.*, I, 30.

17, *Ibid.*

18. *Ibid.*, I, 34.

19. *Lib* II, 5–8; cf. *Jo* 17, 3.

20. *Ibid.*, II, 7–27 (*exercitatio*) and 28–34, 41–44 (norm of "judgment").

21. *Ibid.*, II, 35–38.

22. *Ibid.*, II, 52–53. On the Plotinian cast of this, see *Early Theory*, pp. 52–57 and 173–182.

23. *Ibid.*, II, 54, and II, 1–7; see *Early Theory*, pp. 203–257.

24. *GenMan* II, 3 and 19. See *Early Theory*, pp. 156–158. On the consonance between Augustine's general sign theory and his view of biblical hermeneutic, see Mayer, *Zeichen* II, 279–349, especially his summary, pp. 347–349.

25. *Ibid.*, II, 4–5.

26. *Ibid.*, II, 5–6 and 30–32; see *Early Theory*, pp. 162–166.

27. *Ibid.*, I, 40, and II, 26–27 and 40. See *Early Theory* pp. 173–182.

28. *Ibid.*, II, 23 and 32; see *Early Theory*, pp. 161–166.

29. *Ibid.*, II, 5 and 30–32.

30. *Ibid.*, II, 6.

31. *Ibid.*, I, 29 and 32; II, 6 and 10. See *Early Theory*, pp. 158–159.

32. *Quant* 70–72.

33. *Quant* 77; cf. *Ep* 18, 2.

34. *Quant* 78; cf. 81.

35. *Enn* IV, 3, 18; see *Early Theory*, pp. 163–165.

36. *Immort* 13; Ep 18; *Lib* II, 41–44; *GenMan* I, 13 and 25.

37. *Lib* II, 41–44; *GenMan* I, 11 and 26.

38. *Quant* 10–23 and 27–28.

39. *Lib* II, 54; *GenMan* I, 26. The scriptural reference is to *Wisdom* 11, 21. See Mayer, *Zeichen* II, 130–147.

40. *Immort* 25; *Lib* II, 41–44; *GenMan* I, 12 and 17. See Tscholl, "Die Geistige Schönheit," *Augustiniana* 16:11–53 (1966), (GS pp. 82–124).

41. *Lib* II, 34 and 41–44.

42. *Immort* 4–6; *Lib* II, 41–44; *GenMan* I, 8–10 and 13.

43. See texts in note 42 above.

44. *Immort* 4; *GenMan* I, 13. Svoboda, *Esthétique*, p. 96, traces this idea of "deterioration" to *Enneads* V, 8, 1, and V, 9, 3 and 5. However exact his pinpointing of these sources may be, this is a standard Plotinian view.

45. *Lib* I, 5; *GenMan* I, 10.

46. Svoboda takes note of this development, *Esthétique*, p. 94, but without drawing any inference on the "despiritualizing" corollaries it must eventually have for Augustine's aesthetic.

47. *Lib* II, 35 and 38. See Mayer, *Zeichen* II, 105–130.

48. *Quant* 54; *Lib* II, 35, 38, and 41–44.

49. *Ibid.*

50. *Quant* 76, 80; *Lib* II, 54; *GenMan* I, 25–26 and 32; *Mor* II, 7–9. Implicitly operative in all this is, of course, Augustine's distinction between the *aptum* and the *pulchrum*.

51. Hence the familiar "ladder" structure of *Quant* 70–78 and *Lib* II, 7–39.

52. *Quant,* 76.

53. *Mor* I, 66.

54. *GenMan* II, 16.

55. *GenMan,* I, 33.

56. *Mor* I, 18. Cf. *Quant* 12, 27; *Lib* I, 3 and 19–20, where Augustine comes very near to equating the pursuit of truth with the quest for moral goodness; also *Lib* II, 35–38, where our happiness is said to reside in the possession of the Truth, a Truth which is evidently identical with Goodness and Beauty. For the pitfalls, anthropological as well as aesthetic, involved in all this, see below, Chapter 7, note 2.

57. *GenMan* II, 36 and 41.

58. *Conf* VIII, 26–27, and X, 8.

59. *Immort* 1.

60. *GenMan* II, 6 and 30; cf. II, 32.

61. *Ibid.,* II, 40.

62. *Quant* 24–26, 30, 54, 61, and 73; *Lib* I, 31–32; *Mor* I, 20–21 and 37.

63. *Quant* 3; *Mor* I, 75, condemns *adoratores* of pictures and funerary monuments: hardly an "aesthetic" evaluation. Cf. *Quant* 72, and below note 85.

64. *GenMan* II, 23.

65. *Ibid.,* I, 33.

66. See above, note 35.

67. *Quant* 54; cf. 76; *Lib* II, 41; *Mag* 38–40 and 45.

68. *Ep* 7, 3–6; note the connection with a pre-existent state where Augustine thinks the soul would not be dependent on sense-images.

69. *Ibid.,* see also above, note 62.

70. *Quant* 32–33; *Lib* II, 8–12 (where Augustine invokes the "judgment" of the "inner" sense, thereby relativizing the outer-sense judgment, see II, 12); *ibid.,* 41–44: here the judgment of reason is contrasted with the pain or delight registered by the senses. For this same biological "reactionism," see *Quant* 71. This more deprecatory attitude toward sense-reactions is now regularly supported by the ancient-world commonplace, that such operations belong on that plane common to men and beasts.

71. While not denying his earlier suggestion that dance conveys a *significatio,* Augustine (*Lib* II, 42) now connects the numerically beautiful outward movements of the dance with the sensual *delectatio* they produce.

72. *Quant* 12 and 25; *Lib* I, 4–6 and 10; II, 5–6; *GenMan* II, 5 and 30; *Mor* I, 1, 3, 11–12 and 30; *Mag* 37.

73. *GenMan* II, 5. Cf. *Mor* I, 12, where the clouds (*nubes*) associated with our fallen "unwisdom" (*stultitia*) are linked as well with

the providentially provided "opacity" (*opacitas*) of authority's symbolic transmissions of truth. Compare Mayer, cited above in notes 2, 39, and 47, as well as his summary on the sign theory of this entire period, *Zeichen* II, 442–450.

74. *GenMan* II, 5.

75. *Lib* II, 5–6, 38, and 41. Cf. *Mag* 1–2, 21, 37–38, and 46. Compare *Early Theory*, pp. 258–278, and Mayer, *Zeichen* I, 311–330; *Zeichen* II, 199–278.

76. *Acad* III, 3. See *Early Theory*, pp. 236–250.

77. *Quant* 76; cf. the "breasts" metaphor as it operates in *Acad* III, 3.

78. *Ibid.*

79. *Quant* 10–23 and *passim.*

80. *Quant* 70–71; *GenMan* I, 43; *Mor* I, 7.

81. *Quant* 34, 50–51; cf. *Sol.* II, 34–35, and *Lib* I, 24.

82. *Quant* 33–34.

83. *Ibid.*, also *Mag* 36. Cf. Augustine's use of *admonere, commonere* in *Lib* II, 38, *Mag* 25; of *commemoratio* in *Mag* 1; and of both terms as though equivalent in *Mag* 19.

84. *Ibid.*, 72.

85. *Ibid.* The original text runs as follows: Ergo attollere in tertium gradum, qui jam est homini proprius, et cogita memoriam non consuetudine inolitarium, sed animadversione atque signis commendatarum ac retentarum rerum innumerabilium, tot artes opificum, agrorum cultus, exstructiones urbium, variorum aedificiorum ac moliminum multimoda miracula; inventiones tot signorum in litteris, in verbis, in gestu, in cujuscemodi sono, in picturis atque figmentis; tot gentium linguas, tot instituta, tot nova, tot instaurata; tantum librorum numerum, et cujuscemodi monumentorum ad custodiendam memoriam, tantamque curam posteritatis; officiorum, potestatum, honorum dignitatumque ordines, sive in familiis, sive domni militiaeque in republica, sive in profanis, sive in sacris apparatibus; vim ratiocinandi et excogitandi, fluvios eloquentiae, carminum varietates, ludendi ac jocandi causa milleformes simulationes, modulandi peritiam, dimetiendi subtilitatem, numerandi disciplinam, praeteritorum ac futurorum ex praesentibus conjecturam.

Magna haec et omnino humana. Sed est adhuc ista partim doctis atque indoctis, partim bonis ac malis animis copia communis. The text is taken from the edition in *BA* 5 (Paris, 1948), pp. 376–378. Augustine regularly uses the term *signum* to cover this entire array of corporal-temporal embodiments of the intelligible world of ideas. This, accordingly, will be the meaning of "symbol" in all my subsequent discussion of his aesthetic theory. I find Mayer, *Zeichen,* of the same view.

86. *Ibid.*,72–73.

87. *Ibid.*, 73.

88. *Ibid.*, 26, 31–34.

89. *Ibid.,* 4, 24, 33, 73. Cf. *Lib* II, 6, 14.

90. *Ibid.,* 4, 30, 34, Cf. *Lib.* II, 6.

91. *Ibid.,* 4.

92. *Ibid.,* 24–26.

93. *Ibid.,* 3, 54–55.

94. *Ibid.,* 76.

95. *Mor* I, 52; cf. 77; *Quant* 22.

96. *Quant* 78.

97. *Ibid.,* 76.

98. *Ibid.,* 80–81; cf. note 50 above.

99. Note the reference to incarnation in terms of *susceptus homo,* with the accompanying warning that God alone is *colendus (ibid.,* 76–77). See *Early Theory,* pp. 267–278, and Mayer, cited above in note 75.

100. *Ibid.,* 76.

101. *Ibid.,* 24, 61.

102. *Ibid.,* 76; cf. above, notes 76–78.

103. See the evidence for this change of accent in Peter Brown, *Augustine of Hippo* (Berkeley, 1967), pp. 146–157 (hereafter cited as *Augustine*), and in Mayer also, *Zeichen* II, 181–183. Augustine's tendency at this time to sketch the "ages" of man's spiritual progress in biblico-historical terms (*GenMan* I, 35–48; cf. *Mor* I, 12, 63, 80), would also argue for Brown's view. And yet the more ahistorical, "vertical" ascent will recur in the *De Musica*: one wonders whether Augustine, at this stage in his career, saw these two views of the spiritual journey as mutually incompatible.

104. *Quant* 76.

105. *Ibid.,* 73.

106. *Ibid.,* 78.

107. *Mor* II, 27–35; cf. I, the lengthy development of this theme from 12 to 57 and the summary from 71 to 73.

108. *Ibid.,* I, 4, 10–11.

109. *Ibid.,* I, 48–51, 67. *Mor* I, 51, shows Augustine's awareness of problems involved in following the "second law" of charity.

110. *Ibid.,* I, 52–56.

111. *Ibid.,* I, 52, 77. For earlier hints of this more benign, though still ambivalent, attitude toward the sense-world, see *Lib* I, 33–34; II, 50, 53; *Mor* I, 37, 39, 42.

112. The distinction finds clearest formulation in the *De Doctrina Christiana,* I, 4–37. On all this, see John Burnaby's classic study, *Amor Dei* (London, 1938), pp. 113–132.

4. *The* De Musica

1. *Retr* I, vi.

2. Written in the same period as the *De Musica,* this little work shows, among other things, that Augustine's estimate of the *disci-*

plinae is not significantly different from that in the Cassicacum *Dialogues*.

3. See the discussion in Marrou, *Culture Antique,* note C, pp. 570–579.

4. Augustine first assures us he had "only begun" (*inchoaveram quippe tantummodo*) the *De Musica* while at Milan. "Those same six books," he goes on to add, "I wrote on my return to Africa" (*eosdem sex libros . . . regressus in Africam scripsi, (Retr* I, vi). He later underscores the point: he "wrote six books *de musica*" on his return to Africa (*deinde . . . ut supra commemoravi* [in *Retr* I, vi] *sex libro de musica scripsi, (Retr* I, xi, 1). The *deinde* means to situate the *De Musica* after the *De Genesi contra Manichaeos.* Augustine subsequently informs us he wrote the *De Magistro per idem tempus*: during the same timespan as the *De Musica* (*Retr* I, xii).

5. H. Edelstein, *Musikanschauung,* p. 123.

6. *Esthétique,* pp. 75–76.

7. *Ibid.*; for a fuller discussion of the grounds for Edelstein's view, see Appendix B.

8. See Appendix B for fuller details.

9. See Appendix B.

10. *Culture Antique,* appendix, note D, pp. 580–583. It is piquant to notice how much of the condemnatory language contained in these *emendatio* sections is closely paralleled, but used in exactly the opposite sense in the *De Magistro*: Augustine is forestalling what may have been Adeodatus' nascent suspicions that their long *exercitatio mentis* is nothing more than play (*ludamus*) with "puerile little questions" and "playthings of little worth" (*pueriles quaestiunculae; vilia ludicra*), *Mag* 21. Compare the terms *nugacitas, puerilia, vilis via* of *Mus* VI, 1.

11. It would seem, as Svoboda notes, *Esthétique,* pp. 65–66, that Augustine's original plans included another work on "harmony" or "melody" (*de melo*); see *Retr* I, vi, and *Ep* 101, 3.

12. *Mus* I, 1–12. My translations from the *De Musica* are generally adaptations of Robert C. Taliaferro's in *FC* 2, with help from the text and translation in *BA* 7, by Guy Finaert and F. J. Thonnard.

13. *Ibid.,* I, 5–7.

14. *Ibid.,* I, 13–26.

15. *Ibid.,* VI, 2–22.

16. *Ibid.,* VI, 22–23.

17. *Ibid.,* VI, 34–36.

18. *Ibid.,* I, 28; V, 28; VI, 24 and 47.

19. *Ibid.,* I, 27–28; VI, 23.

20. *Ibid.,* V, 1; VI, 18.

21. Cf. *ibid.,* V, 28, where Augustine speaks of now advancing from these "traces" (*vestigiis*) to the very sanctuary (of music), where it is stripped of all body (*ubi ab omni corpore aliena est*).

22. *Ibid.,* IV, 37.

23. *Ibid.*, II, 20–25; III, 16; IV, 2–3 and 30–31.

24. *Ibid.*, III, 12, 16; IV, 9, 30; V, 10; VI, 18.

25. *Ibid.*, V, 1, 9–12.

26. *Ibid.*, II, 1–2; III, 3–4, 5, 19; V, 20, 27.

27. *Ibid.*, IV, 1, 30–31.

28. *Ibid.*, V, 10.

29. *Ibid.*, III, 3–4, IV, 30–34.

30. *Ibid.*, VI, 32; cf. 35.

31. *Ibid.*, IV, 30.

32. *Ver* 45–46.

33. *Mus* IV, 31.

34. *Lib* II, 38; cf. *Mag* 38 and 46.

35. Edelstein, *Musikanschauung*, p. 120, has seen Scripture's privileged place among "authorities"; he has not fully taken the measure of authority's general relation to the "way of reason."

36. *Mus* VI, 52.

37. *Ibid.*, VI, 36; cf. VI, 22.

38. *Ibid.*, VI, 2; see Edelstein, *Musikanschauung*, pp. 120–121.

39. The same hymn is used in Augustine's later meditation on "time" in the *Confessions*, XI, 35.

40. *Vita* 35.

41. See *Mus* II, 22–26; IV, 3–6, 12; V, 19.

42. *Ibid.*, II, 22.

43. *Ibid.*, IV, 4.

44. *Ibid.*, IV, 5.

45. *Ibid.*, IV, 6.

46. Augustine spins out various metrical arrangements of this verse (the original being from Horace, *Epodes* II, 1) from *Mus* V, 18 to 29.

47. See the work cited above, Introduction, note 25, pp. 146–174.

48. Confer my *Odyssey*, pp. 135–144.

49. *Mus* VI, 2–5; cf. 16.

50. *Ibid.*, VI, 7.

51. *Ibid.*

52. *Ibid.*

53. *Ibid.*, VI, 8–12. For a preliminary development of this curious theory, see *Quant* 41–61. It is perhaps the point at which Augustine's hierarchic relation—or disrelation—of soul to body exhibits the greatest strain.

54. *Early Theory*, p. 166 and the note.

55. *Mus* VI, 13.

56. *Ibid.*, VI, 14. It should be remembered throughout that for Augustine, as for Plotinus, the soul is never completely "fallen," it is both "fallen and unfallen." See *Early Theory*, pp. 166–168.

57. *Ibid.*, VI, 13.

58. *Ibid.*, VI, 23–24.

59. *Ibid.*, VI, 25–28.

60. *Ibid.*, VI, 29.

61. *Early Theory,* pp. 170–171.

62. *Mus* VI, 30.

63. *Ibid.*, VI, 30–31.

64. *Ibid.*, VI, 33. Robert C. Taliaferro's translation, in *FC* 2, p. 358, implies that God does indeed "grudge" these numbers, but I cannot think this is the force of the *cur* beginning the sentence. Compare Guy Finaert's version in *BA* 7, p. 433, which I have followed.

65. *Ibid.*, VI, 34.

66. *Ibid.*, VI, 36–37.

67. *Ibid.*, VI, 38.

68. *Ibid.*, VI, 39.

69. *Ibid.*, VI, 40. This represents Augustine's own gloss on the text from *Ecclesiasticus.*

70. *Early Theory,* pp: 173–183.

71. *Enn* V, 1, 1, 1–8.

72. Compare this deceptive appearance of "more" with such frequent Augustinian paradoxes as "plenteous want" (*copiosa egestas, Ver* 41), "mortal life, living death" (*Conf* I, 7), etc.

73. *Enn* III, 7, 11, 12–29.

74. *Mus* VI, *passim,* but see especially the clusters in 7, 13–14, 37–40, 42–43, and 48.

75. *Early Theory,* pp. 174–183.

76. *Mus* VI, 41. Note that Augustine seems (deliberately?) to refrain from saying that pride uniformly, or necessarily, motivates symbolic activity. It is not clear how regularly he would see such motivation as operative. But a necessary connection would preclude all possibility of the "rehabilitation" of art activity attempted below, *Mus* VI, 43ff.

77. *Ibid.*, VI, 42.

78. *Ibid.*, VI, 41.

79. *Ibid.*, VI, 43.

80. *Ibid.*, VI, 44; cf. I *Jo* 2, 15–16. Again, see *Early Theory,* pp. 169–173.

81. *Ibid.*, VI, 45. Augustine's sensitivity to praise, even when it amounts to "necessary approval," still shows in *Conf* X, 59–64.

82. *Ibid.*, VI, 46.

83. *Ibid.*

84. *Ibid.*, VI, 56–58.

85. *Ibid.*, VI, 46. Note the clear anticipation of Augustine's classic *uti-frui* distinction.

86. See especially *Enn* V, 8, 1.

87. *Enn* III, 8, 4.

88. On Plotinus' ambivalent attitude toward matter, see A. H. Armstrong's article "Plotinus" in *Cambridge History of Later Greek and Early Mediaeval Philosophy* (Cambridge, 1967), especially pp. 256–257; cf. *Early Theory,* pp. 117–121.

89. *Mus* VI, 48.

90. *Ibid.*, VI, 49.

91. Nor is this reflection a *hapax*: Augustine's earlier speculation on the same paradoxical "diminution of consciousness" (*Mus* VI, 13) led him into a parallel series of reflections on the soul's final condition. Cf. *Quant* 55, 76 and 79, and above, Chapter 3, note 12.

92. *Mus* VI, 13.

93. *Enn* IV, 3, 18, and V, 8, 3. See *Early Theory*, pp. 162–166.

94. *Mus* VI, 50.

95. *Ibid.*, VI, 51–55. F. J. Thonnard, in the *BA* 7 edition (Paris, 1947), p. 471, note 1, opines that the finale of this reflection is of Plotinian inspiration. He cites (pp. 528–529) *Enn* I, 2, in substantiation. I find myself sympathetic to that view.

96. *Ibid.*, VI, 46.

97. *Quant* 24, 61.

98. *Util* 24; see *Early Theory*, pp. 250–257.

99. *Republic* 519C–520E.

100. *Vita Plotini* 11, 9, and 1, 7. See, however, the sympathetic appreciation of Plotinus' attitude on this matter in John Rist, *Plotinus: The Road to Reality* (Cambridge, 1967), pp. 153–168. A. H. Armstrong sagely cautions me that we have here the report of Porphyry, hence conceivably bearing the stamp of Porphyry's own value judgments. Still, he admits, Plotinus remains, among the pagan Platonists of his time, the least "community-minded."

101. *Mus* VI, 44. See the translation in *BA* 7, p. 435.

102. See *Early Theory*, pp. 258–278.

103. *Mus* VI, 7.

104. See my *Odyssey*, especially pp. 113–119, 158–185.

105. *Ver* 88. Translations of the *De Vera Religione* are those of John H. S. Burleigh in *Augustine's Early Writings* (London, 1953).

106. *Ibid.*, 89.

107. *Ibid.*, 88.

108. *Ibid.*, 88.

109. *Ibid.*, 89.

110. *Ibid.*, 38; cf. 43.

111. *Ibid.*, 54–64; cf. 18–19, 74–78.

112. *Ibid.*, 40.

113. *Ibid.*, 45.

114. *Ibid.*, 64. We shall see that Augustine supposes much the same theory of imagination in his *Confessions*.

5. Art in the Confessions

1. See my *Odyssey*, pp. 3–22, for a discussion of the literature on the question.

2. *Culture Antique*, p. 61.

3. *Retractatio*, pp. 665–672.

4. *Retr* II, vi, 1. On the multiple sense of the term *confessio,* see Solignac's valuable Introduction to *Les Confessions, BA* 13, pp. 9–12.

5. See Pierre Courcelle, *Recherches sur les "Confessions" de Saint-Augustin,* 2d. (Paris, 1968), pp. 29–32; also, *Les Confessions de Saint-Augustin dans la tradition littéraire* (Paris, 1963), pp. 559–607.

6. This does not mean to deny that rhetoric can be artistic; for a brilliant analysis of this dimension of the *Confessions,* see Kenneth Burke, *The Rhetoric of Religion* (Berkeley, 1970); (hereafter cited as *Rhetoric*) also John J. O'Meara's sensitive observations in "Augustine the Artist and the *Aeneid,*" *Mélanges Christine Mohrmann* (Utrecht, 1963), pp. 252–261.

7. *Conf* I, 1.

8. *Meno* 80DE.

9. *Conf* X, 16; see my *Odyssey,* pp. 122–130.

10. *Ibid.,* X, 17.

11. *Ibid.,* X, 19.

12. *Ibid.*

13. Implied here is the same view of the soul's fall from contemplative beatitude as Augustine proposed in the *De Musica.* This, however, is not a necessary supposition of my argument precisely at this stage; Augustine fully intends that his view will become clearer only further on. On the *Confessions* as "exercise of the mind," see my *Odyssey,* pp. 15–16.

14. *Ibid.,* XI, 35.

15. *Ibid.,* XI, 39.

16. *Ibid.,* XI, 39, and X, 40. See note 13 above.

17. *Ibid.,* I, 8, 13.

18. *Ibid.,* I, 14–15.

19. *Ibid.,* I, 30.

20. *Ibid.,* II, 9–17.

21. *Ibid.,* IV, 11–12.

22. *Ibid.,* IV, 13.

23. *Ibid.,* III, 2–4.

24. *Ibid.,* VIII, 6–8.

25. *Ibid.,* IV, 22.

26. *Ibid.,* IV, 9.

27. *Ibid.,* IV, 22.

28. Here too Augustine's theory of the soul's fall is hinted at, but the reader is not required to subscribe to that interpretation quite yet. For Augustine's theory of signs in the *Confessions,* see Mayer, *Zeichen* I, 41–169; also the article cited above in the Introduction, note 23, on "Signifikations-Hermeneutik." It could be clearer in Mayer's exposé in *Zeichen* I that Augustine is interpreting his life experience of signs through the lens of a theory formed subsequently and inspired (as Mayer shows) largely from Plotinus.

29. *Conf* I, 8 and 13.

30. *Ibid.*, I, 8.

31. *Ibid.*, I, 10

32. *Ibid.*, I, 13.

33. See below, note 51.

34. *Conf* III, 7.

35. *Ibid.*, III, 9.

36. *Ibid.*, III, 10–11.

37. *Ibid.*, IV, 27.

38. *Ibid.*, V, 10–11.

39. *Ibid.*, V, 23–24.

40. *Ibid.*, VII, 16–23.

41. *Ibid.*, VII, 16.

42. *Ibid.*, VII, 23.

43. *Ibid.*, VII, 23. Augustine is here echoing a version of the theory of imagination presented in the *De Vera Religione*, 64. See above, Chapter 4, note 114.

44. *Conf* VII, 24.

45. *Ibid.*, VII, 25.

46. *Ibid.*, IX, 23.

47. *Ibid.*, IX, 24.

48. *Ibid.*, IX, 25.

49. *Ibid.*, X, 2.

50. *Ibid.*, X, 3–4.

51. *Ibid.*, X, 9–10; see also X, 11: *unus ego animus*, "I, the single mind." Augustine is now unfolding the view of man implicit in his description of language learning in I, 8 and 13.

52. *Ibid.*, X, 18–21.

53. *Ibid.*, X, 22.

54. *Ibid.*, X, 25.

55. *Ibid.*, X, 29.

56. *Ibid.*, X, 31.

57. *Ibid.*, XI, 5–8.

58. *Ibid.*, XI, 5.

59. *Ibid.*, XI, 10. Implicit here, I suggest, is the view of *sacramentum* lying behind Augustine's reflection on the Incarnation, VII, 24–25.

60. *Ibid.*, XI, 11. Again, in contrast to the "transfiguration" image of *Acad* I, 3, these clouds are scarcely seen as "luminous"; and yet, curiously, the divine light seems to be piercing "through" them.

61. Cf. *ibid.*, XI, 41.

62. *Ibid.*, XII, 9.

63. *Ibid.*, XII, 12; cf. XII, 23.

64. *Ibid.*, XII, 9.

65. *Ibid.*, XII, 16.

66. Here, as Augustine later makes clear (below, XIII, 9) there dwell not only angels, but (potentially?) human souls.

67. *Ibid.*, XII, 2.

68. See A. H. Armstrong, "Spiritual or Intelligible Matter in Plotinus and St. Augustine," in *AM* I, 277–283.

69. *Conf* XII, 24.

70. *Ibid.*, XII, 23, 29.

71. *Ibid.*, XII, 27–32.

72. *Ibid.*, XII, 32 and 35.

73. *Ibid.*, XII, 33.

74. *Ibid.*, XII, 34.

75. *Ibid.*, XII, 27 and 34.

76. *Ibid.*, XII, 35.

77. Note the occasionalist flavor implied in such expressions as *quae mihi ardenter confitenti* (XII, 27), *quae aliter et aliter . . . occurrunt* (XII, 33).

78. *Ibid.*, XII, 27–35.

79. *Ibid.*, XII, 36 and 42. One should distinguish: Augustine's theory here is far more applicable to the Christian's life of prayer than to the theologian's effort to elicit from Scripture a *regula fidei*. In this latter connection, Augustine's practice, as well as the rules he lays down in the *De Doctrina Christiana*, are both much soberer than the *Confessions'* theory would seem to encourage.

80. *Ibid.*, XII, 37; cf XII, 41.

81. *Ibid.*, XII, 38–39.

82. *Ibid.*, XIII, 1–3. For my overall view of Book XIII, the reader might usefully consult *Odyssey*, pp. 158–185. I must confess my inability to know what exactly to make of A. Holl's study of Book XIII, *Die Welt der Zeichen bei Augustinus*, (Vienna, 1963).

83. *Ibid.*, XIII, 3.

84. *Ibid.*, XIII, 7.

85. *Ibid.*, XIII, 9.

86. *Ibid.*, XIII, 10.

87. *Ibid.*, XIII, 5.

88. *Ibid.*, XIII, 9.

89. *Ibid.*, XIII, 14.

90. *Ibid.*, XIII, 15.

91. *Ibid.*, XIII, 14.

92. *Ibid.*, XIII, 15

93. *Ibid.*, XIII, 14.

94. *Ibid.*, XIII, 16. Augustine here remains faithful to his interpretation (*GenMan* II, 32; cf. 23) of the "coats of skin" as signifying the mortal bodies of our fallen condition.

95. *Ibid.*, XIII, 18.

96. *Ibid.*, XIII, 23. This remark occurs in the context of Augustine's discussion of action and contemplation, but its application here remains valid.

97. *Ibid.*, XIII, 18.

98. *Ibid.*

99. *Ibid.* It should be pointed out that these spiritual "heavens"

stand, in Augustine's mind, for the intelligible world (the "forms" alluded to in XIII, 33; cf. below note 114) through which the mind achieves its (indirect) knowledge of God. Cf. *Conf* VII, 16, and VIII, 1.

100. *Ibid.*, XIII, 18.

101. *Ibid.*, XIII, 19.

102. *Ibid.*, XIII, 27.

103. *Ibid.*, XIII, 26.

104. *Ibid.*, XIII, 27.

105. *Ibid.*, XIII, 28.

106. *Ibid.*, I, 13.

107. *Ibid.*, XIII, 28 and 34.

108. *Ibid.*, XIII, 30.

109. *Ibid.*, XIII, 34.

110. This condition of luminous transparency we are now fully entitled to understand as what Augustine intended earlier, when describing our condition in the resurrection as clothed in "garments of light" (*veste luminis*, XIII, 9); cf. 14.

111. *Ibid.*, XIII, 28.

112. *Ibid.*, XIII, 29.

113. *Ibid.*, XIII, 32.

114. *Ibid.*, XIII, 33. See note 99 above and Solignac's observations in *BA* 14, pp. 629–634. Cf. *Odyssey*, pp. 170–172.

115. *Ibid.*, XIII, 34.

116. *Ibid.*, XIII, 33.

117. *Ibid.*, XIII, 36.

118. *Ibid.*

119. Augustine argues that the interpreter of Scripture must consider the *omission* of this blessing (e.g., on the occasion of the creation of plant life) as significant as its conferrals on "water animals" and men: *ibid.* XIII, 35–37.

120. *Ibid.*, XIII, 37.

121. *Ibid.*, XIII, 22–25.

122. *Ibid.*, XIII, 22.

123. *Ibid.*, XIII, 23.

124. *Ibid.*, XIII, 23 and 25.

125. *Ibid.*, XIII, 38–42.

126. *Ibid.*, XIII, 50.

127. *Ibid.*, XIII, 46. Augustine actually puts this the other way round: God will see in "our" seeing.

128. *Ibid.*, XIII, 53.

129. See above, Chapter 4, note 85.

130. *Conf* I, 20. Some of Augustine's severity may issue from the widespread practice in his time of reverentially "allegorizing" even the crudest episodes in pagan literature. (I am again indebted to A. H. Armstrong for this observation.)

131. *Ibid.*, I, 24–25.

132. *Ibid.*, I, 22.

133. *Ibid.*, I, 24.

134. *Ibid.*, I, 24–26.

135. *Ibid.*, I, 20.

136. *Ibid.*, I, 22.

137. *Ibid.*, I, 21.

138. *Ibid.*, I, 25.

139. *Ibid.*, I, 26. Cf. the "whirlpool of filth" (*vorago turpitudinis*) of I, 30. Note that these designations apply to human society insofar as it compounds its penal condition, a condition resulting from the primordial sin that brought on the soul's fall, by sins committed in "this mortal life."

140. *Ibid.*, I, 25–26.

141. *Ibid.*, I, 28.

142. *Ibid.*, I, 29.

143. *Ibid.*, IV, 17; III, 15; XIII, 43.

144. Cf. *ibid.*, VII, 19 and 22, where all things are said to be "good" in virtue of this order. The *pulchrum-aptum* distinction has become momentarily blurred.

145. *Ibid.*, IV, 7; cf. I, 12 and 15, and XIII, 50.

146. *Ibid.*, V, 2; cf. VII, 18–19, where the slide from beauty to goodness occurs again.

147. *Ibid.*, X, 38.

148. *Ibid.*, I, 4; *dulcedo sancta*. Again, is this beauty, or a kind of spiritual "good"?

149. *Ibid.*, I, 12.

150. *Ibid.*, II, 12. Here, too, Augustine moves from God as beauty to God as his "true good."

151. *Ibid.*, III, 10.

152. *Ibid.*, VII, 23.

153. *Ibid.*, II, 13. *Suavitas*: cf. notes 144, 148, and 150 above.

154. *Ibid.*, II, 18.

155. *Ibid.*, II, 12; X, 38.

156. *Ibid.*, V, 2.

157. *Ibid.*, XI, 6: *quo conparato nec pulchra sunt nec bona sunt nec sunt.*

158. *Ibid.*, II, 3. Here Augustine contrasts the "beauties" of sexual attractiveness (the "fleeting beauties of the lowest of things" (*novissimarum rerum fugaces pulchritudines*) with the "embrace (*amplexus*) of God's own Beauty. He admits, however, that these lowest forms of beauty can be turned to "good use." Cf. II, 10, where this same contrast is drawn between the "lowest and last" and the "highest" of beauties. Again, beauty is being portrayed as object of the soul's desire for bliss.

159. *Ibid.*, II, 11; they are "mean and base" (*abjecta et iacentia*), when compared with the "higher and beatifying" beauties of the spiritual world.

160. *Ibid.*, IV, 15–16.

161. *Ibid.,* X, 51–53.

162. *Ibid.,* X, 54–55.

163. *Ibid.,* X, 51.

164. *Ibid.,* X, 52: "alluring and perilous sweetness" (*inlecebrosa ac periculosa dulcedo*). Observe again (notes 159–164) Augustine's persistence in equating "beauty" with the "good" that answers to the soul's desire for happiness.

165. *Ibid.,* IV, 18; cf. 19.

166. *Ibid.,* X, 8.

167. *Ibid.,* IX, 25; cf. III, 14.

168. *Ibid.,* XI, 7.

169. *Ibid.,* VII, 23.

170. *Ibid.,* X, 53.

171. *Ibid.* This, I am compelled to think, may be one of those image clusters that turn out to be more revealing than Augustine's conscious mind might have wished. He is playing upon the *Vetus Latina* translation of *Psalm* 58, 10; it prompts him to complain that artists do not "guard their strength (*fortitudo*) for God," but "sow it" instead (*spargunt*) into "luxurious weariness" (*in deliciosas lassitudines*). It scarcely requires a sinister imagination to detect, in that expression, a reference to post-coital languors. Comparison with *Conf* I, 28, reinforces the suspicion: there, as here, it is question of *pedes, gressus,* and the soul's movement further away (*longior*) from the God "within" toward the "external" delights of adulterous loves (cf. the soul's *fornicatio,* I, 28). Augustine evokes (I, 28) the image of the Prodigal, in direct connection with Plotinus' urging (*Enn* I, 6, 8), that like Odysseus, we should flee to the beloved fatherland: to his imagination, the Prodigal parable works as a kind of Christian "Odyssey." But the Prodigal, we know, "dissipated" (I, 28, *dissiparet*) the *substantia* given him by his father. That *substantia* Augustine equates with the *fortitudo* of *Psalm* 58, 10 (see *Enarr* 70, *sermo* 2, 6, 49, where *Psalm* 58, 10, leads to the Prodigal story; also *Enarr* 58, *sermo* 2, 1, where the same verse evokes the entire nexus of *longior, gressus,* and *vehicula* found in *Conf* I, 28).

But, Augustine frequently reminds us, the Prodigal dissipated his substance, or *vires* (*effudit, disperdit, erogavit, exaninitur* are *other* expressions used) among whores (*cum meretricibus, Serm* 96, 2; *Enarr* 70, *sermo* 2, 6; *Serm* 95, 5; 131, 12; 138, 5), whence the sexual connotation alluded to above.

What accounts for the allusion to *lassitudines?* *Sermo* 330, 1, speaks of the farmer who "wastes what he sows" (*profert, spargit, abjicit, obruit* are the expressions employed) and passes on (330, 3) to a similar set of images referring to the Prodigal, who is said to be *fame fatigatus* ("weary from hunger").

What brings the image into final focus, I suggest, is the underlying connection with Homer's *Odyssey: Enarr* 123, 9, 5ff. depicts the Prodigal as drawn to plunge himself in the "jaws" or "gullet" of this world's sweetness (*dulcedo*) in a fashion strongly reminiscent of the way Plotinus depicts Odysseus, enticed by Circe and Calypso to forget the steadfast purpose of his homeward journey. The charms of these two ladies extended much beyond the "delights of the eyes" and "great beauties of sense" Plotinus discreetly refers to, and Augustine certainly knew that much. Mingled in here, though, there is likely a side reminiscence of the sirens and lotus islands, whose function in Homer's *Odyssey* is also to make the soul "forget" its homeward journey.

I also suspect, without wishing to labor the point, that at the center of this whole image cluster may well be Plotinus' other image, from *Enn* III, 7, 11, of the "seed" uncoiling its inner resources, "squandering" them "outside itself" as it goes forward to a "weaker greatness'; see above, Chapter 4, notes 70–73. All this implies a somewhat dizzying, and at times even bizarre, feat of image fusion, admittedly; but I find it well within range of Augustine's creative powers.

172. *Ibid.*, X, 49–50.

173. *Acad.*, III, 43; cf. *Quant* 73 and 76.

174. *Enn* I, 6, 7; note that the Odyssey image occurs *ibid.*, 8.

175. *History of Dogma* (New York, 1961), trans. Neil Buchanan, V, 64.

6. The Artistry of the Confessions

1. *Eloquentia Pedisequa* (Nijmegen, 1949). See also J. Finaert, *Saint-Augustin rhéteur* (Paris, 1939).

2. *Rhetoric.*

3. Introduction, note 8.

4. *BA* 13 and 14. For incidental but significant remarks on aspects of Augustine's artistic sensitivity, see also Brown, *Augustine*, pp. 35–39, 158–181, and Mandouze, *L'aventure*, pp. 461–464 and 678–708.

5. *Conf* V, 2. An adaptation of Pusey's, my translation, preserves the semi-archaic forms "thee" and "thou," to stress that Augustine is addressing God with the childlike trust implied by the intimate Latin *tu*.

> Ipsi convertantur,
> et ecce ibi es in corde eorum,
> in corde confitentium tibi
> et proicientium se in te
> et plorantium in sinu tuo post vias suas difficiles:
> et tu facilis terges lacrimas eorum,
> et magis plorant et gaudent in fletibus,
> quoniam tu domine,
> non aliquis homo, caro et sanguis,
> reficis et consolaris eos.

6. *Ibid.,* IX, 25.

> Si cui sileat tumultus carnis
> sileant phantasiae terrae et aquarum et aeris,
> sileant et poli
> et ipsa sibi anima sileat
> et transeat se non cogitando . . .
> et loquatur ipse solus non per eas
> sed per seipsum,
> et audiamus Verbum ejus . . .

7. *Ibid.,* X, 38.

> Sero te amavi,
> pulchritudo tam antiqua et tam nova,
> sero te amavi.
>
> .   .   .   .   .
>
> Vocasti et clamasti et rupisti surditatem meam,
> coruscasti, splenduisti, et fugasti caecitatem meam,
> gustavi et esurio et sitio,
> tetigisti me, et exarsi in pacem tuam.

8. See above, Chapter 2, note 47.
9. *Acad* I, 3–4; Cf. *Sol* I, 17, 22.
10. *Conf* VIII, 27.
11. *Ibid.,* X, 8.
12. See above, Chapter 2, note 50.
13. T. S. Eliot, *The Wasteland,* III, "The Fire Sermon" (*in fine*).
14. Charles Baudelaire, Preface to *Les Fleurs du Mal,* quoted in T. S. Eliot, *The Wasteland,* I, "The Burial of the Dead" (*in fine*).
15. *Conf* VIII, 17.
16. *Ibid.,* III, 7–8.
17. *Ibid.,* VIII, 12.
18. *Ibid.,* VIII, 16. The Latin, sense-lined accordingly:

> Narrabat haec Pontitianus.
> Tu autem, domine, inter verba eius
> retorquebas me ad meipsum,
> auferens me a dorso meo, ubi me posueram.
> dum nollem me attendere,
> et constituebas me ante faciem meam, ut viderem, quam
>   turpis essem,
> quam distortus et sordidus, maculosus et ulcerosus.
> Et videbam et horrebam,
> et quo a me fugerem non erat.
> Et si conebar a me avertere aspectum,
> narrabat ille quod narrabat,

et tu me rursus opponebas mihi
et inpingebas me in oculos meos,
ut invenirem iniquitatem meam et odissem.
Noveram eam,
sed dissimulabam et cohibebam et obliviscebar.

19. See *Early Theory,* pp. 65–86, for fuller evidence on what follows.

20. *Conf* IV, 1, to V, 2. The climax of this development is quoted above, note 5.

21. *Rhetoric.*

22. *Ibid.,* pp. 55–58.

23. *Ibid.,* pp. 62–65.

24. *Ibid.,* pp. 87–88.

25. *Ibid.,* p. 126.

26. *Ibid.,* pp. 129–133.

27. *Ibid.,* p. 69.

28. *Conf* VII, 26.

29. *Rhetoric,* p. 160.

30. *Language as Symbolic Action* (Berkeley, 1966), pp. 44–62; see also pp. 5, 22, and 28.

31. See R. A. Markus, "St. Augustine and Signs," in *Augustine: A Collection of Critical Essays,* ed. R. A. Markus (New York, 1972), pp. 61–85, especially his remark on p. 72, on Augustine's tendency to view "language . . . as running parallel to the stream of experience and alongside it, so to speak, rather than within it." Note the connection between the view of language and of man exposed in Gareth B. Matthews' essay, "The Inner Man," in the same collection, pp. 176–190.

32. *Conf* I, 20–24.

33. *Ibid.,* I, 24–26; cf. also I, 29 (on "good form" as all-important) and III, 2 and 5 (on the immoral influence of lascivious literature).

34. *Conf* I, 23: the connection between *curiositas* and imitative action still holds firm; see above, Chapter 4, notes 68–75.

35. *Conf* I, 23 (à propos of Homer).

36. *Ibid.,* I, 22.

37. *Ibid.,* I, 24. There may also be the fear in Augustine's mind that Scripture will also be interpreted as "myth," i.e., so many false tales.

38. *Ibid.,* I, 27.

39. *Ibid.,* III, 2.

40. *Ibid.,* III, 2–4.

41. *Ibid.*

42. *Poetics* 6 and 9.

43. *Conf* III, 2.

44. The interpretation of the Aristotelean *catharsis* implied here owes much to suggestions found especially in Samuel H. Butcher,

Aristotle's Theory of Poetry and Fine Art, 4th ed. (London, 1911). Gerald F. Else, *Aristotle's Poetics: The Argument* (Cambridge, Mass., 1957), differs from Butcher in several provocative respects, but I have not found his views convincing.

45. See Mandouze, *L'aventure,* pp. 71–77, for one of the best distillations of what this term implies.

46. See, for some examples, *Early Theory,* pp. 48–64, 170–171, and 178–179.

47. *Conf* V, 15.

48. *Ibid.,* VI, 11–16; cf. 22.

49. *Ibid.,* VIII, 13–18. See above at note 18.

50. *Ibid.,* VIII, 25–27. See G. Bouissou's note, *BA* 14, pp. 543–546.

51. *Ibid.,* IV, 9.

52. Cf. *ibid.,* I, 28; also *Early Theory,* pp. 73, 188, 225; and *Odyssey,* esp. pp. 12, 33, 43, 104, 186–190.

7. Augustine's Later Aesthetic

1. Gustave Bardy, "Les méthodes de travail de Saint Augustin," in *AM* I, 19–29.

2. *Esthétique,* p. 195. Svoboda's "tendentiousness" shows principally in his repeated efforts to draw from the texts he summarizes the conclusion that Augustine's aesthetic theory becomes more *spiritualiste* as time goes on (pp. 169, 195–196). "Ethical and religious" preoccupations tend more and more to "dominate" the bishop's thinking on these matters (p. 192), which means, for Svoboda, that the quest for truth (pp. 144, 167) or for the beatifying good (pp. 140, 147) explain Augustine's extracting less "profit" of an aesthetic sort from the subjects he is dealing with than (presumably) he might earlier have done (pp. 150–151, 161, 167). The result, as Svoboda sees it: properly aesthetic considerations are progressively relegated *au second plan* (p. 151), "subordinated" to ethical and religious concerns which are set well above (*bien au-dessus*) aesthetic values (p. 164). (Note the curious exception for *Civ, Esthétique,* p. 178.)

My claim here is that Svoboda, in surveying these later works, has only just come to see what was *always* true for Augustine's aesthetic i.e., the coordination that holds between truth, good, and beauty at all the levels of being's hierarchy, a coordination which accounts for Augustine's sliding from any one of these categories to the others. (See *Esthétique,* p. 140, where Svoboda comes close to perceiving this.) Qua hierarchic, such coordination necessarily entails a corresponding subordination: higher levels of truth-good-beauty are always to be preferred to their lower-level counterparts. But the coordination on each level makes it a matter of relative indifference whether Augustine refers to the creatures concerned as true, good, or beautiful; hence he can as easily urge us to seek higher spiritual "goods" over lower bodily "beauties," as higher "beauties" over lower "goods." The "subordination" of aesthetic values Svoboda frequently claims to have uncovered turns out, accordingly, when more closely inspected, to be no more than Augustine's persistent subordination of "lower" to "higher" values generally, all of them equally "aesthetic," "ethical," and "religious."

In justice it should be said that, despite this tendentiousness in interpretation, Svoboda's survey of the relevant texts is, if anything, over-scrupulous, running to the slightest of Augustine's parenthetical allusions to *decus, pulchrum, ornamentum,* etc. His summaries are also, with few exceptions, objective and trustworthy insofar as the content of Augustine's observations is concerned. There are occasions where closer attention to context would have been desirable. Dom Lambot's more recent authentications (*Stromata* I, Brussels, 1950) leave the issues where they were in Svoboda's time. See, e.g., Sermons XXIV, 3–4; CIV, 3–5, 7; CLXXVII, 8–10.

3. *Civ* XXII, xxx. Cf. ibid., IX, xvii, and *Trin* I, 16.

4. *NatBon* 3, 8–9; *GenLitt* III, 37; V, 43; XI, 28; *AdvLeg* I, 6–8; *Civ* XI, iv; xviii, 1; xxiii, 1 (vs. Origen; cf. xxii also); XVI, viii, 2); *Enchir* 10–11; *Enar* 144, 13; 148, 9–10 (where, *pace* Svoboda, *infernum* refers to this "lower world" of corporeal reality); *Serm* 125, 5; *Ep* 138, 2–5. In this last text Augustine presents a revealing application of his *pulchrum-aptum* distinction: God, like a medicinal "artist," fashions the beauty of the temporal "whole" by prescribing what is "apt" for each successive time period. Note the familiar "theodicy" or *de malo* context constant since the *De Ordine.*

5. On bodily beauty, see *Faust* XX, 7; XXI, 6–7, 9–10; *NatBon* 8–9, 13–14; *SecMan* 15; *GenLitt* III, 25; V, 43; *Civ* V, xi; X, xiv; XI, iv; XXII, xxiv; *Enar* 34 S I, 13, 79, 14 (where Augustine asks the "aesthetic" question *Quare autem amas . . . nisi quia pulchra,* but in an outspokenly *beata vita* context); 84, 9; *Serm* 19, 5; 68, 2; 141, 2; 158, 7; 241, 2; 243, 7. Note, in these texts, how regularly the "theodicy" context, when present, swiftly yields to the "ascensional" context proper to Augustine's (ethical? religious? both, of course) view of the soul's quest for "happiness." See above, note 2.

On beauty's numerical character, a theme which frequently leads Augustine to speak of the entire temporal-historical sequence as a "poem" or "song," see *Faust* XX, 7; XXI, 6–7; *Trin* III, 16 (cf. *ibid.* VI, 11–12; XIII, 4); *GenLitt* IV, 7–12; V, 44; *Civ* V, xi; XI, xxii; XI, xviii and xxx; XII, xix; *Serm* 243, 4; *Ep* 166, 12–13. The stress on "unity" as the fount of all number is frequent here, but its presence in *Serm* 46, 37; 103, 4; 138, 3–4 (see *Esthétique,* pp. 190–191) is so obviously due to Augustine's focus on the divisive character of the Donatist heresy that it becomes difficult to weigh the properly aesthetic importance of the theme. (Compare the context of *GenLitt* IV, 7–12, and Svoboda's remarks, *Esthétique,* p. 151.)

6. See again most of the texts and contexts referred to in the

first portion of note 5, above: one comes to expect this stress when the ascensional *beata vita* context is active. See also *NatBon* 23; *Trin* VIII, 9; IX, 11; XV, 7; *GenLitt* IV, 1; VII, 9; *JoParth* 9, 9; *Civ* I, xviii, 1; XII, iv–v and viii; XV, xxii; XVII, xvi, 1; *Enar* 9, 3; 41, 7; 79, 14; *Serm* 19, 5; 68, 2; 158, 7; *Ep* 118, 23; 120, 20. Cf. also Svoboda's further *Sermon* references to the superior beauty of God, of Christ as God, of the angels, and of the "interior" beauty of souls adorned with virtue, *Esthétique*, pp. 187–190. On Svoboda's contention that Augustine regularly finds the incarnate Christ "ugly," see below, note 15.

7. *NatBon* 13–18; *Enchir* 10–11.

8. See texts cited in notes 6 and 7, above.

9. *CMend* 36; *Civ* X, xiv, Cf. *Enar* 64, 8 (*amputa*) and 79, 14 (*viscum*).

10. *Trin* I, 16–20.

11. *Ibid.*, XIV, 24–26.

12. *Civ* X, xvi.

13. *Trin* VIII, 4 (where Augustine presents an ascending survey of beauties but under the label of "goods"; whence Svoboda, *Esthétique*, pp. 147 and 151, points out that he "speaks now of good (*bien*) "as he spoke in times past of beauty." On such verbal argumentation, see above, notes 2 and 5); *JoParth* 1, 14; 2, 11; 4, 5; *InJo* 3, 21; 15, 21; 32, 3; *Civ* X, xvi; XV, xxii; cf. XII, viii; *Ep* 118, 23; *Enar* 136, 5; *Serm* 19, 5; 69, 2; 158, 7; 194, 4. Augustine continues to speak of this "other" as a world of spiritual and intelligible beauties, even after a quite distinct development beckons for his attention, i.e., the specifically Christian motif of the "new earth and new heaven" peopled by "risen bodies." See below, note 47.

14. See texts cited above note 6; also *InJo* 3, 21; 40, 4; *Doc* IV, 61; *Serm* 9, 16; 159, 2–3; 337, 1; 343, 6–7; Denis 18, 4–5; Caillau I, 47, 1; Morin-Guelf. 26, 2. Augustine's regular distinction between (audible and visible) words and their higher, invisible meanings emerges from the same thought pattern: see *Serm* 28, 4–5; 32, 6; 47, 30; 98, 3. Note that Svoboda, p. 188, has God "abandoning" the (consequently ugly) soul, when it is the soul who has done the abandoning. For the sermons designated as Denis, Caillau, and Morin-Guelf., see *Miscellanea Agostiniana* I (Rome, 1930).

15. The position Augustine adopts on the "beauty" of Christ may not have all the "aesthetic" import Svoboda ascribes to it; it is also far less clear than Svoboda portrays it.

Augustine was forced (as Svoboda appreciates, p. 154) into this line of speculation by an exegetical problem: whereas *Psalm* 44, 3 speaks prophetically of Christ as *speciosus prae filiis hominum*, "more beautiful than the sons of men," *Isaiah* 53, 2, seems equally clear in the contradictory sense: "We saw him, and he had neither beauty nor comeliness": [*neque*] *speciem neque decorem*. (See *JoParth* 9, 9; *Enar* 103 S I, 5; and *Serm* 95, 4, where Augustine puts these two texts into a virtual debate.) How was Augustine to reconcile these equally inspired accounts?

One solution would be to make the *Psalm* refer to Christ as God (and in *this sense* "au-dessus des hommes" as Svoboda vaguely puts it, p. 155), while making *Isaiah* refer to Christ as man (as Svoboda puts it more clearly *ibid.*, p. 187). And there are texts that argue for Augustine's having adopted this solution, for a time at least: *Civ* XVII, xvi; *InJo* 10, 13; *Enar* 43, 16; 83, 11; less clearly so, *JoParth* 9, 9.

Another solution would make both texts refer to the incarnate Christ: his "beauty" would then be the surpassing interior beauty of justice, visible to the eyes of the heart; his ugliness would refer to his "outward," bodily appearance. (See Svoboda's passing suggestion, *Esthétique*, p. 155.) Again, there is one occasion, at least, where one could think Augustine is opting for this solution: *Enar* 44, 14; but the text is far from being apodictic.

Svoboda suggests a third possibility: that when Augustine became older, he was more willing to attribute beauty to Christ (*Esthétique*, pp. 155 and 188). Svoboda's proposal remains vague to me (one must presume he means bodily beauty, else why speak of a change of view?), and the texts he adduces, along with the chronological conjectures he is forced to make, weaken his case considerably. Note that this theory, if true, would call into question the curve of "spiritualization" Svoboda is arguing for, a corollary he does not seem to have noticed.

There may, however, be a genuine development in Augustine's thought on this question; but what is needed is a much more assured chronology of both his *Sermons* and *Enarrationes* than such scholarly Trojans as Kunzelmann, Kalb, Rondet, and LaBonnardière have been able, up until now, to furnish (see Mandouze, *L'aventure*, pp. 599–615, for a fairly recent state of the question). Until such time, then, I would like to propose only a line of inquiry. A number of Augustine's texts suggest that there came a moment when he linked the *Isaiah* text with that of *Psalm* 44 by means of *Philippians* 2, 6–8, where St. Paul contrasts the "form" of Christ's divinity with the *forma servi*, the form of a "servant," or "slave," that He assumed at the incarnation. Paul goes immediately on to show this "self-emptying" as climaxing in the crucifixion, and we are brusquely thrown into the Passion context to which the liturgy of the Church applies Isaiah's description of the "suffering servant." This may well have given Augustine an idea different from any of the above; at all events, there are texts wherein he traces Christ's "ugliness" to his humiliated aspect during his Passion and Crucifixion. *Enar* 127, 8: "He appeared ugly (*foedus*) while in the hands of his persecutors," whose "eyes" needed "cleansing"; but even we believers do not love his *membra crucifixa*, but rather his interior "charity" toward us; *Serm* 210, 4: again, *inter manus persequentium non habuit speciem;* and 254, 5: *Foeda species, crucifixi species,* "His ugly appearance was the appearance of one crucified." Note here that Augustine goes on to say that this ugliness brought forth the beauty (*pulchritudinem*) of the resurrection. There are additional texts where the Crucifixion is on the scene, but not so clearly accounting for Christ's "ugliness": *Enar* 44, 3; 103, S I, 5; *Serm* 95, 4: "What is more beautiful than God? What more deformed than one crucified?"; 138, 6. Finally, *Serm* 27, 6; 44, 1–2; 285, 6 might fit any of the various solutions above.

16. *SecMan* 15; *InJo* 1, 17; 37, 8; *Civ* XII, xxv (but note that here the artist seems to work from the "external" form); cf. *Enar* 34 S II, 2; 98, 12; *Serm* 93, 16.

17. See his extended treatment of this in *Trin* IX, 9–11.

18. *Trin* VIII, 4–5; IX, 9–11; XII, 2; *InJo* 15, 21; *Jul* IV, 65–66 (Svoboda's additional reference to IV, 75, seems to be in error; see *Esthétique,* p. 168); *Civ* VIII, v–vii; XI, xvi and xxvii, 2. Note that while *Trin* VIII, 4, and *Enar* 98, 12, distinguish between the (obviously "sensible") judgments of the practiced and unpracticed eye, the norm for correctness remains the intellectual judgment. Cf. *Enar* 18, S II, 1, where Augustine exhorts his flock to sing, not like the birds, but "knowingly."

19. In the sense of *disciplinae.* Svoboda's persistent lack of discrimination in using the term "art" vitiates many of the observations he makes on Augustine's later aesthetic, also. Despite the severity that would *limit* the appropriate readership of his *De Musica,* note (as Svoboda fails to do, pp. 141–142) that Augustine (*Ep* 101, 1–4) still holds for the continuing validity of his earlier "way of the *artes.*" (The same is true of *Retr* I, iii, 2, and I, xi, 1, on the *De Ordine* and *De Musica* respectively; compare Svoboda, pp. 185–186.) Augustine complains that so many professionals, and their students (*ibid.*; also *CatRud* 10, *Serm* 70, 2) study the *artes* for pleasure, riches, praise, and suchlike "vanities"; but this implies, among other things, that they spurn or ignore the "true" value of the *artes* as a way of ascending from corporeal to incorporeal reality. For this reason, he would prefer young Christians to be nourished on Scripture (*Serm* 133, 4). His fundamental evaluation of the *artes,* remains, accordingly, the same as always. On "art" in the more modern sense of the term, see below note 22.

20. On the value of rhetoric, used in the service of truth, see *CatRud* 13; *Cresc* I, 12 (cf. *InJo* 124, 8); *Civ* XXII, v asserts that the apostles themselves did not study the liberal *artes,* but *Doc* IV, 20–26 gives examples of how eloquent they could be without having studied rhetoric. See also *Doc* IV, 2, 6–7, 9–10, where Augustine's guidelines to the Christian rhetorician show the value he accords to this *ars.* But truth must be served, not merely the pleasure of hearing sweet-sounding words: *Doc* IV, 27, 30–34, 55–57; *Serm* 28, 4–5; 32, 6; 47, 30; 98, 3; 156, 1. If the orator pleases, however, the audience may keep listening and find the truth. See *Esthétique,* p. 167, for an extreme

example of Svoboda's attitude toward this Augustinian focus: Consentius has written to Augustine asking whether Christians may not use an occasional lie to entrap the Priscillianists, liars themselves, Consentius claims—do we not have scriptural precedents commending such holy dissimulation? Augustine responds in an effort to show that such biblical figures as Esau did not really lie and argues at one point that if certain of Consentius' examples were to be construed as genuine lies, then the rhetorician's use of various figures, hyperbole for example, must be construed as lying: a *reductio ad absurdum*, as the bishop confidently sees it. To which Svoboda by some inverted logic concludes that in such matters of art, we have another instance to show that "truth is," for Augustine, "the superior norm." For the substantial question involved, see again above, note 2.

21. *Civ* XVII, xiv; *Doc* IV, 19; *Enar* 147, 5; 150, 2; *Serm* 34, 6; 365, 1. Note, despite Svoboda's introductory demurrals, the positive character of such remarks as link singing with *hilaritas* (*Serm* 34, 1) and *amor* (*Serm* 33, 1; 34, 6). The remaining *Enarrationes* alluded to (pp. 158–160) by Svoboda, as well as the remaining *Sermon* allusions (pp. 192–193) have little or no aesthetic bearing.

22. In *Civ* XXII, xxiv, Augustine surveys the blessings God has conferred on the "misery of humankind, in which the justice of the punishing [God] is praised." The blessings include, first, propagation, with the corporal beauties of the human body and of the sensible creation taking third and fourth place (all later, quite unspiritual emphases whose force escapes Svoboda). The second class has to do with the gifts of man's mind, among them the "marvels, the stupefying products" of his "artistic" fecundity. This is shown in the forms of vesture, architecture, statues, and paintings, in the achievements of agriculture and navigation, in theatrical productions, cuisine, hunting, and taming of animals, and finally in language, rhetoric, music, mathematics, astronomy, and dialectic: a pell-mell enumeration in which *ars* embraces indiscriminately the useful and fine arts, and the liberal *artes* as well. Augustine's enthusiasm recalls the parallel oratorical flight in *Quant* 72; he ends with a comparable evaluation: "all of these are but the solace of the wretched and condemned . . . blessings of a condemned state."

23. Here the gap between Svoboda's "summary" and subsequent evaluation becomes serious. On painting: he acknowledges (*Esthétique*, pp. 137–138) that *Faust* XXII, 17, refers to representations used in reprehensible cults of the dead or of "demons" but draws the remarkable conclusion that such associations make it unremarkable that Augustine "shows himself as enemy to *all* paintings" (italics mine). *InJo* 24, 2, contrasts admiring a beautiful script (where we are called to the further step of understanding what is written) and a beautiful painting where merely seeing is admiring (*hoc est totum, vidisse, laudasse*). This, Svoboda speculates, may betray Augustine's dim awareness that "in the plastic arts form is more important than

in a literary work," but he makes it clear he is just guessing. (For my own less recondite suggestion, see below.) *Civ* XI, xxiii, 1, repeats Plotinus' comparison of evils to the "black" colors in a painting: hardly a pregnant aesthetic observation about painting itself. In *Serm* 316, 5, Augustine qualifies as *dulcis* the picture of Saul, the future apostle, guarding the cloaks of those who were stoning Stephen, the first martyr; Svoboda wonders if this shows that Augustine "changed, toward the end of his lifetime, his opinion on paintings," this being the "only instance" where he gives approval to a painting (*ibid.*, p. 192). One is tempted to ask what this might do to the curve of "spiritualization" Svoboda speaks of, but alas: the *pictura* in question is quite conceivably the *word* painting of the scene that Augustine has just finished reading from the *Acts of the Apostles*.

Regarding sculpture: Svoboda (*ibid.*, p. 144) has Augustine (*UnBapt* 5–6) railing against those who "venerate statues," and invoking St. Paul's words (*Romans* 1.23ff.) on idolatry. Later he "attacks sculpture" on the same grounds as do the *Psalms;* "they condemn the veneration of statues" and mock them as deaf and mute (*ibid.*, 156). Svoboda's expression disingenuously betrays him also in his summaries of *Civ* XVIII, xxiv, and *Serm* 197, 1 (*ibid.*, pp. 182 and 192 respectively), and a fair-minded inspection of all these texts reveals that Augustine is uniformly talking about "divine images" in the sense of idols. What *would* Augustine's estimate have been of "sculpture" in our modern acceptance of that term? As with painting, we simply cannot know for sure.

The only text I can find where idol associations seem clearly excluded is *Civ* XII, xxv, where Augustine speaks of the form which potters and artists impose "who paint and fashion forms like the body of animals," a form "given from without"; this he contrasts with the "internal" form God's creative artistry effects in natural entities. Couple this with the remark from *InJo* 24, 2 (see above, this note) and one might hesitantly suggest that Augustine may have seen the plastic arts—painting and sculpture—as imposing an "external form," a visible representation of the original but serving no further symbolic function. *Hoc est totum, vidisse, laudasse*: not Plotinus' theory, but Plato's "copy of a copy" notion from *Republic* X? Possibly; but that is all we have a right to say.

24. *JoParth* II, 13; *Civ* I, xxxii–xxxiii, and II, vii–viii and xx; cf. II, xxv, 1; VI, vi, 2; VIII, xiii–xiv, xxi, 2; *Enar* 96, 7; 102, 13; *Serm* 198, 3; Denis 14, 3, and 17, 7. Augustine's opinion of "theater" (and Svoboda's evaluative comments, *Esthétique*, p. 192) must be appreciated against the background (and meaning of the term) illuminated by Van der Meer, *Augustine the Bishop*, pp. 48 and 50–54.

25. See Brown, pp. 299–312.

26. *Faust* XV, 5; XX, 9 (where they compare favorably with Manichee fictions); *CatRud* 10; *Civ* II, viii and xiv; IV, x, xvii; XVIII, xv–xvi; XIX, xii, 2 (both quite parenthetical observations).

27. *Civ* VI, v–vi; cf. also the texts cited above, note 26.

28. *Faust* XV, 5 (cf. XX, 9).

29. *Enar* 36, S II, 8 (cf. 85, 9). Svoboda, *Esthétique,* p. 157, lists a number of *Enarrationes* where Augustine interprets the call to "jubilation" as implying a praise beyond all that words can convey. See also the texts cited above, notes 5 and 6.

30. See the texts cited below, notes 31–33; cf. Jean Pépin, "Saint Augustin et la fonction protreptique de l'allégorie," *REA* 5:243–286 (1955).

31. *Ep* 55, 21; *Civ* XX, xxi, 2.

32. *Enar* 147, 5.

33. *Faust* XII, 7; *CatRud* 13; *CMend* 24, 28; *Civ* XX, xxi, 2; *Doc* IV, 15.

34. *Immort* 17; see *Early Theory,* pp. 138–145.

35. See E. Gilson, *Christian Philosophy,* pp. 45, 52–58.

36. *Trin* VIII, 9. I simplify the lines of Augustine's argument somewhat, for the sake of exposition. Cf. *CatRud* 17.

37. *Trin* VIII, 13.

38. *Ibid.*

39. See my "Augustine's Rejection of the Fall of the Soul," in *Augustinian Studies* 4:1–32 (1973).

40. See *Lib* III, 53 (cf. 52) where Augustine shapes the objection: how to account for the "ignorance" and "difficulty" we experience in living the virtuous life and thus pursuing our beatitude.

41. Burnaby, *Amor Dei,* pp. 143–144.

42. *Trin* XIV, 4–14. Augustine's way of expressing this "essentiality" is more roundabout: he is bent on finding what aspects of man are included in his "image" character. I take this as a quest to uncover God's creative idea of man, i.e., the divine idea originally constitutive of man's true "essence."

43. *Ibid.,* XV, 44–45.

44. *Ibid.,* XI, especially 1 and 8–9.

45. See H. I. Marrou, *The Resurrection and St. Augustine's Theology of Human Values* (Villanova, 1966; hereafter cited as *Resurrection*).

46. *Civ* XIII, xvi–xviii; cf. *ibid.,* X, xxix, and XXII, xxvi–xxvii. Note how adroitly Augustine plays off Plotinus' teaching on this point against Porphyry's.

47. *Civ* XIII, xx–xxiii; XXII, xix, 1; xxi, xxx, 1.

48. See, for example, *Trin* II, 13, and III, 4–5. St. Paul's teaching in I *Cor* 15, 42–51, obviously has a good deal to do with Augustine's thinking on this question; cf. also *Matt* 22:22–23 where Christ speaks of our being, in the risen state, "like the angels," thus encouraging such expressions as *mutatio* (or *commutatio, immutatio*) *angelica.* See Marrou, *Resurrection,* pp. 18–19 and the notes.

49. *Civ* XXII, xix, 1–2; xxiv, 4; xxx, 1; *Enchir* 87–92; *Retr* I, xi, 2–3 (emending *Mus* VI, 7 and 13); *Serm* 240, 3; 243, 4–7. Svoboda

dutifully records the *Retractations'* corrections to the relatively disincarnate view of resurrection in the *De Musica* (*Esthétique,* pp. 186–187; cf. *ibid.,* pp. 86–87, on *Mus*) apparently unconscious that his curve of "spiritualization" has been seriously questioned. The risen body has now become outspokenly incarnate (even "material": *Enchir* 87–92); in *Civ* the formerly "spiritual" beauty of the other world has become corporeal as well, yet Svoboda succeeds in giving this development a reverse twist: for Augustine, "true corporeal beauty is . . . the beauty of risen bodies" (*Esthétique,* p. 180). The fact is that the Christian teaching on resurrection has reconferred on corporeal beauty its right to be called "true" beauty.

50. *Civ* XXII, xxix.

51. *Ibid.* Augustine cannot find sure grounds in Scripture for either a firm yes or a firm no; but observe the suggestive insistence on the "spiritual" power of our corporeal eyes and the correlated transparency, not only of other spiritual bodies, but of the entire "new heaven and new earth."

52. *Civ* XIII, xx–xxiii; *Retr* I, xi, 2–3; *Serm* 362, 19.

53. *Civ* XXII, xix, 1–2; xxiv, 4; xxx, 1 (cf. *Retr.* I, xvii, and II, iv, 3); *Enchir* 87–88.

54. See Marrou, cited above, note 45, esp. pp. 35–38.

55. *Doc* I, 37. Cf. the rigor of Augustine's original formulation of the distinction, *ibid.,* 20.

56. *Trin* IX, 13.

57. *Trin* XI, 10.

58. *Doc* I, 34 (God's love of us is a love of "use"); *Trin* X, 17 (all *frui* is reducible to *uti*).

59. *Doc* I, 4, expresses this caution about delighting in the "amenities" encountered on our "journey."

60. *NatBon* 3 (where Svoboda sees but misinterprets the fact that beauty and good are spoken of together without any clear distinction between them, *Esthétique,* p. 140; cf. *InJo* 15, 21). Much the same correlation identification occurs in *Trin* VIII, 4; X, 1–2; *AdvLeg* I, 6–9; *Enchir* 5, 10–11. *InJo* 32, 3, shows Augustine missing an excellent opportunity to probe how personal love may actually transform the quality of sexual desire; and *Retr* I, i, 3 simply draws the logical conclusion of all this, by equating true *Philocalia* with *Philosophia.* And yet, Augustine's repeated appeals to the *pulchrum-aptum* distinction shows an underlying sensitivity to the difference of attitude required toward beauty and good; his encounter with Julian of Eclanum compels him to distinguish between the attitudes of "concupiscence" and aesthetic admiration when confronted with a beautiful human body; and finally, his enthusiastic portrayal of risen bodies as beautiful but not exciting concupiscence seems almost to "release" him to proclaim the genuineness of corporeal beauty as never before. For these themes, which often interweave, see *Civ* XII, iv; XXII, xxiv; *Jul* IV, 65–66 (cf. *Serm* 159, 2: the real force of both

these texts Svoboda simply misapprehends, *Esthétique,* pp. 169 and 191–192); *Ep* 138, 2–5 (but cf. note 4 above); *Serm* 240, 3; 243, 4–7; *Retr* I, xi, 1–3. See also notes 2, 4, and 49 above.

61. *Civ* XIX, xiii, xvii; cf. *ibid.,* v, viii, xix.

62. *Serm* 156, 16.

63. See Burnaby, *Amor Dei,* pp. 53–82.

64. *GenLitt* VI, 32; VIII, 1–5; IX, 20–23. It has completely escaped Svoboda that this major work is so much more "incarnate" than *GenMan* as almost to negate the "spiritualist" tendencies of the earlier work at important points. His reference back to *GenMan* (*Esthétique,* p. 150) only accents again his all too frequent unawareness of "context."

65. *Ibid.,* VIII, 8–10; XI, 45–46, 55; *Civ* XIII, xxi.

66. *Trin* XII–XIII; cf. *Doc* I, 38–63. See Marrou, *Culture Antique,* pp. 561–569.

67. *Civ* XXII, xxx.

8. Toward a Contemporary Augustinian Aesthetic

1. For one of the most sensitive attempts at *Wiederholung* of the Augustinian aesthetic that I know, see Henri Davenson [pseudonym for H. I. Marrou], *Traité de la musique selon l'esprit de Saint-Augustin* (Neuchatel, 1942). On some of the wider questions entertained here, compare the views of Anton Maxsein, *Philosophia Cordis* (Salzburg, n.d. [1967?]).

2. *Resurrection,* p. 2.

3. Cited above, Chapter 5, note 175.

4. Again, see Brown, *Augustine,* pp. 146–157, and Burnaby, *Amor Dei,* pp. 45–82.

5. The term is Gerard Manley Hopkins'; for much of what it has come to imply in my thinking, see William Lynch, *Christ and Apollo* (New York, 1960), esp. pp. 1–12, 133–160 (hereafter cited as *Apollo*). See also Lynch's earlier studies of theology and the imagination in *Thought,* 29 and 30 (1954–55).

6. The reference is to Wordsworth's earlier "To a Skylark," written in 1805.

7. See the 1825 version of "To a Skylark."

8. Percy Bysshe Shelley, "To a Skylark."

9. Gerard Manley Hopkins, "To a Caged Skylark."

10. *Conf* X, 57.

11. See the discussion of this concept in Suzanne Langer, *Feeling and Form* (London, 1953), *passim,* but especially pp. 79–103. The reader will surmise how stimulating I have found this work, along with her *Problems of Art* (London, 1957). Cf. pp. 44–58 and her earlier *Philosophy in a New Key* (Cambridge, Mass., 1942). As with virtually all the references cited in this chapter, however, I have taken

the liberty of recasting many of her suggestions in the light of my own "Augustinian" preoccupations.

12. See the works of Stewart and Friedländer cited above, Chapter 1, note 44. Eric Havelock takes a different view in his *Preface to Plato* (Oxford, 1963): having undertaken to show that Plato was bent on exorcising the spell of poetic thinking in favor of "scientific" thought, he must own up to a certain disappointment at the aesthetic residue in Plato's theory of forms; see pp. 254–275.

13. *Early Theory,* pp. 116–121, 284–285; and *Odyssey,* pp. 81–89.

14. *Odyssey,* pp. 177–185.

15. See *Early Theory,* p. 288.

16. I have tried to develop some aspects of this proposal in "Action and Contemplation in St. Augustine," in the work cited above, Chapter 6, note 31, pp. 38–58.

17. Compare Aristotle's suggestions in the *Nichomachean Ethics,* e.g., III, 6–7; IV, 2–3, that the accomplished moral agent must have an "eye" for the morally *kalon* or "beautiful"; also, St. Thomas Aquinas's pregnant suggestions about the need for a certain "connaturality" to guide the moral insights or the virtuous man. Jacques Maritain, *Creative Intuition in Art and Poetry* (New York, 1953), pp. 80–90, develops some valuable applications of this principle to the aesthetic area.

18. *Apology,* 28 BE.

19. Lynch, *Apollo,* pp. 1–12.

20. Augustine is not entirely insensitive to this: see his remarks on the kind of *stoliditas* he does *not* mean, in *Mus* VI, 15. There is, too, a sense of "stretch" undeniably running through the reports of "vision" recorded in *Conf* VII, 16 and 23 (Milan), and IX, 23–25 (Ostia).

21. Martin Heidegger, *On the Way to Language* (New York, 1971), trans. Peter D. Hertz, p. 131, refers to silence as the "soundless tolling of the stillness" of what he considers to be "authentic" speech. I am suggesting that the relationship could just as easily be reversed, that silence can be the "chiming" of speech itself. See the suggestions of Heidegger, *ibid.,* pp. 98 and 108.

22. T. S. Eliot, *Four Quartets,* "Burnt Norton," lines 139–140, 149–150; and "East Coker," lines 68–71.

23. *Phaedrus,* 251A, 254B, 254E. I have tried to meditate on the significance of Plato's stress on this attitude and on its connections with our appreciation of the world as product of the divine artist, in the article cited above, Chapter 2, note 44, esp. pp. 13–23.

24. *Conf* VII, 16. Augustine uses a variety of terms to express this more properly aesthetic attitude, even while working in the context of his *beata vita* dynamic. See, for some examples: *GenLitt* V, 43 (*admirationis horror*); *Civ* XXII, xxiv (*stupor mentis; mirabilia stupenda*); *Enar* 41, 7 (*stuperi, mirari, admirari*); 144, 13 (*terreri*);

145, 12 (*mirari; exhorrescere; contremiscere; stupenda*); 148, 10 (*expavescere*).

25. See the entry (dated 8.4.59) in Dag Hammarskjöld's *Markings* (New York, 1964), trans. Leif Sjöberg and W. H. Auden, p. 174.

26. *Civ* XXII, 24. See the references in Pontet, *L'exégèse,* pp. 565–566. The quotation is from Dylan Thomas's "Fern Hill."

27. See the suggestions in this sense of G. Madec in "Connaissance de Dieu et action de grâces," in *Recherches Augustiniennes* II (Paris, 1962), pp. 273–309, especially pp. 302ff.

28. See LeBlond, *Conversions,* pp. 5–164.

29. Note the surrender motif, not only in *Conf* VIII, 27, but also in the *cessavi de me paululum* of *Conf* VII, 20.

30. *Ibid.,* VII, 20.

31. William Wordsworth, "Tintern Abbey."

32. *Republic,* 518C.

33. *Early Theory,* pp. 121–124.

34. *Acad* I, 3.

35. *Sol* I, 12–14; cf. the title of the work, *Fides rerum quae non videntur.*

36. *Mus* VI, 32; cf. 35.

37. *Util* 24; see *Early Theory,* pp. 253–257.

38. See especially the Emmaus episode, *Luke* 24:13–35. It would be valuable to research whether Augustine ever considered the transfiguration experience as a kind of anticipation of faith's "luminous" insightfulness after the resurrection.

39. *Sol* I, 8.

40. See above, Chapter 7, note 36.

41. The expression is Gilbert Ryle's in his *Concept of Mind* (London, 1949). Cf. Gareth Matthew's essay, cited above, Chapter 6, note 31.

42. *Conf* X, 3–4.

43. See John Hick, *Faith and Knowledge,* 2d ed. (Ithaca, 1966), esp. pp. 3–42. I have also profited, in this connection, from many aspects of Michael Polanyi's *Personal Knowledge* (Chicago, 1958) and *The Tacit Dimension* (New York, 1966).

44. *Luke* 24:41.

45. Samuel Taylor Coleridge, *Biographia Litteraria* (Oxford, 1958), II, 6.

46. See above, Introduction, note 14.

47. See, on this theme, R. Formesyn, "Le *Semeion* Johannique et le *Semeion* hellénistique," in *Ephemerides Theologicae Lovanienses* 38:856–894 (1962), esp. pp. 890–893; also Donatien Mollat, "Le *Semeion* Johannique," in *Sacra Pagina,* ed. J. Coppens *et al.* (Paris and Gembloux, 1959), II, 209–218. For anticipations of this, see Augustine's *In Jo* 19, 5, *Subtexit . . . nubilo lucem suam*; and 34, 4, *tegitur, non ut obscuretur, sed ut temperetur.*

48. Karl Rahner in "The Eternal Significance of the Humanity

of Jesus," *Theological Investigations* III (Baltimore, 1967), trans. Karl-H. Kruger and Boniface Kruger, 35–46, has some compelling observations in this sense. So too his essay in *ibid.*, IV (Baltimore, 1966), trans. Kevin Smith, 221–252, on "The Theology of the Symbol." Cf. J. Alfaro, "Christo Glorioso Revelador del Padre," in *Gregorianum* 39:222–270 (1958).

49. See above, note 1.

50. T.S. Eliot, *Selected Essays, 1917–1932* (New York, 1932), p. 200.

51. See, for example, William James's essays, especially "The Will to Believe," "The Sentiment of Rationality," and "The Moral Philosopher and the Moral Life," in *The Will to Believe* (New York, 1899).

52. See E. Gilson's remarks on this in "The Future of Augustinian Metaphysics," in *A Monument to Saint Augustine*, M. C. D'Arcy *et al.* (London, 1930), pp. 289–315.

53. *Acad* II, 22.

54. See Joseph Pieper's commentary on the *Phaedrus* of Plato: *Enthusiasm, or the Divine Madness* (New York, 1964), trans. Richard and Clara Winston, especially pp. 47–89.

55. *Art as Experience* (New York, 1958), pp. 192–195.

56. *Romans* 8:22 and 19.

Appendix A

1. See especially Augustine's interpretations of *Genesis*, e.g., *Conf* XIII, 17–19; *GenMan* II, 5, and compare with his notion of the "opacity" of authority's transmissions, e.g., *Mor* I, 11–12. Cf. *Early Theory*, pp. 250–257, 272–273, and my *Odyssey*, pp. 163–164.

2. *Conf* VII, 20; cf. *Early Theory*, pp. 65–86.

3. *Conf* VII, 27.

4. The Gospel expressions are drawn from the *Itala* text which Ambrose and Augustine probably were using: cf. *Das Neue Testament in Altlateinischer Ueberlieferung* by Adolf Jülicher (New York, 1954–).

Index of Subjects and Names

Index of the Works of St. Augustine